T0356678

Praise for

# CRUSHING CHAOS

"Manny Arango doesn't pull punches in *Crushing Chaos,* and that's exactly why you need it. This book gets right to the point—your life doesn't have to stay messy, but you've got to be ready to put in the work. Arango is honest, funny, and straight-up practical. He gives you real steps to crush the chaos and make room for God's order in your life. You'll laugh, you'll grow, and you'll be glad you picked this book up."

—Travis and Jackie Greene, lead pastors of
Forward City Church, South Carolina

"Manny Arango is a masterful storyteller with the depth of a skilled theologian and the insight of a pastor. *Crushing Chaos* is a much-needed guide for navigating the turbulence that so often surrounds us. Arango doesn't just diagnose the problem— he also leads you on a journey to rediscover the ancient rhythms of order God established from the very beginning. This book is raw, insightful, and filled with biblical truths that will challenge your thinking and transform your life. If you're ready to confront chaos and step into God's peace, *Crushing Chaos* is a must-read."

—Chris Durso, pastor at SoHo Bible Study and
author of *The Heist*

"We've been in the chaos before—addiction, crumbling marriage, feeling ready to walk away. *Crushing Chaos* isn't just another self-help book. Manny Arango brings deep biblical truth with the raw honesty of someone who's walked through chaos. If you're tired of surface fixes and ready for real transformation, Arango will guide you there. This book isn't about escaping chaos—it's about embracing the peace and order God designed for your life."

—JIMMY AND IRENE ROLLINS, authors of *Two Equals One*

"We have a rare gift in Manny Arango who has given the church a theological master class, storytelling masterpiece, and shepherding manual in his newest book, *Crushing Chaos*. In a world filled with chaos politically, spiritually, emotionally, and relationally, Arango takes us back to the garden and reintroduces us to our God who has been establishing order and peace for His people from the very beginning. Each chapter offers fresh revelation from God's Word and applicable strategy to crush the chaos in our own lives. Arango reminds us that our inheritance as children of God is a sound mind, peace that passes all understanding, and joy unspeakable and full of His glory."

—NATALIE RUNION, founder of Raised to Stay, worship leader, songwriter, speaker, and bestselling author

# CRUSHING
# CHAOS

# CRUSHING CHAOS

*Calm Your Storms. Order*
*Your Life. Find Your Peace.*

## Manny Arango

**Foreword by Scot McKnight**

WATERBROOK

WaterBrook
An imprint of the Penguin Random House Christian Publishing Group,
a division of Penguin Random House LLC
1745 Broadway, New York, NY 10019
waterbrookmultnomah.com
penguinrandomhouse.com

This is a work of nonfiction. Some names and identifying details have been changed.

Italics in Scripture quotations reflect the author's added emphasis.

Interior illustration: @ Spencer Fuller/Faceout Studio (dragon)

Library of Congress Cataloging-in-Publication Data

Names: Arango, Manny, author.
Title: Crushing chaos : calm your storms, order your life, find your peace /
Manny Arango ; foreword by Scot McKnight.
Description: First edition. | [Colorado Springs, CO] : WaterBrook, [2025] |
Includes bibliographical references.
Identifiers: LCCN 2024043171 | ISBN 9780593601600 (hardcover) | ISBN 9780593601617 (ebook)
Subjects: LCSH: Christian life—Biblical teaching. | Chaos (Christian theology)
Classification: LCC BS680.C47 A73 2025 | DDC 248.4—dc23/eng/20241208
LC record available at https://lccn.loc.gov/2024043171

Printed in the United States of America on acid-free paper

9 8 7 6 5 4 3 2 1

First Edition

The authorized representative in the EU for product safety and compliance is
Penguin Random House Ireland, Morrison Chambers, 32 Nassau Street,
Dublin D02 YH68, Ireland. https://eu-contact.penguin.ie

BOOK TEAM: Production editor: Jessica Choi • Managing editor: Julia Wallace • Production manager: Maggie Hart • Copy editor: Tracey Moore • Proofreaders: Bailey Utecht, Carrie Krause, Marissa Earl

Book design by Diane Hobbing

For details on special quantity discounts for bulk purchases, contact specialmarketscms@penguinrandomhouse.com.

This book is dedicated to Chaos and Order. To the chaos of my childhood—without you, I wouldn't be who I am today or have the requisite empathy to write this book.

And to my wife who has patiently waited and prayed as I've journeyed from Chaos to Order—this book is dedicated to you. Thank you for being my peace, constant and unmoving. I'm better because of you.

# Foreword

There are good reasons to capture the cosmic problem with humans and the world order with the word *Chaos,* and not just because it derives from one of the Bible's first (and very cool) Hebrew terms. We are prone to dig our heels in with traditional and historical terms, like *sin* and *transgression* and even our *Adamic nature.* Chaos was tamed by God and reordered into the beauty of all creation flowing as designed by our Creator. The primordial problem with creation, then, was not sin against God but the presence of Chaos. It's the fundamental problem behind all fundamental problems.

Chaos is systemic in that it impacts all of creation, all our governmental systems, all our economic systems, all our (yes) church systems, and all our relationships. Chaos, then, is not something entirely subdued. It's the original problem that lurks in the corners like some goblin, waiting to rise into a presence that disrupts the good order of God. Nothing speaks systemic Chaos more than the oceans—dark, gloomy, mysterious, fathomless, filled with death. Only one can tame the ocean, and that is the Water Walker, Jesus, who reached out His hand to a sinking follower and then calmed the chaos above (storms) in order to calm the chaos below (the turbulent waters).

Chaos is spiritual in that it distorts God's love into magical thinking, disrupts the flow of God's grace toward us into what must be earned, and disengages us from God, from ourselves, and from those we are to love. Chaos is spiritual because it transforms the gospel about Jesus Christ into a weapon that can be used to manipulate, control, and dominate. Chaos turns Christ into a weapon against the world rather than the revelation of God's grace and love and justice and beauty.

Chaos is personal because it invades our innermost selves, coercing us to think we are unworthy, unable, unwilling, undesirable, and ugly—but we are not. God loves us. Christ died for us. Christ was raised for us. Christ is coming back for us. The Spirit is with us, in us, for us, and empowering us. God has done all this for us because God wants our innermost selves to be redeemed, transformed, and empowered to love, to bring chaos into beauty, and to shift the conversations away from domination and violence toward goodness and justice and peace.

Chaos is personal because we are prone not only to wander, as the old hymn has it, but moreover to wander into the wild and the wilderness—where chaos rules, where order is not to be found, and where we can be "free" to live in the wild out of reach of God's Order.

Chaos is a story, one we cannot live and flourish in, but it has become a compelling story for too many today. Chaos whispers to us that we each can do our own thing, that "you be you, I'll be me, and we can get along." Chaos knows that you are not you without us and that we cannot flourish on our own—that Walden is no place to live for those made to love one another. (I'm told Thoreau's mother did his laundry.) Chaos takes us into the wilderness to ruin us, to weaken our need for love, and to diminish our yearnings for justice and peace. Chaos brings anxiety; God's ordering in Christ brings the true peace.

In this book, Manny Arango has given us the gift of a word, and by it, through it, and with it paves a new path through the disorders of our modern world, naming them for what they are—chaos—and taking us into the beauty of God's redemption and empowering presence. *Crushing Chaos* is courageous, creative, and compelling. The dragons of disorder can be ordered only when Chaos is crushed by the Lion who, paradoxically, doubles as the Lamb. Manny's book turns the whole Bible into a story of God taming Chaos, of God turning Chaos into Order, and of an ordered creation finding its best Order in Christ. Chaos then is scriptural, but Order is even more so.

Most of all, *Crushing Chaos* names what ails, disrupts, ruins, wounds, crushes, divides, and deconstructs us. At one time, long ago when I was a college student, a professional asked what had become of *sin*. People liked the title of his book,[1] but America was not ready to embrace the truth: Sin was real. Manny is asking the same question with the primordial word and the primordial problem, with the word *Chaos*. He's also proposing the primordial redemption: Order. Ordering is God's work, and it is not as simplistic as creating "out of nothing." Ordering turns chaos into beauty and darkness into light; ordering turns empty seas into waters teeming with fish, empty skies into skies filled with birds, and open spaces into communities populated by those energized by God's image to care for this world and the persons in it. Ordering then is the flip side of Chaos. If Chaos is the systemic, spiritual, and personal problem we face today, the solution is not government control; it is not one man running the world. It is God ordering it and God's created images sub-ordering what God is ordering.

Ordering sees this world as God's temple—as an earth shaped by God for you and me to bring the fruits of our labor into order as a way of worshipping God and loving one another. Creation's true Order is a person, Jesus Christ, who crushed Chaos on the cross and who rose to establish an Order based on grace, love, justice, and peace. No word captures our world better than *Chaos,* and the only solution to it is God's true, lasting, and flourishing Order.

—*Scot McKnight*
PROFESSOR IN SEARCH OF GOD'S ORDER

# Contents

## SECTION 3: COME HELL OR HIGH WATER

## SECTION 4: THE PRINCE OF PEACE

# A
# WORLD
# OF
# CHAOS

## Chapter 1

# Panic in the Lobby

> Now the earth was formless and empty,
> darkness was over the surface of the deep,
> and the Spirit of God was hovering over the
> waters.
>
> —GENESIS 1:2

> The main emphasis [of creation] is not on a
> process from nothing to something, from
> nonexistence to existence, but on a process
> from confusion to distinction, *from chaos to
> order.*
>
> —JAMES BARR, "WAS EVERYTHING THAT GOD CREATED
> REALLY GOOD?," EMPHASIS ADDED

Anxiety coiled itself around a young girl while she was standing in our church lobby on a Wednesday night. Minutes before our weekly worship service, she was fighting to breathe and relentlessly wiping tears from her face. I offered up prayers, seemingly in vain. My job was to protect and love these young people, but I felt powerless over the chaos of panic that had engulfed her.

Eventually her wave of anxiety subsided, but I never forgot

this moment. I had preached dozens of messages about anxiety and panic. We had devoted prayer and ministry time specifically focusing on anxiety, but clearly, we hadn't cracked the code on the path to peace. After months of reflecting on this moment, I remembered that the creation account in Genesis has a whole lot to say about Chaos and that it describes the original state of creation as a deep, wild, raging ocean of Chaos. The opening words of the Bible declare:

> In the beginning God created the heavens and the
> earth. Now the earth was formless and empty, darkness
> was over the surface of the deep, and the Spirit of God
> was hovering over the waters. (Genesis 1:1–2)

God created the heavens and the earth, and the earth was "formless and empty." In Hebrew, those terms are *tohu*[1] and *va-vohu*,[2] which translate into English as "wasteness . . . that which is wasted, laid waste . . . a desert . . . emptiness, vanity . . . nothing"[3] and "emptiness, voidness,"[4] respectively. Other translations are "place of chaos," "wilderness," and "barren."[5] And the Hebrew term *tehom* ("deep") can be translated as "abyss."[6] (We'll look at these terms in more detail in later chapters.)

Simply put, Scripture's first words declare that creation was a chaotic, untamed mess and that the Spirit of the Lord God was brooding over the surface of this barren, unintelligible, chaotic ocean abyss. Pretty epic visual, if you ask me. However, God didn't bring peace to this chaos. God began organizing the creation and moved the earth from chaos into *order*. God began to separate, pull apart, gather, and bring structure to the chaos of creation. Look at this description in Genesis 1:6–7:

God said, "Let there be a vault between the waters to *separate* water from water." So God made the vault and *separated* the water under the vault from the water above it.

What did God do? *God separated.*
Read this next description in verse 9:

God said, "Let the water under the sky be *gathered* to one place, and let dry ground appear."

What did God do? *God gathered.*

The beginning of creation reveals a God who knows how to rearrange, organize, unclutter, clean, uncomplicate, simplify, and structure life. God's solution for the Chaos found in Genesis wasn't to bring *peace;* it was to establish *Order.* Ironically, peace is always a natural by-product once Order takes root in the cosmos, and I have discovered that God's strategy for responding to Chaos hasn't changed.

Order was the missing key in our ministry approach, as anxiety was simply a result or by-product of chaos. I had spent all my time focused on the check engine light of anxiety instead of popping open the hood and actually checking the engine. Anxiety is just a symptom of the real, undiagnosed chaos living deep within us. I had been preaching about peace, essentially medicating pain and providing temporary quick fixes, instead of addressing the root of the problem. The good news is that there's a cure for Chaos, and my discovery of that cure is what this book is all about. The cure for Chaos is *Order.*

There's an Order to life that's revealed in the Scriptures.

Take sex for example. The Bible's vision: Sex goes *after* marriage, not before. Confusing this sequence will inevitably create chaos.

Unnecessary heartbreak.
Soul ties with multiple individuals.
Insecurity. Possessive behavior.
Children born outside of wedlock.
Baby-mama drama. Child support.

This is absolute chaos.

And it creates abundant opportunities for anxiety to thrive. It doesn't matter how much we pray for peace—peace will never be permanent in the soul of the person who rejects God's order.

Our families, churches, and institutions can flourish only when they are well ordered. God's order for families involves mothers *and* fathers who are present, engaged, and invested in the flourishing of their children. Mothers *and* fathers who exercise healthy authority over their children to guide, teach, and protect them. When this order is ignored or rejected, chaos ensues. Allow me to give an example around fatherhood.

According to a 2022 United States Census Bureau report, about one in five children are currently growing up without a father in the home,[7] and the negative results speak for themselves. Removing the father from the head of the home creates chaos within society.

"Research suggests that fatherlessness is a significant contributor to mental health issues in children . . . and 71% of all children who abuse substances come from fatherless homes. . . . Another study found that 75% of adolescent patients in substance abuse centers are from fatherless homes."[8] In addition, "63% of youth suicides . . . and 85% of children who exhibit behavioral disorders" come from homes without fathers present.[9] Fatherlessness not only affects mental health but also impacts financial outcomes, educational outcomes, and criminal activity.

Fatherlessness is directly linked to anxiety, depression, suicide, poverty, incarceration, and a host of other challenges.[10] The facts paint a clear picture: When humanity deviates from God's order, chaos always results. God's order includes a healthy, present, invested father. A good dad defends his children from the chaos of society. Wherever there's fatherlessness, there will also be chaos.

My dad was incarcerated for eighteen years and battled a drug addiction for decades. I grew up in a chaotic home, within the wider culture of a chaotic neighborhood, and I bucked against the order of male authority figures my entire teenage life. I hated the idea of order and submitting to my father's authority because it was so foreign to the way I grew up, but then I realized I'd never actually mature if I didn't embrace Order and reject Chaos. It didn't matter how many earnest prayers I offered to God, desperately asking Him for peace; until I embraced His Order, I continued to struggle with depression and suicidal thoughts because my depression was being fueled by the fatherless chaos I was raised in. Depression was simply a symptom of a chaotic life that lacked the foundation, structure, and identity that fathers are designed by God to provide.

Order extends way past sequence and authority. The Bible outlines a rhythm for life. We're designed to work for six days and rest for one day. Chick-fil-A style. Closed on Sundays.

Yahweh commanded the people of Israel in the Old Testament to allow their land to rest every seven years—no crops, no planting, no harvesting. Modern scientists have proven that this practice of allowing the soil to rest has incredible health outcomes for humans and the environment. Genesis teaches that you and I were made from the dirt of the ground, and we also require rest if we're going to experience optimal fruitfulness. Adam was created from the dirt, which in Hebrew is called *adamah*.[11] Adam's name literally means "dirt man."

Jesus teaches that the seed of God's Word should be planted in the soil of our hearts (Matthew 13:23). Paul teaches that the fruit of love, joy, peace, patience, kindness, goodness, faithfulness, gentleness, and self-control should be growing from the soil of our very beings (Galatians 5:22–23). The Bible acknowledges that we are soil (Genesis 2:7). We are dirt, not metal. However, in the Chaos of our modern world, we have become machines—cranking out projects and grinding and being productive. Maybe many of us are anxious and living chaotic lives because there's no rhythm to our work. Both machines and farms produce. But those processes of production look radically different. Embracing Sabbath doesn't mean that we produce less; it means that we produce differently. Sabbath is a rhythm, and rhythm is a nonnegotiable element of God's Order.

Sequence. Authority. Rhythm.

I wonder how many of us have been praying for peace but are sabotaging our ability to receive, produce, or sustain peace because our lives reject God's sequence, authority, and rhythm. I wonder how many of us have rebuked anxiety but have yet to reject the forms of chaos that produce anxiety in our lives. The

Bible provides a path out of Chaos, but it requires that we recover an ancient way of reading the Scriptures.

Modern interpretations of the creation account in Genesis focus so heavily on the fact that God created ex nihilo, or "out of nothing," that we miss what ancient audiences would've emphasized and appreciated most about the biblical text. The authors of the Bible and their audiences assumed that Yahweh created everything out of nothing. That conclusion wasn't their dominant point of emphasis.

Genesis 1:1 communicates this straightaway: "In the beginning God created the heavens and the earth." Think of this verse as the summary of the entire creation narrative, ten words that uphold the idea that God created everything out of nothing. However, once the text starts detailing the process of how this Creator brought everything into existence, the emphasis shifts. The writer of Genesis starts to describe a chaotic primeval ocean, not a blank canvas of nothingness.

Once verse 2 begins, the starting point for creation is no longer a blank slate of "nothing" but rather a deep and dark abyss of Chaos. And everything after verse 1 describes a sovereign Creator who masterfully rescues the creation from Chaos and establishes divine Order so that humans can flourish.

I hope we can recover this ancient emphasis. Because the same sovereign Creator who pulled creation out of the Chaos *then* wants to rescue our lives from Chaos *now*. The Bible provides a path from Chaos to Order, and as I began to discover that path for myself and teach it to others, I started seeing less and less anxiety.

This is why I stopped preaching about peace and anxiety. Instead, I rediscovered this way of reading and interpreting

Genesis like an ancient person—seeing God as bringing Order out of Chaos. I returned to the ancient path, and I began preaching and teaching on Order and Chaos. I started teaching people how to properly order their lives, and somehow, we stopped having panic attacks in the lobby.

When we change our theology, everything else changes as a result. My dad has struggled with a drug addiction my entire life. As you can imagine, living with an addict is quite chaotic. But when I was somewhere around the age of twelve, my dad gave his life to Jesus and got baptized. From that moment on, he began to pray that God would miraculously deliver him from the chaos of addiction. I can vividly remember being twenty-two years old and my dad rejecting an opportunity to participate in a one-year Christian rehab program known as Teen Challenge.

Teen Challenge was offering my dad a process. Order. A daily routine. Community rules. A Bible memorization plan. Structure. A way to unravel the web of addiction he was trapped in.

I'll never forget my dad's words in that moment. He said, "I have faith for God to miraculously deliver me. I'm believing God for a miracle. I just need the right pastor to lay hands on me and the power of God will deliver me instantly."

My dad refused the process of discipleship because he wanted the instant power of deliverance. He wanted ex nihilo deliverance. He wanted his rescue to arrive "out of nothing" and God to wave a magic wand and conquer his chaos. And my dad's theology has kept him stuck in the chaos of addiction. I wonder if he would've made a different decision had he seen God as the Creator who carefully and steadily moved the cosmos out of Chaos and into Order in those opening days of

Genesis. I couldn't convince him of the Chaos-crushing God of the Bible, but maybe I'll be able to convince you.

If there's chaos in your life, please rest assured: The God of the Bible is neither intimidated nor stumped by it. He knows exactly how to conquer the chaos and create order in your life. And although He doesn't wave a magic wand over you to cure your anxiety instantly, He will lay out a path toward order so your anxiety begins to correct itself. God *can* bring peace into your life instantly and out of nothing. God *can* create freedom and sobriety for my dad instantly and ex nihilo. He *can*.

But there's a reason He tends not to. And that is what we will explore through the next couple of chapters.

## Chapter 2

# Peace in the Temple

By the seventh day God had finished the work
he had been doing; so on the seventh day he
*rested* from all his work.

—GENESIS 2:2

Come to me, all you who are weary and
burdened, and I will give you *rest.*

—MATTHEW 11:28

In the traditional view that Genesis 1 is an
account of material origins, day seven is
mystifying. It appears to be nothing more than
an afterthought with theological concerns
about Israelites observing the sabbath—an
appendix, a postscript, a tack on.

In contrast . . . without hesitation the
ancient reader would conclude that this *is a
temple text* and that day seven is the most
important of the seven days.

—JOHN WALTON, *THE LOST WORLD OF GENESIS ONE,*
EMPHASIS ADDED

I've spent more nights in a Red Roof Inn than I'd like to admit. About a decade ago, I was driving from North Carolina to Boston and got caught in a blizzard. Somewhere between Richmond and D.C. I got into a pretty bad car accident, and Red Roof Inn became my dwelling place for about three nights.

The room smelled funky.

The sheets were scratchy.

The bathroom was gross.

My nerves were rattled, and my mind kept rehearsing the accident over and over. It was the least restful sleep I've ever gotten because it's nearly impossible to rest in the midst of chaos. That Red Roof Inn taught me that *where* you rest will dictate *how* you rest and that there is an ideal resting place for humanity.

It's difficult to rest in chaos because you and I were designed to dwell within an ordered temple space that the Bible calls the Garden of Eden. We were not designed to be wandering nomads. There's a massive clue that the Garden of Eden is a temple, but it's possible to see that only when we read the text based on its ancient context.

Genesis 2:2 tells us that on the seventh day Elohim *rested:* "By the seventh day God had finished the work he had been doing; so on the seventh day he rested from all his work." For the ancient reader, this was the natural climax of the entire creation story. God's rest proved that the creation project had been a success and that the space had been sufficiently ordered.

If this verse feels anticlimactic, just know that the issue lies with us modern readers, not the text. This part is where the ancient saints would've taken a lap around the sanctuary, like in the Pentecostal church I grew up in. Ancient audiences un-

derstood that deities rested only once their temples were ordered and sanctified. Rest was the final confirmation that the
space was sacred. Rest was synonymous with divine approval.
John H. Walton, respected and renowned Old Testament professor emeritus at Wheaton College, asserted that in the ancient world, "Deity rests in a temple, and only in a temple. This
is what temples were built for. We might even say that this is
what a temple is—a place for divine rest."[1] In the ancient world,
gods rested only in temples, nowhere else. Because *where* you
rest will dictate *how* you rest.

And the process of preparing a temple for the deity was known
as *ordering* the temple space. Since God doesn't rest within
Chaos, His temple must be ordered—into a highly detailed and
intentionally designed space where everything has a function.

In the ancient world, readers would have understood the creation account of Genesis as a process that turned the Chaos of
*tohu va-vohu* into the sacred temple of Yahweh—they would
have recognized the relationship between Chaos and Order.
Modern readers understand Genesis very differently, seeing it as
the formation of the universe. Our goal is to uncover the original
message of Scripture to its original audience. Therefore, if the
ancients saw in Genesis the construction of Yahweh's cosmic
temple, their interpretation should have massive implications for
us. Oftentimes, we're so busy trying to harmonize the Bible with
our modern science that we don't realize we're forcing Scripture
to answer questions its authors were never even asking.

Robert J. V. Hiebert echoes this exact idea:

> Creation in Genesis 1:1–2:3 has more to do with bring-
> ing order to that chaos and populating voids than with
> generating all matter. That does not mean that this pas-

sage is inimical to the idea of God creating all matter. It is just that the issue does not seem to be relevant to this biblical author and his contemporaries. The mystery of ultimate origins is addressed by subsequent revelation that acknowledges that absolutely everything, even the primeval deep, must have its origin in God.[2]

Creation ex nihilo, or "out of nothing," is affirmed in other passages of Scripture, such as Psalm 33:6 and Hebrews 11:3. However, in the context in which Genesis was written, the main concern of the writers as well as the audience was the establishment of an ordered, functional world as opposed to an uninhabitable chaotic world. The ancient person was deeply concerned with the triumph of Order over Chaos. The ancients wanted Chaos to be utterly crushed, and this concern is reflected in the literature they produced.

We have more in common with ancient audiences than we realize. We, too, are consumed by Chaos. We, too, long for Chaos to be crushed and for Order to triumph. However, we've lost connection with the ancient world. We must learn to interpret the Scriptures according to an ancient perspective so we can find biblical truth that will crush the Chaos in our lives.

So far, we have two massive clues that the Garden of Eden is a temple. First, the garden is the product of God's ordering, Chaos-conquering process. Second, God is resting at the conclusion of this process, and deities in the ancient world rested only within temples, as confirmation that the space had been sufficiently ordered. However, it is the third clue that's most significant for you and me as we embark on this journey to conquer chaos and find peace:

In the ancient world, temples weren't simply the resting

place of the gods. They were also the resting place of the *images* of the gods.

Nearly every temple in the ancient world had an image inside. The temple of Zeus had an image of Zeus in it. Same with the temples of Hermes, Apollo, and Artemis—they housed images of their gods. Therefore, the final proof that God was constructing a temple in the opening movement of the Bible is His declaration in Genesis 1:26: "Let us make mankind in our image, in our likeness, so that they may rule."

*Image. Likeness. Rule.*

These are buzzwords.

These are temple words.

Images of God are designed to reside and find true rest only within the temple of God. Because *where* you rest will dictate *how* you rest. This verse provides function, purpose, and meaning for every single human being. However, most people have not ordered their lives around this functional reality—that they were made in God's image for the purpose of imaging and reflecting His glory throughout the cosmos.

When I was in the eighth grade, I attended a Christian school and memorized the very first question and corresponding answer of the Westminster Shorter Catechism. I've never forgotten these words, and they have ordered my life in the most profound way:

**What is the chief end of man?**
Man's chief end is to glorify God . . . and to enjoy him forever.[3]

The chief end of humankind is to glorify God and enjoy Him forever. As image bearers we are uniquely designed to glorify God, to reflect His majesty and His reign and rule throughout all creation. Our chief end is *not* to pursue and find our own happiness. When happiness becomes our main objective, it will create chaos. Our chief end is *not* to discover our destinies. When individual achievement becomes our primary focus, it creates chaos. Our ultimate goal is *not* to amass wealth and die fulfilled. It isn't to express our sexuality or live out our sexual desires or find our soulmates. When those objectives usurp the chief end for which we were created, we multiply chaos on this planet. The chief end of humankind—the reason we were created—is to reflect the One whose image we bear. And until that becomes the one thing we're obsessed with, we will be consumed with everything else and everything else will consume us. We will be less than truly human.

Our primary function as humans is to reflect the image and likeness of almighty God and to order our lives according to the reality that we are image bearers. That is the predominant reason we were created. It is our central function and our chief end. It is of first importance and occupies the place of primary priority.

We unleash chaos when we

are ignorant of our true function,
rebel against our true function,
attempt to redefine our function.

And we rob ourselves of rest. Because *where* you rest will dictate *how* you rest.

If we fail to operate according to our function as image bearers, we get released from the temple we were designed to dwell in because we have not carried out the purpose we were placed there to fulfill. And whenever we try to make an alternative environment our home, we become restless and tired and burnt out because we were designed only to rest in temples.

John Walton argues that God brings Order to the cosmos by bringing function to it. "Creation was an activity of bringing *functionality* to a nonfunctional condition rather than bringing material substance to a situation in which matter was absent."[4] Chaos is marked by a refusal to accept our God-ordained function.

We weren't designed for the Red Roof Inn. We weren't designed for chaos. And you can try to abide in the chaos if you'd like, but you'll never enjoy true rest until you embrace your true function and come back to your true home. Because, again, *where* you rest will dictate *how* you rest.

Once Adam and Eve are driven out of the temple they were created to dwell in, humanity moves further and further away from God's presence. When their son Cain commits the first murder, God comes down to communicate the consequences to him: "Now you are under a curse and driven from the ground. . . . You will be *a restless wanderer* on the earth" (Genesis 4:11–12). Cain is devasted by this news. The Bible says that he replies to the Lord, "My punishment is more than I can bear. Today you are driving me from the land, and I will be hidden from your presence; I will be *a restless wanderer* on the earth" (verses 13–14). God could've chosen any punishment for murder, so it's fascinating that He causes Cain to be a restless wanderer.

Someone with no home, no rest, and no access to the temple of God. A *restless wanderer.*

Maybe that describes your current state. Restlessly wandering from one job to the next. From one relationship to the next. From one church to the next. No roots. No sense of security or permanence. And maybe your soul is tired and you're burnt out from wandering aimlessly through life, constantly creating new passions and new interests based on some new function you've created for yourself. The Bible says that Delilah put Samson to sleep on her lap before shaving off the seven braids of his hair (Judges 16:19). This is the trap of Satan—to offer us sleep but never rest.

Many of us believe a vacation will fix the restlessness of our souls. But you don't need sleep; you need the security and safety of the home you were made for. Because *where* you rest will dictate *how* you rest. One young man I used to mentor swore he couldn't sleep without smoking weed because of his anxiety. As his pastor, I promised him that although he was attaining sleep, he hadn't achieved rest and that if he found true rest he'd inevitably get sleep. I promised him that the peace *of* God flows from being at peace *with* God. And I reminded him that Satan can never offer us rest, so like Delilah, he lulls us to sleep in order to subdue us and rob us of true rest.

Here's the good news of the gospel of Jesus Christ: You can come home. You can return to the temple you were created for. Jesus says in Matthew 11:28, "Come to me, all you who are weary and burdened, and I will give you rest." Remember, *rest* is temple language. Jesus isn't merely promising rest; He's promising access to the temple we were created for. Jesus's promise of rest is an invitation to return to the presence of God and to dwell with Him.

Jesus says "Come to me" because He is the flesh-and-blood temple. Jesus referred to Himself as a temple in John 2. In a heated discussion at the literal stone temple in Jerusalem, Jesus said to the religious leaders, "Destroy this temple, and I will raise it again in three days." Incredulous, "they replied, 'It has taken forty-six years to build this temple, and you are going to raise it in three days?' But the temple he had spoken of was his body" (verses 19–21). Jesus saw Himself as the temple of God, a dwelling place where God could reconcile with restless wanderers like you and me.

*Where* you rest will dictate *how* you rest.

You can come home. You can return to the temple you were made to occupy. If you're tired of wandering, weary from walking away from God, tired of searching for your true function, and burnt out from hiding, you can come home. And home isn't a place. It is a person. Home is Jesus, the temple of God.

Despite what you've done, Jesus is inviting you home, but there's one prerequisite: You must return to the original function you were created to fulfill. Only image bearers who are functioning according to their design have a secure spot in the temple God has prepared for us. And the incentive to surrender to God's design is that it will finally bring rest to your soul.

There's a second functional purpose for humans being made in the image of God. In the ancient world, rulers and emperors made statues in their images to extend their rule. A sovereign's image was the sign and symbol of their authority. God's image, in the form of Adam and Eve, is the manifest symbol of His rule and reign. The way the kingdom and Order of heaven begin to crush the Chaos of the earth is through the image-bearing humans who reflect the King's values. The temple of Eden was designed to be an embassy of heaven here on earth, with image-bearing ambassadors exporting the wisdom, language, culture, and worldview of heaven to the four corners of the world. That was Adam and Eve's function. And it is ours.

Modern readers understand and use the word *rest* in dramatically different ways than our ancient counterparts. When we think about rest in the modern world, we think of sleeping in on the weekend, relaxing on the beach, or vacationing during the holidays. However, the God of the Bible doesn't get tired. The Maker of heaven and earth neither sleeps nor slumbers.[5] Therefore, the rest that Genesis 2:2 describes must have a deeper meaning.

For the gods of the ancient Near East, rest was synonymous with taking up residence in their temples so they could rule. Rest meant that all enemies had been conquered and the work of *ordering* and *organizing* the cosmos could now transition into the work of *running* and *sustaining* it. Rest meant that Chaos had been properly dealt with.

When a king rested on his throne, that wasn't a vacation; it meant that decisions, verdicts, laws, and orders would soon emanate from the throne. When Genesis tells us that Elohim rested and took up residence in the temple of creation, it means that the King of the universe was ready to rule and reign. Jesus doesn't rest in the Gospels until Chaos has been crushed—but we'll deal with that in depth later. When a new president of the United States of America takes up residence in the White House, it has not merely become their dwelling place where they sleep or relax. The White House is the central hub where the president and the cabinet run the nation. This is the weight that Genesis 2:2 carries. Elohim rested, and that simple fact proves that the cosmos was successfully ordered as a temple for God's presence so that He could reign and rule.

There's a cyclical relationship among order, rest, and authority. Rest flows from order, and authority flows from rest. Walton describes it this way: "The role of the temple in the ancient world is not primarily a place for people to gather in worship like modern churches. It is a place for the deity— sacred space. It is his home, but more importantly his headquarters—the control room."[6] A kaleidoscope of images is present:

> Rest. Dwelling place. Temple.
> Palace. Throne.
> Headquarters. Control room.
> Function. Order. Rest. Authority.

These ideas are deeply intertwined.

In the ancient world, the words *image* and *idol* are essentially interchangeable. Idols were always made in the image of the deities they represented. So, naturally, as image bearers, we are uniquely drawn to idolatry—to worship the reflection as opposed to the reality. We're drawn to exalt ourselves and our opinions, to exercise autonomy, and to try to re-create ourselves in our own images. We want to create identity for ourselves and live according to our truth. But this is vanity. My reflection doesn't have autonomy. My reflection can only reflect the truth of the person standing in the mirror.

We are currently living in a society of people adamantly opposed to being reflections of God; they even deny the existence of the One they image and therefore fail to reflect and image Him properly. And when created things attempt to be their own creators, making vain attempts at autonomy, Chaos always abounds. Our lives must carry the tenor of humility and submission because we're merely reflections in the mirror.

I dare not usurp the authority of God and begin creating and defining myself, for that would be failing to order my life according to the reality of an image bearer.

When I was a child and teenager, my mom would always give me the same pep talk before I left the house. It went something like this: "You don't represent yourself; you represent me and your father and this family, so conduct yourself accordingly." In our current culture, everyone represents themselves. We live in a culture of expressive individualism—which is simply idolatry and an exaltation of the self as god—and it has created Chaos. We were primarily designed not to express our individuality but to reflect the glory of God and to represent His reign and the cultural values of heaven.

These three functions are imperative. First, reflecting the glory of God is the chief end of the human race. Second, we are all called to extend God's rule as ambassadors of *His* kingdom. Third, we must choose to reject the temptation of idolatry. We are images, not idols.

When we fulfill our function as image bearers dwelling within the temple of God, something ironic takes place: We ourselves become temples, and the Holy Spirit begins dwelling within *us*. Talk about a curveball. When we dwell within Him, He dwells within us.

When we humble ourselves and take our places in His temple, He exalts us to be temples of the Holy Spirit. When we order our lives according to the reality that we are image bearers, we then become more than image bearers—we become temples for the divine presence. When we dwell in His temple, He decides to dwell in ours.

Paul reminds us that this is the ultimate goal: to order our lives in such a way that we become resting places for the divine presence. He tells the church at Corinth in 1 Corinthians 6:19–20, "Do you not know that your bodies are temples of the Holy Spirit, who is in you, whom you have received from God? You are not your own; you were bought at a price. Therefore honor God with your bodies." This is the ultimate goal of those made in His image. Because *where* you rest will dictate *how* you rest. And God wants to rest in us.

When Genesis begins, it describes creation as chaotic and wild, and therefore the Spirit of God is hovering above the creation. Once God brings order, there's a significant transition. God shifts from *hovering above* to *resting within* the creation and walking in it during the cool of the day with Adam and Eve (Genesis 3:8). This may seem like a minor change for the modern reader, but to an ancient audience, this was a monumental shift. God will gladly hover above chaos but will rest within a space only when order has been sufficiently established. That is the shift we're after in this book. We want God to move from hovering above our chaos to resting within the ordered spaces of these flesh-and-blood temples we call our bodies.

We know firsthand that it is impossible to rest within chaos. We know that *where* we rest will determine *how* we rest. So, the ultimate question of functionality is this: Have we become proper dwelling places for the Most High God? Have we each made Him our resting place so that we might become a dwelling place for the divine?

If your life is full of chaos, then rest assured that God is hovering above you, speaking to you the same way He spoke to the creation in Genesis. He's not barking orders but gently whispering commands. And if you obey, order will begin to peek through the clouds of chaos, and you'll recover your true identity. You'll find rest in Him. And then He'll rest in you.

You simply have to trust and obey.

I promise you that order and rest are waiting on the other side of your obedience.

## Chapter 3

# Monsters in the Bible

> God created the great sea monsters (*tannin*)
> and every living creature that moves, of every
> kind, with which the waters swarm. . . . And
> God saw that it was good.
> —GENESIS 1:21, NRSV

> Whereas in Canaanite just as in Babylonian
> mythology, the dragon or dragons of *chaos*
> preceded the regnant divinities, in Genesis 1
> the monsters are created by God himself.
> —WILLIAM FOXWELL ALBRIGHT,
> *YAHWEH AND THE GODS OF CANAAN*

I grew up being taught that God made everything in creation perfect and then placed Adam and Eve in a perfect garden paradise. However, the Bible describes Yahweh's creation or garden temple as "good," never as perfect, and so many unmet and unrealistic expectations are rooted in this misunderstanding.

We assume that God will give us perfect spouses, perfect employees, perfect pastors, and perfect churches. But I've learned that instead of giving us perfection, God blesses us with good marriages, good employees, good pastors, and good churches that all require work and cultivation.

We suppose that since God is capable of perfection, He would surely express that perfection in what He creates, but God prefers good over perfect. He could have made a perfect garden for Adam and Eve, but perfection would've made them lazy. Instead, God creates a world for them that requires lots of work and lots of cultivation.

Again, Yahweh never calls anything in the creation narrative perfect; He calls everything He made good. Everything. No exceptions. That includes the tree of the knowledge of good and evil. And the crafty Serpent. And the fruit that Adam and Eve are forbidden to eat.

This is a curveball. There are elements of Chaos residing in God's temple, and it seems to be okay with God. There's some Chaos in the garden, yet God calls it good. That's odd, to say the least.

How can everything be good yet there's still Chaos? Because the right amount of Chaos is good for humanity. It gives us something to do, a mission to accomplish.

Genesis gives us a massive clue that Chaos is an intentional part of God's design for His creation. While describing the creation process, Scripture uses a very specific Hebrew word, *tannin,* which triggers only one image and one symbol: Chaos.[1]

We see the word *tannin* for the first time in Genesis 1:21:

God created the great sea monsters (*tannin*) and every living creature that moves, of every kind, with which the waters swarm. . . . And God saw that it was good. (NRSV)

You read that correctly. Great sea monsters.

*There are monsters in your Bible.*

And they're not a consequence of the Fall. They are not bad. They're an intentional piece of the cosmic puzzle. Oh yeah, and they're huge. They're larger than life and all over the biblical text.

The King James translates *tannin* as "great whales" in this verse.

The New International Version translates *tannin* as "the great creatures of the sea."

And the English Standard Version goes with "the great sea creatures."

These translations fall short and rob us of language that we need if we're going to understand the Bible according to its original context and learn how to navigate our modern Chaos. The NRSV and the NASB1995 nail it with their translations of *tannin* in Genesis 1:21, capturing the true meaning that the original audience would have had in their minds.

We find *tannin* present in Genesis because the biblical authors were products of their cultures. The creation account in the Bible was written not in a vacuum but rather in conversation with the creation accounts of Israel's neighbors. Like listening to one end of a phone call, we oftentimes approach Genesis completely unaware of the other creation accounts the biblical authors were responding to and engaging with. These authors borrowed language, symbols, and imagery from their neighbors, but they used familiar images to introduce radically different theology.

When the Babylonian creation story, known as the Enuma Elish, was discovered during an excavation of ancient Nineveh in 1873,[2] it changed everything about how we engage with the creation account in Scripture. For the first time, we could understand the worldviews and cultural contexts of the original audiences of Genesis. Uncovering the *world* that produced our Bible has helped us better understand the *words* on the Bible's pages.

Scholars and professors began to realize that the images and symbols in the Bible weren't exactly unique and that the world-views of Israel's neighbors had an inevitable influence on the symbols and images the authors employed as they communicated the truth of Scripture. The people of God were products of their culture; they didn't exist in a vacuum. However, their theology was radically unique.

Both Genesis and all the other major creation accounts in the ancient world included these *tannin,* which were synonymous with Chaos. The Israelites were very familiar with these creatures and undoubtedly would've known many of them by name. The *Lexham Bible Dictionary* plainly states that "the biblical writers regularly use the sea, serpents, and various sea monsters to represent forces of cosmic chaos that must be held in check by the power of Yahweh."[3] Simply put, *tannin* were the ancient mascots of Chaos. Dragons. Sea monsters. Wild beasts. Sea serpents. All symbols of unfathomable Chaos.

In Ugaritic, an ancient Canaanite language, the *tannin* was named Lotan. Lotan is depicted as a multiheaded dragon and was eventually destroyed by the storm god named Baal. Israel knew all about Lotan the Chaos Dragon and Baal. And Lotan even appears in the Hebrew Bible as Leviathan. Scholar and writer Dr. Jaap Dekker explained, "Leviathan is the Hebrew name of a dragon called *lītānu* (or Lotan) that occurs in mythological texts from the ancient city of Ugarit. He is one . . . who represents the power of the sea and against whom the god Ba'al must fight."[4]

The Babylonian *tannin* is named Tiamat[5] and is always depicted as a sea serpent or dragon. Tiamat is the goddess of the sea and is eventually destroyed by a Babylonian hero and storm god known as Marduk. Scholars unanimously agree that Babylonian mythology traced the origin of the universe to the struggle between these two forces: "Marduk the god of order and Tiamat the goddess of chaos."[6] Israel knew all about Tiamat the Chaos Dragon, and the Hebrew Bible follows this familiar pattern of juxtaposing Order and Chaos.

In ancient Egypt, the *tannin* was a giant serpent named Apep.[7] Apep had the titles Lord of Chaos, Serpent from the Nile, and Evil Dragon.[8] Eventually, this monster of chaos was defeated by Ra, the Egyptian sun god. Israel most certainly knew all about Apep the Chaos Dragon.

Every culture throughout the ancient Near East included *tannin* in their stories of origin or creation. These creatures and their stories permeated the ancient world—stories where the creator had to tame the Chaos monster to start the creation process.

And then a new narrative appeared. A foreign idea—that Yahweh, an omnipotent God, doesn't need to battle or tame anything to create the cosmos. Yahweh doesn't treat anything like His equal by fighting it. Yahweh has no barriers that impede His desire to create.

Genesis introduces a radically foreign concept: an omnipotent Creator.

This theological claim doesn't end in Genesis. When we look at the book of Revelation, it is the archangel Michael who is dispatched to make war against the great Dragon of Chaos known as Satan (12:7). At no point does Yahweh get off His throne to combat the Chaos Dragon. Because Yahweh has no equals, no rivals, and no competition. He is wholly other. Utterly transcendent. And worthy to be praised.

The storm god Baal personally conquers Lotan.
Marduk, the patron god of Babylon, slays Tiamat.
The sun god Ra combats Apep.

In pagan creation stories, it is the unique role of the chief deity to combat Chaos.

This is a prime example of how the biblical authors introduced radically different theological conclusions while employing the exact same symbols as their neighbors. Ancient Israel wouldn't have been shocked when they heard about a talking *tannin* who decided to unleash Chaos into the creation in Genesis 3. They had a category for talking serpents that still had legs and limbs: Chaos monsters.

Abraham didn't need to be taught how to offer a child sacrifice, and Moses's brother, Aaron, didn't need a tutorial on how to fashion golden calves as idols, because they were products of the ancient world they inhabited. In the same way, Israel didn't need an explanation for the *tannin* found in Scripture. The people of Israel were products of their culture, and they had categories for talking serpents and sea monsters and dragons. What may seem foreign to us would have been incredibly familiar to them.

The Chaos monsters in the cosmos prove that Adam and Eve have work to do, chaos to tame, order to spread, and adversity to overcome. Their role as image bearers gives them function, but the presence of the *tannin* gives them work and mission. And the talking *tannin* in the garden means they must be wise, alert, and on guard. The Garden of Eden is not a vacation. There's chaos to conquer, a wilderness to subdue.

God designed Adam to work in the garden. Genesis 2:15 says, "The LORD God took the man and put him in the Garden of Eden to *work it* and *take care* of it." It isn't immediately obvious to modern English readers engaging with an English translation of the Hebrew Scriptures, but this is priestly language.

To work it and take care of it. To tend it and till it.
To keep it ordered. To defend it from Chaos. To cultivate it.

Numbers 3:7–8 commands the Levitical priests to work in the temple and keep it.

In 1 Chronicles 23:32 (NRSV), the priests are tasked with working in the temple and keeping it.

Ezekiel 44:14 (NKJV) is all about the priests being charged to work in the temple and keep it.

To work it and to keep it. This is garden language. This is temple language. This is *priest* language.

Adam and Eve were designed to carry on the work that God started in the garden. Genesis 2:8 says that "the LORD God had planted a garden in the east, in Eden," which officially makes God the first gardener in history. He then commissions Adam and Eve to be priests and gardeners alongside Him in the garden.

Working it and keeping it. Tending it and tilling it.
Planting. Cultivating. Pruning. Harvesting.

Taming the Chaos. Keeping the Order.
Guarding it against the monsters and dragons and serpents
of Chaos.

I've fallen into some YouTube wormholes a time or two.
Carpet-cleaning videos have become a favorite, which naturally prompts the algorithm to suggest car-detailing videos.
Hours of my life have been spent down a good YouTube rabbit
trail, and one such time I stumbled into an entire corner of the
internet devoted to gardening. Urban farms. Vertical gardening. Aquaponics. Container gardening.

Regardless of the method, one thing is consistent: Gardening requires order. The wilderness is chaotic and messy, but
gardens are well-tended, highly organized, and ordered spaces.
God placed Adam and Eve in the garden to maintain the
Order He had established and to push the garden's boundaries
to slowly overtake the chaotic wilderness with the Order of
Eden.

What does it mean to be a priest in God's garden temple? It
means we're busy tending to the gardens of our souls so that
we can tend to the gardens of our world.

Internal gardening. External gardening. In that order.

Well-gardened souls are well-ordered souls, and that means
we embrace two things. First, we must place the members of
our souls into proper hierarchy. When the Bible talks about
the soul, it is referring to the mind, emotions (heart), and the
will. If the heart usurps authority and sits at the top of the
soul's totem pole, we become driven by our emotions—
unpredictable and unstable. The heart is a great servant but a
terrible leader. When the emotions take the lead, the soul is

full of chaos. In equal measure, when emotions are suppressed or ignored, the soul is full of chaos.

As a pastor, I know someone's soul is disordered when they cannot forgive offenses. Instead of rationally and logically applying the truth of Scripture to their life, they're led by their emotions and hold on to bitterness. They'll even use emotionally manipulative tactics to justify the sin of unforgiveness. The root of the issue isn't forgiveness; it's that their emotions have yet to be dethroned as the ruler of their soul.

The mind belongs at the top of the soul's hierarchy. Paul says that we are to be transformed by the renewing of our minds and that we are to adopt the mind of Christ (Romans 12:2; Philippians 2:5). When the soul is healthy, the renewed mind is empowered to lead the heart and the will. The rational, wise, strategic, intentional, and renewed mind takes the lead when the soul is ordered and healthy.

The will belongs at the bottom of the hierarchy because it is the seat of one's behavior. Once I surrender my mind and emotions to the lordship of Jesus, then I can use the power of my will to say no to sin and my flesh. We will dive deep into the importance of the will in a couple of chapters.

Mind. Heart. Will.

That's the proper hierarchy.

Anything else is chaotic.

Second, let's remember that we are made in the image of God. And God is a triune being—three in one. Father. Son. Spirit. The Trinity exists in perfect *shalom*. Most people have been taught that *shalom* means "peace," but that's not completely accurate. It means "wholeness and harmony."[9] All three members of the Trinity dwell together in wholeness and harmony. The Son never disagrees with the Father. The Father never disagrees with the Spirit. The Spirit never disagrees with the Son.

When Adam sinned against God, he experienced brokenness for the first time. Brokenness is the opposite of *shalom*. In the modern Christian tradition, we tend to focus only on Adam's fragmented relationship with God, but he experienced other layers of brokenness too—in his relationship with Eve and, moreover, in himself. Internal brokenness. For the first time, Adam's spirit, soul, and body experienced incongruence and fracturing.

A well-ordered soul is a soul where the mind, heart, and will have been brought back into harmony and wholeness—into *shalom*. In the early sixteenth century, Christians were trying to find a word that communicated the process of how God restores our oneness, wholeness, and harmony. They began to call Jesus's work on the cross the moment that we were made "at one" again.

At one. Which is how we get the word *atonement*. Jesus's work on the cross was designed to heal the fractured reality of our disconnection not only from God but also from others, as well as the internal disconnection from who we were designed to be that we have all felt in our souls. Any atonement theory that fails to address internal brokenness is incomplete.

A well-gardened soul is an ecosystem where all the members of the soul work in congruent harmony. Where one's mind agrees with one's heart. Where their spirit agrees with their flesh. Where their will agrees with the divine presence resting within them. Chaos of the soul happens when internal conflict and turmoil create unrest within a person.

Gardening one's soul is a process. Conquering chaos within. Conquering chaos without. Planting the seeds of Eden and growing the fruit of the Spirit from the soil of a well-tended soul.

We need more missional Christians who see themselves as gardeners. We've had preachers and evangelists who create converts but who aren't themselves healthy or whole. We need gardeners. Gardeners create disciples and cultivate greatness within others. They care more about health than growth because health inevitably leads to growth. Gardeners exemplify health and wholeness and plant the seeds of God's Order within the Chaos of our world. We need these men and women who have embraced the Order of God, have applied it to their own souls, have experienced the complete atonement of God, and are billboards of biblical *shalom*.

It is not shocking that when Mary Magdalene went to the tomb on that first Resurrection Sunday, she encountered the risen Lord, the High Priest, the second Adam, and "did not realize that it was Jesus . . . thinking he was the gardener" (John 20:14–15).

Mary was so wrong yet so right.

Jesus wasn't the literal gardener hired to tend and till that property, but He sure was and still is the figurative gardener who tends and tills the soil of our souls. He's the sower who announces to His workers that the harvest is plentiful yet the gardeners few. Mary didn't recognize whom she was talking to, but she somehow grasped the vocation He was fulfilling and properly saw Him as gardener, priest, and second Adam.

We, too, are gardeners. Tending to the soil of our souls. Harvesting souls where Jesus has planted seeds. Yielding to the pain of His pruning. And standing guard to protect our souls and our world against the mayhem that seeks to plunge us back into Chaos and threatens God's good Order.

Yahweh doesn't dare dishonor Himself by treating anything in the created order as an equal. Yahweh has no rival. No equals. So, who will combat, conquer, and crush the Chaos clearly present within the cosmos?

Yahweh allows Adam and his bride, Eve, to come face-to-face with the agent of Chaos because Eden isn't a vacation. This couple has a garden to defend and an enemy to crush.

Now let's turn our focus to the inevitable collision between God's agents of Order and the agent of Chaos who's in the Garden of Eden with them.

## Chapter 4

# A Dragon in the Garden

The LORD God said to the serpent, "Because
you have done this,

> "Cursed are you above all livestock
>     and all wild animals!
> You will crawl on your belly
>     and you will eat dust
>     all the days of your life."

—GENESIS 3:14

Not cursed to go on its belly until the end of
the story (Genesis 3:14), the serpent (*nakhash*)
should be understood as a dragon.

—L. MICHAEL MORALES, *EXODUS OLD AND NEW*

I was on the edge of my seat, mouth agape, for at least three
straight minutes as Leonardo DiCaprio survived being mauled
by a wild grizzly on the big screen. The scene was so captivat-
ing that Leo won his first and so far only Oscar based in large
part on his unforgettable battle with this wild bear.

Humanity is obsessed with stories like this. The film, in case
you're unaware, is called *The Revenant,* and its director, Alejan-
dro Iñárritu, reportedly watched over a hundred videos of bear

attacks just to film this scene with the necessary bone-crunching force and brutality. And it worked—the scene is iconic.

But there's a reason it worked: because struggles like this resonate with us. Humans love creating and consuming stories about our cosmic battle with beasts and monsters.

*Godzilla. Jaws.*
*Anaconda. King Kong.*
*Cocaine Bear. Monsters, Inc.*
*Smaug.*

The list is endless.

Whether we're killing werewolves or warding off vampires, humans are obsessed with battling beasts. Monsters have been the primary adversary in the tales humans have told since we started telling stories. This isn't a modern Hollywood phenomenon. This is not a trend. It's ingrained in our nature. Most ancient civilizations also told stories about monsters and beasts. The oldest written tale like this is *The Epic of Gilgamesh,*[1] which you probably learned about in high school since it provides the bedrock of human mythology and literature. If not, maybe you saw Gilgamesh depicted in Marvel Studios' *Eternals.*

What's *The Epic of Gilgamesh* about? What were humans obsessed with in 2000 B.C.?

The oldest written story is about humans defeating monsters. Gilgamesh must defeat Humbaba—a fire-breathing dragon demon—and faces off with multiple beasts and monsters throughout his epic journey to attain immortality.

Before humans were writing, we were drawing stories in red pigment on cave walls. Limestone caves on the island of Sulawesi in Indonesia house the oldest-known human narrative drawings. And what do those drawings depict? Humans hunting pigs and buffalo.[2] Humans defeating beasts.

Whether we're drawing in caves, writing in cuneiform, or filming on camera, we tend to tell a strikingly consistent story. It's the story of our epic battle against the beasts and monsters that threaten the survival of the human species. And it's no coincidence that this is the primary plot conflict of the biblical narrative—defeating the Beast that defeated us. The first announcement we get in Scripture of Jesus's assignment centers on this plot conflict. Yahweh promises that one of Eve's children will finally get revenge on the Serpent that deceived humanity.

That is what we are all wired for. It is the common dream that drives our species. We all want to kill the beasts, slay the dragons, overcome the monsters, and restore peace and order to the temple of creation. We're all standing in front of our own trees of knowledge, facing off with our own beasts and trying our best to defeat them. Which means the original story of Adam and Eve has something to teach us.

When most modern audiences read of humanity's temptation in the Garden of Eden, we imagine Satan as a small, slithering garden snake. The only issue with this is that it probably doesn't line up with what the Bible's original audience envisioned. Crawling on its belly is a wildly illogical punishment for a snake who's already doing so. Could the text of Genesis be begging modern readers to ask a question that would've been obvious to an ancient audience? I think so.

What would the people of Israel have pictured in their minds when Moses told them about a serpent in the Garden of

Eden whose consequence for deceiving humanity was a loss of legs and limbs? What symbol would've most likely occupied their minds?

They would've imagined Adam and Eve standing before a dragon.

That's right—a dragon. A serpent with limbs is a dragon.

But why does that matter? Why is this seemingly small detail worth knowing? Why should we care what image was in the minds of the original audience?

Because images aren't just images. They are symbols that must be interpreted, and those interpretations contain ancient wisdom for the modern reader. The Bible paints a consistent and compelling picture for us of what kind of beast stood before Adam and Eve in the garden temple of Eden.

The prophet Isaiah tells us about an interesting creature named Leviathan and uses interchangeable words to describe this monster of the sea. Isaiah 27:1 reads:

> The LORD will punish with his sword—
>> his fierce, great and powerful sword—
> Leviathan the gliding serpent,
>> Leviathan the coiling serpent;
> he will slay the monster (*tannin*) of the sea.

The NRSV has a slight variation that's worth noting:

> The LORD with his cruel and great and strong sword will punish Leviathan the fleeing serpent, Leviathan the twisting serpent, and he will kill the dragon (*tannin*) that is in the sea.

This one verse uses the words *Leviathan, serpent, dragon,* and *monster* interchangeably and synonymously. The Bible is laying out breadcrumbs, inviting us back into Eden to behold the Beast that stood before Adam and Eve.

Multiple passages throughout the Scriptures make this same link between serpents and dragons or *tannin*. Amos 9:3 discusses serpents as if they are creatures that live in the chaos waters. Here is what God says through this prophet:

> Though they hide from my eyes at the bottom of the sea,
>     there I will command the serpent to bite them.

For many modern readers of Scripture, it can be difficult to comprehend how the language of the Bible is so fluid. In today's world, serpents are serpents and dragons are dragons. But in the ancient world, these images were completely interchangeable because they represented the same idea—*Chaos.*

The book of Revelation describes Satan using the exact same imagery as the prophets Isaiah and Amos. John depicts Satan not as a slithering garden snake but as a mighty dragon:

> Then another portent appeared in heaven: a great red dragon. . . . The great dragon was thrown down, that ancient serpent, who is called the Devil and Satan, the deceiver of the whole world—he was thrown down to the earth, and his angels were thrown down with him. (12:3, 9, NRSV)

Great dragon. Ancient serpent. The devil and Satan. Deceiver of the whole world.

I think John has in mind the Leviathan passages of the Hebrew Bible as well as Genesis 3 as he's writing Revelation 12, and he's not the only ancient mind to connect these dots. Early church father Saint Jerome of Stridon did too:

> The Jews say that God has made a mighty dragon called Leviathan which lives in the sea; and when the ocean recedes, they say it is because this dragon is turning over. But let us say that this is the dragon that was cast out of Paradise, that beguiled Eve, and is permitted in this world to make sport of us.[3]

Jerome states matter-of-factly that the dragon named Leviathan tempted Eve.

If the Serpent that stood before Adam and Eve in the garden was a dragon, that changes everything—because dragons were the universal mascot for Chaos in the ancient world.

If temples represent Order, then dragons symbolize Chaos.

Which means Adam and Eve were deceived by a Chaos monster and thus became partners in bringing Chaos into the cosmos. So often we simply conclude that Genesis 3 is the moment that sin entered our world, but I think it may be helpful to introduce some ancient language into our vocabulary. The ancients would've seen Genesis 3 as the moment that the untamable force of Chaos broke into our culture.

This is helpful because it reframes our thinking: Anxiety isn't a sin, but it's a form of chaos. Poverty isn't a sin, but it creates chaos. Suffering and sickness aren't sin. But the reason God tells Job about Leviathan when He finally responds is because suffering can easily produce chaos.

While growing up, I used to imagine that the mysterious

creature that appeared in the Garden of Eden was a venomous viper or deadly boa constrictor. But recently I've been picturing the satanic Serpent as a massive sea dragon, and I think that's a bit more consistent with the rest of Scripture.

Once the original audience found out that the dragon in the garden could speak, the debate would be over. Those freed nomads wandering around the desert would've heard Moses's creation story and made the connection that Adam and Eve were being tempted by a Chaos monster—which changes everything.

It means that Satan was luring Adam and Eve into partnering with Chaos. That Satan's Chaos had limits until humanity unleashed it into the cosmos. That we're the real monsters. That the monster in my mirror is a bigger threat than the monster under my bed. That Chaos is not only out in the cosmos but also taking up residence within us.

It means we are the Chaos monsters.

And you want to know what's scarier than Leviathan? A world full of humans that have become the Chaos.

Humanity was safe so long as Chaos was external, in the cosmos. So long as it was outside us, it was okay. But once the Chaos got inside us, we became the monsters, and so the Bible beckons us back to Order:

Tame the beasts.
Defeat the monsters.
And crush the Chaos Dragon in the garden.

This should give us a brand-new perspective on the promise that God makes to Adam and Eve once the Dragon has been cursed in Genesis. In Genesis 3:15, God says:

I will put enmity
   between you and the woman,
   and between your offspring and hers;
he will *crush your head,*
   and you will strike his heel.

This moment is the very first promise of a Savior in the Scriptures. Scholars refer to this as the *protoevangelium,* which comes from the Greek words *protos* meaning "first" and *evangelion* meaning "good news" or "gospel." This initial announcement and description of Jesus in the canon of Scripture should carry a lot of weight. In the same way a first impression of someone leaves an indelible mark, this is something like our first impression of Jesus. And here's what's very clear:

Jesus will be a dragon killer.

Jesus will crush the head of the *tannin* who's responsible for deceiving Adam and Eve. Jesus will inevitably battle, combat, and crush the main antagonist of this unfolding drama. He will avenge us. And since snakes, dragons, and beasts all represent Chaos, Jesus will be crushing Chaos and creating Order.

This is the obvious conclusion that any reader of Genesis would make if they were aware of the cultural and historical context surrounding the imagery that symbolized Chaos in the ancient world. However, somewhere along the way, we lost connection with the ancient world, so we've failed to see Jesus this way. But now that we know what we're looking for, I promise you that we will approach the Gospels looking for a dragon-taming, Chaos-crushing divine Warrior. And the best news is that Jesus crushes Chaos *for us* and provides a road map for how to maintain and sustain the victory He won over the dragon of Chaos during His three years of earthly ministry.

It will take us a while to get to the Gospels, but I promise, once we get there, to present Jesus according to this initial revelation of His assignment tucked away in Genesis 3:15.

For now, let's keep unpacking the chaos imagery that permeates Genesis so we can uncover the Bible's wisdom for crushing Chaos.

## Chapter 5

# Rolling in the Deep

> The earth was a formless void and darkness
> covered the face of *the deep,* while a wind
> from God swept over the face of *the waters.*
> —GENESIS 1:2, NRSV

> Nowhere in the seven-day creation scheme of
> Genesis 1 does God create the waters; they
> are most likely *primordial.*
> —JON D. LEVENSON, *CREATION AND THE PERSISTENCE*
> *OF EVIL,* EMPHASIS ADDED

For five days in June 2023, the world watched with bated breath as the news broke that all communication had been lost with the Titan submersible, which was created and operated by the underwater exploration company known as Ocean-Gate. At 8 A.M. on Sunday, June 18, the vessel started what should've been a two-hour descent to the wreck of the *Titanic,* which lies at a depth of thirteen thousand feet,[1] where the pressure is four hundred times greater than at sea level. Needless to say, humans can't survive at these depths. But that sure doesn't stop us from diving beyond our capacity.

By Sunday evening, this story was an international news

headline, and personally it's all I talked about until the US Coast Guard announced on Thursday that the Titan submersible had imploded due to the pressure of the ocean depths. Everyone aboard most likely died instantly.[2]

As I watched everything from random TikTok posters and YouTube influencers to professional news anchors and journalists, one theme kept emerging: This whole catastrophe was completely avoidable. What led these five people to believe that they could handle the pressure of descending that deep in a vessel made of carbon fiber?[3]

I know exactly what voice prompted these five Titan passengers to descend into depths beyond their capacity. It's the same one we've all heard—the voice that deceives us into believing we can handle the pressure of the chaos that inevitably accompanies our sin or circumstances. You thought you'd be fine living up to the pressures that your in-laws, your spouse, or a pastor has placed on you, but you can't, and you're drowning and you feel like you're imploding. Yes, they're happy. But you're drowning and nobody knows.

Some people drown in the chaos of sin. But others of us drown in the chaos of people pleasing. We implode due to the pressures of everyone else's expectations of us.

The major you chose in college. The size of the diamond on your wife's finger. The guest list for the wedding. How fast you guys had kids. The square footage of the house you chose to buy. The car you drive. The hours you have to put in at work to afford the life you've chosen. Did you really make those decisions because they bring glory to God and contentment and fulfillment in your life? Or because it's what everyone expected of you?

You weren't designed to live like this.

Living beyond your means. Drowning in debt.
Buying Christmas gifts for people you see once a year.
Making everyone happy.
Impressing neighbors you don't even know.
Sinking deeper and deeper into numbness and anxiety.

The Dragon convinces us that we can survive at depths he knows will crush us.

A number of us are drowning in the chaos of people pleasing. And some of us actually *are* drowning in the depths of sin.

Sin always convinces us that we have everything under control and can stop whenever we'd like. But the reality is that although at first we begin playing with sin, eventually sin will be the one playing with us. That's the chaos of sin. It drags you into the depths and drowns you. It overwhelms you. And before you know it, you've lost all control.

It started with you looking at a website. But now you're drowning in a porn addiction.

It started with one DM or text message. But now you're drowning in an affair.

It started with you downloading one app. But now you're drowning in gambling debt.

Sin deceives us into believing that we're in control of our own chaos, but the truth is that you cannot control the force of Chaos. Only God can control it, and only He can rescue you. You need a lifeguard far stronger than you to rescue you from the raging waters and the great deep.

If you're drowning in chaos, whether from sin or other people's expectations, God has a lifeline. The force of Chaos has been present since the very beginning, yet God has a proven track record of rescuing His creation from Chaos, and He can rescue you. This is how the creation account of Genesis begins—with God pulling creation out of the watery depths of Chaos. The Bible has wisdom to get you safely back to shore; we just need to interpret Scripture well to extract that wisdom.

Let's examine Genesis 1:2, which reads, "The earth was a formless void and darkness covered the face of *the deep,* while a wind from God swept over the face of *the waters*" (NRSV).

When ancient readers thought of the starting point of creation, they would have imagined not a vast, empty nothingness but a vast, raging ocean of Chaos. An unmistakable buzzword in this verse, the Hebrew word *tehom,*[4] would have immediately alerted them that this Genesis story was about Order and Chaos. In Genesis 1:2, we have references to water—twice.

*Tehom* is translated as "the deep."[5]
*Mayim* is translated as "waters."[6]

This creation account is telling us about two types of related chaos: the raging floodwaters and the deep ocean abyss. According to the Brown-Driver-Briggs lexicon, the word *tehom* refers to the "abyss" or "primeval ocean,"[7] and *The Lexham Bible Dictionary* asserts that it should be understood in connection to the ancient Near Eastern cultures where it originated.[8]

The *tehom* and the *tannin* were interconnected realities in the ancient world. The Chaos monsters (oftentimes simply referred to as sea monsters) were the embodiment of Chaos in the minds of ancient readers and writers, but the sea was the realm of Chaos. What is the *tehom*? It's the home of the *tannin*. Leviathan is a monster of the deep, a monster of the *tehom*. And this connection between *tannin* and *tehom* runs from Genesis all the way to Revelation.

When John describes the new heaven and the new earth, something is intentionally missing from the equation. Revelation 21:1 reads like this: "Then I saw a new heaven and a new earth; for the first heaven and the first earth had passed away, and the sea was no more" (NRSV). Let that sink in. The sea is so indistinguishably linked with Chaos and Leviathan that John simply tells his audience that Yahweh has finally re-created the heavens and the earth and now there's no more sea. For John and his audience, eternal paradise is a creation with no sea. Tell me that Chaos has been destroyed for good without telling me that Chaos has been destroyed for good. No more sea—no more Chaos.

All of this explains why Jesus shows up in the Gospels calming the raging storms on the Sea of Galilee and walking on the surface of the deep with Peter. No wonder the disciples place their faith in Jesus when He does so—they understand that only Yahweh has control over this kind of Chaos. The disciples see that the same power that pulled creation out of Chaos in Genesis is at work in the person of Jesus. We will explore these stories based on their Old Testament context in later chapters. For now, back to Genesis.

The *tehom*, or the deep, represents Chaos.
The *tannin*, or the sea monsters, represent Chaos.
The *tohu va-vohu,* or desert wilderness, represents Chaos.
And darkness represents Chaos.

All these elements are in the opening chapter of Genesis. One might assume that since God is moving the creation from Chaos to Order, He would completely erase and eliminate these elements. However, God doesn't eradicate these clear forms of Chaos.

He gives Chaos *boundaries*.

God brings forth land and creates a boundary to separate the dry ground from the chaos of the deep. He plants a garden and marks off a boundary to clearly distinguish between Eden and the surrounding wilderness. He speaks the light into existence and separates "the light from the darkness" (Genesis 1:4), creating a boundary between the order of the day and the chaos associated with the darkness of night. God's creative process is marked by both separation and boundary establishment. Separation and boundaries—these are key elements of order. Conversely, a lack of boundaries is a mark of chaos.

So far in our journey, we've talked about various elements of divine Order that are traceable in Genesis. We've covered sequence, hierarchy, rhythm, and function. Now it's time to tackle separation and boundaries.

Creating healthy boundaries with my mother has been the most difficult task of my adult life. I love my mom more than words can articulate. She's the person who's responsible for taking me to church as a kid, using the Bible to teach me to read, and prophesying that I'd be in ministry. In a very real way, I owe my mother a debt I could never repay. She's a modern-day Hannah who knew her son was called by God and marked for ministry, so she nurtured that gift in me and placed me in the kind of Christian environments that were conducive to those seeds growing and bearing fruit. I cannot exaggerate this enough—without the influence of my mother,

I don't know that I would be in ministry. She stewarded my young mind and spirit in a way that set me up to have a life-long love of the Scriptures and vibrant faith in Jesus.

However, relationships are complicated and layered. As I mentioned, my father has battled with a drug addiction my entire life, and so often when there's an addict in the scenario, the other family members team up for protection and safety. So, I grew up with my mother as my teammate and ally. It was me and her against the world. Whereas my father was unpredictable and chaotic, my mother was consistent. And I was grateful for at least one parent who was always present. Every sports event. Every speaking engagement. Every performance. My mom and I formed a tight bond because nothing binds people together like trauma, and my dad was a tornado of trauma as I was growing up.

Then I got married. And I had to genuinely wrestle with the reality of the Bible's teaching that "a man leaves his father and mother and is united to his wife, and they become one flesh" (Genesis 2:24). I had to break an attachment with my mother that was forged in the chaos of trauma. Instead, I needed to bond with my wife and unite with her and become one flesh. I was used to being bound together in chaos as a survival mechanism. Yet now I needed to be bound with my bride in covenant—not to survive but to thrive. And I wish I could say that I dove into the pool of marriage and immediately impressed my wife with my ability to swim through the waters of covenant love. But the truth is, I drowned those first few years.

I was drowning in my mother's expectations of our relationship. In the need for my mom's approval. In the same chaos that forged our bond in the first place. In my mom's unrequested and oftentimes unwelcome advice and feedback. In anxiety—utterly overwhelmed.

And then my therapist threw me a much-needed lifeline, sharing a term that truly helped me. He taught me that my mom and I had developed surrogate spouse syndrome and that we had an enmeshed relationship—essentially over-bonding. My mother and I had become *too close.* I didn't even know that "too close" was a thing. But I learned that in an enmeshed relationship, individual agency and freedom get lost. And I was forced to come to grips with the reality that boundaries don't prohibit intimacy; they actually make intimacy healthy and appropriate. So, I had to begin implementing painful boundaries with a woman who had built her entire life around ensuring I'd be successful.

To say that I felt guilty would be the understatement of the decade. I felt like a terrible and ungrateful son for implementing boundaries that clearly hurt my mom's feelings. But I was desperate to escape the chaos, and my soul needed order. And order requires separation and boundaries. Conversely, a lack of boundaries is a mark of chaos. So, I chose health over comfort and a bond of covenant over a bond of trauma. Did I do everything right? Did I get it perfect? No. I wish I could go back and tweak certain decisions. But overall, I stuck to my guns and fought to uphold boundaries that I knew would create order and peace in my life and crush the chaos that was crushing me.

Separation and boundaries are designed to function as a pair. When I was newly establishing boundaries with my mother, all I had the capacity for was separation. So, our communication was incredibly limited because I had to fully become an independent person. Once I had truly separated, it

was time for boundaries. And unlike the common mispercep-
tion, a boundary is designed to facilitate a relationship, not
prohibit one. A boundary functions as the rules of engagement, and the health of the boundary will determine the health
of the relationship. I learned this the hard way: Just because a
relationship is *close* doesn't mean it's *healthy*. And for so much
of my life, I had asked only whether my mom's and my relationship was close, never whether it was healthy.

As someone who has tried my best to intentionally move
from chaos to order and wrestled with the fear and guilt of ruin-
ing a meaningful relationship, I promise you there's hope and
grace. I'm a living witness that the God of Order will help you
walk on the water, and even if you fail, He won't let you drown.

Whether you're drowning in the chaos of people pleasing or
in the chaos of sin, God's grace will pull you out of the depths
of the *tehom* and rescue you from the undertow of the raging
floodwaters. Moreover, no matter what kind of chaos you're
drowning in, you need to establish healthier and stronger
boundaries in your life. Because people pleasing is the result of
not establishing good boundaries with others and sin is the
result of not establishing good boundaries with yourself.

The imploding pressure of people pleasing.

The raging and dizzying chaos of sin.

The solution for both is healthy boundaries.

After a few initial meetings with the therapist who helped
me navigate my relationship with my mom, he recommended
that I read Henry Cloud and John Townsend's iconic book titled *Boundaries*. And he gave the simplest definition of a
boundary—it's recovering the power of your no.

Being able to say no to the people in your life when necessary is healthy and the mark of someone with an empowered

will. If a person has a no in their heart but a yes still finds its way out of their mouth, they're lying. Jesus commands His followers in Matthew 5:37 to "let your 'Yes' be 'Yes,' and your 'No,' 'No'" (NKJV). So, a healthy boundary with others is marked by an ability to say no.

And so is a healthy relationship with yourself. Saying no to sin and temptation and the desires of the flesh is proof that you have a healthy boundary with yourself. And boundaries are a nonnegotiable element of order.

In the same way that God separated the waters and created a boundary between the dry ground and the *tehom* so that life could flourish and thrive, He desires to stand over the chaos of your life and create separation, boundaries, and order. But He won't violate your will. He's waiting for you to finally trust Him. And when you do, He'll be there to rescue you.

Like I said at the beginning of this chapter, the untimely and unfortunate deaths of the five individuals aboard the Titan submersible were completely avoidable. The job of science is to wonder whether things are *possible*, but it's the job of religion to consider whether ideas are *wise*. Wisdom would've stayed at the surface of the ocean. Wisdom knows its limits. Wisdom would forgo visiting a wreckage from the past and romanticizing history. Wisdom always chooses the future because wisdom is *foresight*. And we'll unpack that in the next chapter.

PS: The *tehom* will make another appearance. These fountains of the great deep are going to burst forth during the Flood narrative, and it may make us doubt the character of God. So, Genesis carefully shows its audience that the *tehom* is the original state of creation. We'll dive into the Flood story later, but the foundation we've laid here will serve us well when we get there.

# Chapter 6

# Drowning in the Darkness

*Darkness* is synonymous with *chaos.*
—DOMINIC RUDMAN, "THE CRUCIFIXION AS CHAOS-
KAMPF," EMPHASIS ADDED

I'm an incredibly *indoorsy* person. Yes, I practically coined that term. I like indoor malls, movie theaters, air-conditioning, coffee shops. Restaurants, swank hotel lobbies, a good spa.

If a hobby involves being outside, count me out. Hiking. Running. Hunting. Bird watching. Fishing. No, thank you. Take me to a mall. Please.

The *most* outdoorsy thing I've done in the last couple of years is wander around the Bass Pro Shops location fifteen minutes from my house. I love that place. It's like being outside, but you're inside. Love it. You can probably imagine my instant angst and misery when I found out that one of the graduation requirements at Gordon College was to complete a wilderness survival excursion in the Adirondack Mountains of upstate New York.[1]

I tried to get out of this in every way imaginable. Backpacking through the wilderness of the Adirondacks for twelve days is as close to torture as I've ever experienced in my life.

We read the Bible outside. We ate our meals outside. We

slept outside. We brushed our teeth outside. We worshipped outside. We went to the bathroom outside.

We did everything outside for twelve days.

And the final day of this dreadful experience was a twenty-four-hour "solo." We individually got dropped off in the woods with a tent, tarp, Bible, notebook, and thirty-to-forty-pound backpack. The purpose of the solo was to spend uninterrupted, distraction-free time with God and to hear His voice for ourselves.

I heard absolutely nothing from God.

It started raining, and of course I set up my tarp incorrectly. And by the time the sun went down, I was soaking wet and wrapped in a wet sleeping bag, in a tent, in the middle of nowhere, covered in thick darkness. I couldn't see my hand in front of my face. And I barely slept because I kept hearing noises that I couldn't identify, which made me utterly terrified.

When I rejoined my group, I learned that one of my friends had encountered a bear. I vowed to never go out in the dark wilderness again—but failed to read the fine print on a study abroad program I participated in a couple years later. So, I found myself studying at the Uganda Christian University for an entire semester, only to be blindsided by the news that we were required to complete a one-week "rural homestay."

Middle of nowhere, Uganda.

No running water.

No electricity.

Living with host families.

For a whole week.

I was utterly devastated.

My first night after being dropped off in Kapchorwa, Uganda, I had to go to the bathroom (which was a pit latrine, aka an outhouse) in the middle of the night. I woke up to thick darkness. I opened my eyes and saw nothing. Looked around, saw nothing. I could feel the darkness. I used my hands to find the door and glided them along the walls until I finally made it outside.

Everything was going relatively okay—until I walked straight into a cow. You cannot make this stuff up. The cow freaked out, and everyone in the house woke up. Every single member of my host family came outside to check on me and the cow, and my host dad led me by the hand to the pit latrine. How this man could see I have no idea.

Upon graduating from Gordon College, I had accumulated a lifetime of outdoorsy activities, and since graduating, I have been indoors. With HVAC and mood lighting. But I'll never forget the darkness of being in that tent all night in the Adirondack Mountains or the depth of darkness as I stumbled around outside in the yard searching for a bathroom.

I'll never forget the fear I felt as the noise of the wilderness proliferated outside my tent, the dizzying effect of being disoriented by darkness, and the desperate desire for light and sight. I'll never forget the utter lack of confidence in every step I was forced to take or the chaos of drowning in darkness. I'll never forget walking right into that cow, in the middle of the night, simply because I couldn't see what was directly in front of my face. These stories from my college experience illustrate the final two symbols that the biblical authors use to talk about chaos: darkness and the desert wilderness.

The longer I'm in ministry, the more I watch people walk straight into all kinds of chaos that end up bringing unnecessary pain into their lives. I've witnessed people walk straight into adultery, addiction, debt, and toxic relationships. It's like they couldn't see what they were walking directly toward.

I can't count how many times I've said to a couple, "These behavioral patterns will lead straight to a divorce. That is the path you're on." I can see how they're five years away from a divorce because of the road they're traveling down, but they're blind to it. They're living in darkness.

When I was twenty-two years old, my pastor at the time gave me the most succinct definition for wisdom I've ever heard. We were at a restaurant called Not Your Average Joe's, and I ordered the mustard-crusted chicken. This moment was over fifteen years ago, yet it's just as vivid in my mind as mental snapshots from last week. Pastor Matt looked at me and said, "Manny, do you know what wisdom is?" I shook my head no. And he responded, "Wisdom is foresight."

Wisdom is *foresight*. The ability to make decisions based on a vision of the future as opposed to the feelings of today. Wisdom is the ability to see around the corner. Wisdom prevents us from making shortsighted decisions.

*Foresight.*

It's the ability to see that tomorrow's destruction is typically camouflaged as today's desires. And that Satan's goal is to get us to make decisions without considering consequences, ripple effects, or the domino effect on our daily rhythms. Therefore, it's not shocking to me that the Bible equates darkness with chaos and that the chaos of Genesis 1:2 isn't fully encapsulated by the sea or the raging flood; it also includes the darkness of the wilderness:

> The earth was *without form and void (tohu va-vohu),*
> and *darkness (hosek)* was over the face of *the deep*

*(tehom)*. And the Spirit of God was hovering over the face of *the waters (mayim)*. (ESV)

So far on our journey to decode the biblical images and symbols of Chaos, we've explored the *tehom* and the *mayim* as well as the *tannin*. We've also touched on the wasteland or desert of *tohu va-vohu,* which we'll look at more in the next chapter. However, there is one more Chaos symbol that describes the creation *before* God began His ordering work:

The darkness (*hosek*).

Darkness is so foundational to the chaotic condition of the cosmos in Genesis 1:2 that the very first thing God does to move creation from Chaos to Order is found in verse 3: "God said, 'Let there be light,' and there was light." God speaks the light into existence—which makes light a fundamental element for establishing order and for building our lives according to the Order of God revealed in creation.

In John 1:3–5, it is written that through Jesus "all things were made; without him nothing was made that has been made. In him was life, and that life was the *light* of all mankind. The light shines in the darkness, and the darkness has not overcome it."

In John 8:12, Jesus said, "I am the light of the world. Whoever follows me will never walk in darkness, but will have the light of life."

I don't think Jesus is simply a metaphorical light. John says that Jesus holds creative life power, and when we look at Genesis, the creation process is dependent on that very first act—dispelling darkness, giving it a boundary, and thereby crushing the Chaos. Before there was ever a sun, moon, or stars, which were all created on the fourth day of creation, there was Light. Because there was Jesus, the Son of God.

When John describes the new creation in the book of Revelation, he says there's no more darkness or night, which is John's way of showing us that Chaos has been completely crushed. Not simply given a boundary, but crushed. John's Revelation tells us that "the city does *not need the sun or the moon* to shine on it, for the glory of *God gives it light,* and *the Lamb is its lamp.* The nations will walk by its light, and the kings of the earth will bring their splendor into it. On no day will its gates ever be shut, for there will be *no night* there" (21:23–25).

John explains that God is the source of light for this new creation, which isn't new. It's a callback to the first three days of creation, where the Lamb was the lamp as the cosmos awaited the creation of the sun, moon, and stars.

God established light to subdue the chaos of darkness because everything that brings life grows in the light. And everything that multiplies chaos grows in the darkness.

Lies and shame.

Fear and depression.

Sin and secrets.

All of these grow in the dark.

However, life, order, and wisdom flourish in the light.

Light is so interconnected with creation and order that John said Jesus carried a form of life that was "the light of all mankind" (John 1:4). "*That life was the light*" is what John writes. Light is life, which means darkness is death.

Life, light, and order naturally function together. And death, darkness, and chaos function in a trio as well.

Without light, wisdom and foresight are impossible to attain. Another word that we could use to talk about foresight is *vision*.

The Bible tells us that there's a direct link between vision and restraint. Proverbs 29:18 teaches this principle. Different translations vary slightly, so I'll give you two of my favorites:

> Where there is no *vision,* the people are *unrestrained.* (NASB1995)

> Where there is no *revelation,* the people cast off *restraint.* (NKJV)

This is a simple yet profound lesson: A lack of vision and foresight leads to a lack of discipline and restraint. And a life without discipline or restraint is a life of Chaos. Simply put, when there's *darkness,* there's no *discipline.* And when there's no discipline, there's darkness.

Maybe you've diagnosed yourself as someone who doesn't have much discipline. Keep in mind that discipline is the result of a life that is full of vision and foresight. I promise you, it's a whole lot easier to practice discipline *today* when you're living for *tomorrow.*

This connection between chaos and darkness on one hand and light and wisdom on the other can be found in Paul's writings. Read how Paul links these ideas in Ephesians 4:18: "They are *darkened* in their *understanding* and separated from the life of God because of the *ignorance* that is in them due to the *hardening of their hearts.*"

Darkened. No understanding. Ignorant. Hard-hearted. This is chaos language.

This is the chaos of Genesis 1:2, but it's happening within

us. The storm of Chaos within you and me looks like darkness, foolishness, ignorance, hard-heartedness, blindness, and shortsightedness. Paul writes to the church in Rome, "Although they knew God, they neither glorified him as God nor gave thanks to him, but their *thinking* became *futile* and their *foolish hearts* were *darkened.* Although they claimed to be *wise,* they became *fools*" (Romans 1:21–22).

Futile thinking.

Darkened understanding.

Foolish hearts.

Blindness.

Ignorance.

Again, this is chaos language. Chaos *within* us.

And the same way that the Creator brought forth light in Genesis, He brings Light into our souls. He brings Order, and that Order is Light. And that Light brings vision, foresight, wisdom, and clarity.

## Chapter 7

# Adapting to the Desert

> In the ancient Near East there were two
> primary, equally powerful symbols of chaos.
> One was the primeval flood or ocean,
> frequently portrayed as a dragonlike monster;
> the other was *the barren desert,* sometimes
> portrayed as a dreadful land beast.
> —BERNARD F. BATTO, *SLAYING THE DRAGON,*
> EMPHASIS ADDED

It's obvious that humans cannot live in the sea. However, humans *can* live in the wilderness. And humans *can* live in darkness. Which makes the dark desert wilderness an exceptionally interesting realm of Chaos throughout the biblical narrative. There's a natural temptation to make the desert or darkness our home. We can survive in the darkness, and we can survive in the desert, but these are not ideal environments for humanity.

By the way, in the mind of an ancient Hebrew, the terms *wilderness* and *desert* were synonymous and interchangeable. One of my go-to Bible encyclopedias confirms that "the most common Hebrew term for desert means 'wilderness.'"[1]

The Dragon has convinced most of us that the desert wilderness we're living in is really a garden. There are trees. There's fruit. There are rivers. Garden spaces and wilderness spaces share so much in common. So, we compromise and settle—out in the wilderness—and we lie to and convince ourselves that the desert is a suitable home for our souls.

Adam and Eve were designed for a garden, for a highly ordered environment, but because of their choice to partner with Chaos, they got sent into the realm of Chaos—the wilderness. Yet they weren't *designed* for Chaos. And whenever humans get placed into environments we weren't designed for, we begin to adopt coping strategies. And the better those coping strategies become, the more we convince ourselves that the wilderness is our home. We even begin to prefer it. This is the deception of the desert, combined with the deception of the human heart: convincing ourselves that our chaos is normal because order seems beyond our reach.

*Forbes* released an article years ago titled "Why 'Dysfunctional' Families Create Great Entrepreneurs." In it, Melody Wilding makes a compelling case that the majority of entrepreneurs are experts in navigating the chaos of start-ups because they had to navigate the chaos of dysfunctional families. She builds on the observations and research of Steve Blank, a professor and entrepreneur who coined the term *dysfunctional family theory* to describe successful business leaders with a knack for navigating chaos.[2]

Blank posted an entry on his blog in 2009 titled "Founders and Dysfunctional Families." In an "admittedly very unscientific survey," he observed that between 25 and 50 percent of the successful entrepreneurs he talked to "self-identified as coming from a less than benign upbringing"[3]—that is, "household environments marked by conflict, fighting, harsh discipline, little to no expression of love and substance abuse."[4] Both Wilding and Blank essentially claim that the trauma of these entrepreneurs' childhoods made them immune to chaos and wired them with an exceptionally high threshold for stress, anxiety, change, inconsistency, and the lack of predictability that comes with being an entrepreneur.

This is proof that chaos shapes us. Humans are wired for survival, so we learn to adapt and cope with our chaos. However, just because we've adapted to the darkness or the desert doesn't mean we're healed from the chaos that got us kicked out of the garden. Before ending his blog post, Blank writes:

> The dysfunctional family theory may explain why founders who excel in the chaotic early phases of a company throw organizational hand grenades into their own companies after they find a repeatable and scaleable business model and need to switch gears into execution.
>
> The problem, I believe, is that repeatability represents the extreme discomfort zone of this class of entrepreneur. And I have seen entrepreneurs emotionally or organizationally try to create chaos—it's too calm around here—and actually self-destruct.[5]

Once the company moves into a season of order, these founders get very uncomfortable and bored because they're wired for chaos. They miss the chaos. They prefer it. Because chaos has become their comfort zone and the wilderness has become their home. They've learned how to see in the dark, and the light hurts their eyes. The desert has deceived them, and their coping mechanisms have now become the habits they can't kick. These entrepreneurs don't just survive the chaos; they create it. And that is the problem.

This is an issue not only with entrepreneurs but also with all of Adam and Eve's descendants—it's universal. Just because we learn to survive the desert and cope with chaos doesn't mean we're thriving in the gardens we were designed for. It's very easy to mistake coping and surviving with thriving.

There was a time when my wife and I were watching wilderness-survival reality shows on TV, and I just want to point out a simple truth: When we talk about living in the wilderness, we describe that reality as *survival*. Some of the wilderness experts would build elaborate forts and set up complicated apparatuses and systems for cooking food, washing clothes, and guarding against wild animals. But it doesn't matter how fancy the makeshift shelter or how elaborate the system for catching food—it is still survival. I have been thoroughly impressed by some of those wilderness experts, but it's still *survival*. There is no thriving in the desert or flourishing in the wilderness. There are only short-term wins and long-term ramifications when we attempt to live in survival mode permanently.

God led the people of Israel out into the desert for a purpose and a season. They were never meant to remain in the chaos for forty years. However, the chaos of Egypt had forced them to adopt coping mechanisms that kept them stuck in the desert way longer than originally planned.

I can relate more than I care to admit to the dysfunctional family theory as described by Steve Blank. The dysfunction of my childhood has made me an incredible start-up entrepreneur, but I can also see a track record of self-sabotage and chaos creation when things are too peaceful and too orderly.

Early in my marriage, I would throw the proverbial hand grenade into the dynamics of the relationship and later be so confused by my own behavior. I'd start arguments. Rock the boat. Be overly confrontational. Why? Because things felt too peaceful and confrontation was the only way I felt comfortable establishing intimacy. I was practicing survival mechanisms that work in the chaos of the wilderness, and I had to unlearn the lessons that chaos taught me. I had to come to the painful realization that I was no longer a victim of chaotic circumstances but was now the one creating the chaos. Like an addict, I was hooked on chaos and needed to get free.

Maybe you can relate.

Maybe chaos has become your culture.

Maybe your eyes have adjusted to the darkness.

Maybe you self-sabotage your peace.

Maybe *coping* with chaos has turned into *creating* chaos.

And maybe you want out.

Out of the desert.

Out of the darkness.

Out of the chaos.

I'm a living witness that God can take wild people and make gardeners out of us. You aren't trapped in the chaos of your family of origin, your environment, or your own interpersonal patterns. You can learn anything, and you can unlearn anything. You learned, practiced, and perfected habits of chaos. And you can learn, practice, and perfect habits of order.

Recently, I was introduced to the world of Frank Herbert's Dune series and the movies based on the books. I was immediately hooked—layered character development, thoughtful plotlines, and creative world building all make for a particularly attention-grabbing media franchise. The main protagonist, Paul Atreides, winds up on Arrakis, a desert planet known for its particularly harsh climate. This is the setting for most of the novels and movies.

While Paul Atreides is an immigrant to Arrakis, there's a people group known as the Fremen whose entire culture and way of life are adapted to fit the desert—including the clothes they wear, the way they walk, and even the color of their eyes. Although Arrakis is a fictional planet, the Dune series brilliantly portrays what happens when our coping strategies become our culture. This represents many of us. Our ability to cope with chaos has evolved into the cultural codes we live by. We're almost incentivized to remain in dysfunction because returning to the Order of the garden will require that we unlearn the coping mechanisms that have now calcified into habitual patterns.

The idea of desert wilderness is right there in the opening words of Genesis, but we have to return to the ancient path to see the breadcrumbs.

Again, Genesis 1:2 reads:

The earth was formless and empty (*tohu va-vohu*), darkness was over the surface of the deep, and the Spirit of God was hovering over the waters.

When most English versions translate the Hebrew words *tohu* and *va-vohu*, they opt for phrases like "formless and empty" or "without form and void." However, these buttoned-up translations of this verse miss the power and accuracy of the original language and thus the original message to the ancient audience.

Maybe there's a different way to understand the phrase *tohu va-vohu*. It is used three times in the Hebrew Bible, and we'll look at the other two together.

Isaiah 34:11 reads:

> God will stretch out over Edom
> > the measuring line of chaos (*tohu*)
> > and the plumb line of desolation (*vohu*).

The NRSV puts it this way:

> He shall stretch the line of confusion (*tohu*) over it,
> > and the plummet of chaos (*vohu*) over its nobles.

Neither the NIV nor the NRSV translates *tohu* and *vohu* as "formless," "empty," or "void" in this verse. Instead, they've chosen words like "confusion," "chaos," and "desolation."

Let's look at Jeremiah 4:23:

> I looked on the earth, and lo, it was waste (*tohu*)
> > and void (*vohu*);
> > and to the heavens, and they had no light. (NRSV)

*Tohu va-vohu* tends to get translated as "a formless void"[6] because the idea behind the Hebrew term is barrenness. When a woman is barren, her womb is empty, but something deeper is also happening. A barren womb has yet to become a life-sustaining environment. It isn't simply void of life; it is currently incompatible with sustaining life—in the same way that a chaotic world is incompatible with supporting life.

A barren landscape isn't literally empty or void. It has a story to tell. A story of a wilderness waiting to become an ordered garden or a garden that has experienced the desolation and deformation of chaos. One of my favorite Hebrew lexicons defines the term *tohu va-vohu* as "land reduced to primaeval chaos."[7] Again—a landscape with a story to tell.

So, when Scripture describes the pre-creation state as *tohu va-vohu,* it most likely means it was desolate, chaotic, and wild. We should be imagining a vast desert or wilderness in our minds. This is precisely why Yahweh carved out an ordered garden to be the antithesis of the chaotic wilderness.

Genesis 1:2 is showing us three forms of Chaos in a single verse: the waters of the abyss, the untamed wilderness, and the utter darkness. Which makes sense, because Yahweh directly addresses these three realms of Chaos in the creation account of Genesis. First, He deals with darkness and establishes light. Second, He deals with the chaotic waters so that dry ground can emerge. Last, He plants a garden in the East, in Eden, so humans aren't in the wilderness.

The children of Israel were supposed to journey through the desert en route to the land God wanted to give them—Canaan, the land of promise. God had always intended the desert to be part of their journey, but instead of just passing through, they got stuck in the desert and eventually died there. Like the Fremen of the Dune series, the Israelites adapted to the desert. They got comfortable. And when Yahweh finally commanded them to leave the desert behind and invade the land of Canaan, they refused. Because the chaos of the desert has a gravitational pull. It doesn't let us go easily.

The biblical authors describe the land of Canaan using garden imagery and symbols. It was lush, fertile, and fruitful—a new Eden of sorts. A garden for God's people who were stuck wandering in the wilderness. But a garden is a difficult space to occupy if you've become comfortable in the desert.

In the last seven chapters, we've explored the dominant images and symbols for Chaos and Order throughout the Bible. The Bible relies heavily on symbols and images to communicate abstract concepts and ideas. And since order and chaos tend to fit in that category, we must interpret the symbols to glean the wisdom.

Order is rest. Temples. Image bearers. Gardens. Light. Wisdom. Life.

Chaos is wandering. Dragons. Beasts. Sea. Wilderness. Desert. Darkness. Death.

We've worked hard to enter the ancients' world and learn their language. Now we turn our focus to unpack how the Bible actually uses these images and symbols to help its readers—you and me—dispel the darkness, enter the rest, cultivate the garden, escape the desert, reflect God's image, tame the beast, and crush the Chaos.

# TAMING
# THE
# BEAST

## Chapter 8

# You Son of a Beast

Sin is crouching at your door; it desires to
have you, but you must rule over it.
—GENESIS 4:7

Of all the monster flicks that Hollywood cranks out, no sub-genre seems more popular than zombie movies and TV shows.

*The Last of Us. World War Z. Train to Busan.*
*The Walking Dead. Army of the Dead. Dawn of the Dead.*
*I Am Legend. The Girl with All the Gifts.*

If there's a story we're obsessed with even more than hu-mans overcoming monsters, it's humans overcoming humans who have become monsters. Zombies are monsters but still human. Hybrids. Misfits. Mutants. All infected with chaos. Technically alive but also dead. Human, but not fully. Human, but not according to their original design.

In the TV show *The Last of Us,* a fungus turns humans into zombies. The series derives its name from the fact that this fungus will most likely wipe out the human population. As I watched the show, I immediately realized that this is what hap-pened with the first of us, not the last of us. Adam and Eve were deceived by a Chaos monster, became hosts to a virus called Chaos, and then became monsters themselves.

They became hybrids. Misfits. Mutants. Still human, but not fully alive. Human, but a new and scary kind of human.

When the Chaos Dragon stood before Adam and Eve and deceived them into becoming hosts of Chaos, they lost what was most precious to them—God's ideal design for their humanity. In trying to be their own gods, they became beasts of impulse and instinct, and the remainder of Genesis begs us to ask this question:

What does it mean to be truly human?

When we find the answer to that question, we find the key to establishing Order and conquering Chaos. By recovering our humanity, we recover Order. But by continuing to live as beasts, we multiply Chaos. So, let's dive further into Genesis and find out how to be truly human by slaying the beasts living within us and taming the Chaos that surrounds us.

God lays out the primary plot conflict of Genesis and the entire Bible when He curses the Serpent by declaring:

> I will put enmity
>> between you and the woman,
>>> and between your offspring and hers;
> he will crush your head,
>> and you will strike his heel. (Genesis 3:15)

First, there will be conflict between the Serpent and Eve, which makes sense because the Serpent has just deceived Eve. However, God says there will be conflict in a second grouping: between the Serpent's offspring and Eve's offspring.

Which is really odd and confusing. Because who are the

Serpent's offspring? Are we talking about baby snakes? About demons? These are the natural questions this story poses. Let's follow the breadcrumbs and read the text with ancient eyes so we can recover Order and tame the Chaos.

Genesis 2:19 in the ESV tells us that "out of the ground the LORD God had formed every beast of the field." And then verse 20 says that "the man gave names to all livestock and to the birds of the heavens and to every beast of the field" (ESV).

"Every beast of the field"—that precise phrasing is important. Not the beasts from the soil or the beasts from the ground.

Nope. Beasts of the field.

Genesis 3:1 says, "The serpent was more crafty than any other *beast of the field* that the LORD God had made" (ESV). When God curses the Serpent, we read this phrase again: "Cursed are you above all livestock and above all *beasts of the field*" (verse 14, ESV). The Bible wants us to meld these images together in our minds—beasts and fields—so that we cannot see one without the other.

Genesis 4:8 tells us that "Cain said to his brother Abel, 'Let's go out to the field.'"

Every time we've seen the word *field,* we've also seen *beasts.* So, when Cain invites his brother into the field, we should already know that we're about to encounter a beast. This verse continues by saying, "While they were in the field, Cain attacked his brother Abel and killed him." There it is. The beast of the field has appeared.

Cain is the beast of the field, the offspring of the Serpent. Cain fails to crush and subdue the power of Chaos, the rage and violence boiling within him. Instead, Cain is crushed by Chaos and in turn crushes the life of Abel. Adam and Eve were deceived by a beast, then became beasts. And now they've given birth to a beast—a son that behaves like a beast of the field. This is Chaos multiplied.

The Bible doesn't spell this out for us but rather assumes that we are following the breadcrumbs and interpreting the symbols. It established a pattern and turned the field into a symbol—a place that represents beasts and beast-like behavior. Then the Bible showed us a field and asked us to find the beast. This is how Scripture communicates. It shows; it rarely tells.

Another clue to what's happening with Cain is found in God's advice to him. God says, "Sin is crouching at your door; it desires to have you, but you must rule over it" (Genesis 4:7). That's some incredibly intentional wording. Sin is *crouching*.

Crouching is an interesting thing for sin to be doing. Predators crouch before attacking their prey. Beasts crouch. Animals crouch. Monsters crouch. The text is telling us that the Serpent from the previous story is back. The same beast that deceived Adam and Eve is here again, hiding in plain sight, crouching and ready to attack Cain. Sin is crouching and is in position to turn Cain into an agent of Chaos, just like his parents.

Genesis teaches us that it is very easy for humans to slip into beast mode and begin to exhibit animal-like behavior. You allow the beast to take you into the field and rob you of your humanity

> every time your temper gets the best of you,
> every time your lusts and your passions rule you,
> every time your instincts overtake your intentions,
> every time your primal urges aren't conquered,
> every time gossip and negativity erupt from your heart and
>     flow from your lips.

Let me ask you some hard questions regarding your humanity: Do you practice Sabbath, or has your work turned you into a restless beast? Are you a workhorse, or are you a human?

Do you have possessions, or do your possessions have you? Abel had possessions. Cain's possessions had him, which means they became idols. Has the lust to hoard wealth and material things turned you into an insatiable animal? Are you a monster? A machine? Or a human?

Does comparison consume you? Cain must have been consumed with Abel's life. Are you focused on your own life, or do you secretly desire to have the lives of the people you envy?

Back when I was a youth pastor, I had the privilege of being the chaplain of the Hillside High School football team. I got to be in the locker room with the boys, and we had a weekly Bible study where I spoke to the whole team. At some point, I started doing an abstinence challenge with the boys—whether they were Christians or not I challenged them to participate. Without fail, every year when I announced the abstinence challenge at the top of the season, a large group of boys would say things like this:

"Pastor Manny, we're regular dudes, though; we gotta have sex."

"Nah, Pastor Manny, we're human. Sex is a part of life."

"That's our masculinity, Pastor Manny. You're asking us to give up our masculinity."

Without exception, every young man who resisted my abstinence challenge appealed to his humanity. Every time. They used words like *human* and *masculine* and *normal* to make the case that their loose sexual behavior was acceptable. And every year, I asked them one question in return:

"Who told you that acting like animals made you more human?"

What the boys on the Hillside football team called normal human behavior actually bred more chaos and confusion. Their sexual behavior robbed them of God's ideal design for humanity, and my heart broke for them. So, for six straight weeks every fall, I taught those boys what it truly meant to be human and therefore what it meant to be men. My abstinence challenge always worked because I first restored to them the dignity of being truly human. I taught them that they were created to rule their flesh, not be ruled by it.

My lesson to the boys on the Hillside High School football team is the same lesson God wanted to teach Cain. When God tells Cain that sin is crouching at his door and that Cain needs to rule over it, He is reminding Cain of the original design of all humans—that every human is endowed with the authority to rule over Chaos, over primal urges, and over the beasts of the field.

In Genesis 1:26, God says, "Let us make mankind in our image, in our likeness, so that they may rule." Why were we made in the image and likeness of God? To rule over the beasts. To rule over the wild animals. Whether those beasts are within or without.

God reminds Cain that he still bears the divine image and therefore has the power to tame the beast within him. The divine image in us may be marred and cracked, but regardless, because we're made in the image of our Creator, we still have the power to tame beasts and conquer Chaos. I have found that long before we figure out how to rule over the beast, we first have to believe that we *can*.

Just as God reminded Cain, I want to emphasize that you

are not a beast. You were created to rule. You were created to master yourself. You were created to exercise self-control. You were created to rule over your heart and mind instead of letting them rule over you. You were created to overcome temptation. You were created in the image of God to conquer the beasts and crush the Chaos.

## Chapter 9

# Hagar and Her Wild Ass

> You are from your father the devil, and you
> choose to do your father's desires. He was a
> murderer from the beginning and does not
> stand in the truth, because there is no truth in
> him. When he lies, he speaks according to his
> own nature, for he is a liar and the father of
> lies.
>
> —JOHN 8:44, NRSV

When we get to the New Testament, Jesus affirms that we should be looking at Cain and Abel as symbolic children of either the woman or the Serpent. In John 8, Jesus confirms that the Dragon is a father and His preaching acts as a spiritual paternity test—revealing the hearts of His audiences. The lying, murdering Chaos Dragon from Genesis has certainly fathered offspring, and we're going to continue to track the genealogy of those children so we can retain and restore our humanity and thus establish Order.

The next set of brothers that the Bible focuses on is Ishmael and Isaac. And now that we know where to look for the Serpent's offspring, it should be easier to find them.

The Bible describes Ishmael in fascinating terms. In Gene-

sis 16:12, the Angel of the Lord gives Hagar a prophecy about
him:

> He will be a wild donkey of a man;
>> his hand will be against everyone
>> and everyone's hand against him,
> and he will live in hostility
>> toward all his brothers.

The NRSV says that Hagar's son, Ishmael, will be "a wild ass
of a man," and I just think that's a funny translation. Hence the
title of this chapter.

A wild donkey of a man. Sounds a lot like a beast of the
field, an offspring of the Serpent.

The Bible never outright calls Cain or Ishmael beasts, but it
depicts them in those terms. And since the Bible uses looping
images and repetition to show us what's important, we should
pay attention because the image of the human-beast hybrid is
officially looping and repeating. Remember the pattern.

If the son of the Serpent is a predator, the son of the woman
must get offered as prey. Is there anywhere in the narrative
where Ishmael's brother, Isaac, gets offered as a sacrifice?

Yes—yes, there is. Genesis 22:1–3 says, "Some time later
God tested Abraham. . . . God said, 'Take your son, your only
son, whom you love—Isaac—and go to the region of Moriah.
Sacrifice him there as a burnt offering on a mountain I will
show you.' Early the next morning Abraham got up and loaded
his donkey. He took with him . . . his son Isaac." This is not
only a test for Abraham—it is just as much a test for Isaac.
Abraham is an old man. Isaac is a strong, able-bodied teenager
or young man.[1] If Isaac had wanted to get away, I don't see how

Abraham would've been able to stop him. At some point on their trek up the mountain, Isaac becomes aware that something isn't normal:

> Isaac spoke up and said to his father Abraham, "Father?"
>
> "Yes, my son?" Abraham replied.
>
> "The fire and wood are here," Isaac said, "but where is the lamb for the burnt offering?"
>
> Abraham answered, "God himself will provide the lamb for the burnt offering, my son." And the two of them went on together. (verses 7–8)

The two of them went on *together*. At the beginning of the story, Abraham took Isaac. Now Isaac knows what's going on and has to decide to journey together with his father.

This is a picture of Jesus and the Father. This is a foreshadowing of Gethsemane. The Father willed the sacrifice to occur, but the Son had to be willing to do it *together* for the Cross to be just and not cruel.

The Angel of the Lord calls to Abraham from heaven and forbids him to kill Isaac. This was just a test—and all parties have passed. Abraham sacrifices a ram in Isaac's place, and everyone descends the mountain and goes to see a therapist. LOL.

Cain and Ishmael were the offspring of the Serpent. Abel and Isaac were the offspring of Eve. A pattern is emerging.

> Abel's blood was spilled and sacrificed.
>
> Abel kept flocks that he freely sacrificed to God.
>
> Abel, the son of Eve, foreshadows Jesus—the ultimate son of Eve.

Isaac was placed on the altar as a sacrifice to God.

Isaac was replaced at the last minute by a ram caught in a thicket.

Isaac, another son of Eve, foreshadows Jesus—the ultimate son of Eve.

Isaac finally got down off the mountain (and out of therapy) and married a woman named Rebekah. Isaac and Rebekah had twin boys, and the details should immediately grab our attention. Genesis 25:25 tells us, "The first to come out was red, and his whole body was like a hairy garment; so they named him Esau." Esau was born as a red, furry beast. And if that weren't enough breadcrumbs, just read the Bible's next description of Esau in verse 27: "Esau was a skillful hunter, a man of the field" (ESV).

Esau was "a man of the field"—a beast who couldn't control his appetite and allowed his hunger for food to be his downfall. The Bible shows. It rarely tells. This description is how the Bible communicates that Esau is the offspring of the Serpent. And beasts don't handle being hungry very well, which is why fasting will become one of the ultimate marks of practicing humanity throughout the Scriptures. Animals are obedient to their appetites. Humans are not enslaved by their stomachs but obedient to God.

As if these clues weren't sufficient, the Bible tells us that when Jacob, Esau's twin, finally betrayed his brother and deceived his father, he had to put on animal skins to get his dad to believe that he was Esau. The text says that "Rebekah took the best garments of Esau her older son . . . and put them on Jacob her younger son. And the skins of the young goats she put on his hands and on the smooth part of his neck" (Genesis 27:15–16, ESV).

Jacob needed the skins of young goats on his hands and neck if he stood a chance of impersonating Esau. You have to respect how artful the Bible is with these details. It'd be easy to just tell us that Esau was a beast and the offspring of the Serpent. But the Bible would rather show us that and allow us to uncover that revelation for ourselves.

So, we know the pattern. If Esau is the offspring of the Serpent, his twin brother, Jacob, must be the offspring of the woman, right? Not so fast. If there's one thing the Bible loves more than creating a pattern, it's breaking the pattern. When Genesis 25:26 recounts Jacob's birth, we get a suspicious detail. It says, "After this, his brother came out, with his hand grasping Esau's heel; so he was named Jacob." The Hebrew word for "heel"[2] in this verse is also used in Genesis 3:15, where the Serpent is cursed. There, God promises that the ultimate son of Eve will crush the Beast's head but that the Serpent "will strike his heel." The crafty Dragon turned Serpent is a heel striker, and Jacob is a heel grabber.

When Jacob puts on Esau's garments and Rebekah places the goatskins on his hands, it's a confirmation that Jacob, like his brother, is also a beast. Both young men are sons of the Serpent.

The Bible loves establishing patterns and then breaking them to get our attention. With Jacob and Esau, we have a plot twist. It seems the Serpent has won. But God is never in a catch-22, so He launches a plan to restore Jacob's humanity— and to ultimately transform him into a son of Eve named Israel.

Sometimes the Bible shows us how humans lose their humanity and chronicles their descent into animal-like tendencies. But then sometimes it shows us that God can take a heel-grabbing, deceptive, and crafty beast of a man like Jacob and restore his humanity through an epic journey. Which gives me a whole lot of hope because I, too, have failed to tame the beast and conquer the chaos. So have you. But we're not beyond redemption. God is in the business of not only ordering our world but also ordering us. He is in the business of taking broken humans like us and making us whole.

It's easy to be impressed by singular moments of transformation—like Jacob wrestling with the Angel of the Lord and God changing his name to Israel. However, that climactic moment of change was preceded by a journey where the wise and patient God of the Bible worked behind the scenes to guide Jacob down the road of redemption. In the next chapter, we're going to trace Jacob's steps and walk down that path so that we, too, can recover our humanity.

## Chapter 10

# A Ladder in Luz

You will be called *priests* of the Lord,
   you will be named ministers of our God.
   —ISAIAH 61:6

Then Moses went up to God, and the Lord
called to him from the mountain and said,
"This is what you are to say to the descendants
of Jacob and what you are to tell the people of
Israel: . . . Out of all nations you will be my
treasured possession. Although the whole
earth is mine, you will be for me a kingdom of
*priests* and a holy nation."
   —EXODUS 19:3, 5–6

You are a chosen people, a royal *priesthood,* a
holy nation, God's special possession, that
you may declare the praises of him who called
you out of darkness into his wonderful light.
   —1 PETER 2:9

After pulling a snaky move on his dad and brother, Jacob is
on the run. Scared for his life. Alone and isolated. He has fled

in the hope that his uncle Laban can provide him with refuge and the comfort of family. As a fugitive and foreigner, he stops for the night and has a dream while lying in the middle of a town named Luz in the middle of nowhere. He's done absolutely nothing to deserve a divine visitation. Yet that's exactly what happens, because the grace of God often shows up when we least expect it and least deserve it.

The Bible tells us that "taking one of the stones there, [Jacob] put it under his head and lay down to sleep. He had a dream in which he saw a stairway resting on the earth, with its top reaching to heaven, and the angels of God were ascending and descending on it" (Genesis 28:11–12). With a rock for a pillow, Jacob lies down under the stars and dreams of a ladder that connects heaven and earth. Angels are ascending and descending on this cosmic escalator, and then God promises Jacob that He won't forsake him, that his descendants will be great, and that he'll possess the land (verses 13–15).

By the way, in some scholars' view, all the language in this story hints that Jacob saw the kind of tower the builders at Babel were constructing—a ziggurat.[1] Whether it's a staircase, ladder, tower, or ziggurat, it is a bridge between heaven and earth. A portal between the realm of the Divine and the realm of humans.

This sounds a lot like temple and priest language. Temples are portals between heaven and earth. Priests are bridges between God and humankind. (Incidentally, ziggurats were very similar to temples in the ancient world.)

Why does Yahweh show Jacob a ladder? Because He's calling Jacob to be both a priest and a ladder. Yahweh is attempting to turn this beast into a priest. But this is far more than a personal calling. Yahweh doesn't give Jacob a vision only for himself. Nope. He shows Jacob a vision for a family, a tribe, and a nation. Because hyper-individualism creates Chaos.

Humans are designed to live for one another. We are designed to find identity from the community. Only by adopting a vision for his family could Jacob become accountable to a vision for himself. And only by his finding personal discipline would the vision for the family come to pass.

This is a beautifully symbiotic relationship. Jacob sees a vision for an entire family dedicated to being a portal for the divine presence to invade earth. And that family will turn into a tribe and then ultimately a nation—called to be a ladder that connects God with the nations of the earth. This is the message echoed through the rest of Scripture.

In Exodus 19, when Moses and the descendants of Jacob enter into covenant with Yahweh, God makes it clear that they "will be for me a kingdom of priests" (verse 6). God's goal is for an entire nation—not just the Levites—to be priests, bridging the gap between Yahweh and all the nations of the earth. The prophet Isaiah later echoes the exact same vision (Isaiah 61:6).

And it all starts with Jacob—a runaway snake sleeping on a rock in the middle of nowhere. A man trapped in Chaos. Amid tribalism, jealousy, competition, and sibling rivalries, Yahweh wants Jacob to envision a new way of being human. A priestly way, a temple way, a bridge-building way.

We know that this vision of a ladder isn't bound to a physical structure but actually reveals the vocation and identity of a person because Jesus talks to Nathanael about Jacob's ladder in John 1:51: "Very truly I tell you, you will see 'heaven open, and the angels of God ascending and descending on' the Son of Man."

Why are the angels ascending and descending on Jesus? Because the ladder Jacob saw was always a person. The ideal human. The ultimate bridge. The great High Priest.

How did God recover Jacob's humanity even though he was a snake? In the same way He recovers our humanity: by showing us the ideal human. Jesus. The comprehensive model for this new way of being human in the world.

Jacob saw Jesus. And a true vision of Jesus changes everything.

I've mentioned that Jacob most likely saw a ziggurat in his dream. This is important because Yahweh is intentionally using the image of the tower of Babel here. These two texts from Genesis are in conversation with each other.

The builders of Babel make it clear why they're constructing this tower. Genesis 11:4 tells us that they declare, "Come, let us build ourselves a city, with a tower that reaches to the heavens, so that we may make a name for ourselves; otherwise we will be scattered over the face of the whole earth."

The key phrase here is "that we may make a name for ourselves." Names represent identity and significance, and these tower builders are desperately trying to provide that for themselves. This is peak individualism and arrogance. This is idolatry. It is humanity's vain attempt at usurping God's authority to create identity and significance. However, identity and significance can only be given by God. Only God can make a name for someone. Only He could make Abraham's name great. And only He could change Jacob's name to Israel. God opposes the kind of humans who think they can name themselves and then promote the names they've chosen.

I wonder if you notice another key word in this passage about the tower of Babel: The tower builders want to build this ziggurat so they won't be "scattered." Scared of being restless wanderers like Cain, they're building a *temple* so they can have a home and have rest for their souls. They want to be *home*. They want to be *settled*. So, they attempt to make a counterfeit temple to attract and achieve the rest that they desperately desire. But no true rest can be achieved from counterfeit temples because our rest depends on God's rest, and He doesn't rest in counterfeit temples. He doesn't rest in our idolatry.

Here's the irony: Genesis 11:5–9 shows that instead of attracting rest, the builders get God's attention, and He brings confusion to their languages. They are inevitably scattered by the very chaos they brought on themselves.

Since the tower builders are creating a counterfeit temple, they're essentially counterfeit priests. Our culture is full of those. I remember the first time I went into Urban Outfitters and saw chakra stones casually on display for purchase. I came to the conclusion that the store was officially an access point for the occult. And the friend who teaches you how to use those chakra stones you picked up at Urban Outfitters is a counterfeit priest.

That mentor who's teaching you about negative energies—counterfeit priest.

The family member who's into horoscopes—counterfeit priest.

The co-worker who's introducing you to your zodiac sign—counterfeit priest.

The girl who taught you how to smudge—counterfeit priest.

The guy who introduced crack cocaine to my father—counterfeit priest.

Counterfeit priests help people access the spiritual world in an attempt to find rest for their souls, yet they bypass the one true God. Counterfeit priests build counterfeit temples. If you have people like this in your life, I am not suggesting that you write them off, but don't give weight to their "spiritual" ideas or teaching.

One last detail about these tower builders: They are actually scared of another flood. Genesis 11:3 provides some seemingly random details about the building supplies they chose to use for this tower temple.

The NIV says that "they used brick instead of stone, and *tar* for mortar."

The NRSV says, "They had brick for stone, and *bitumen* for mortar."

Tar and bitumen.

I wonder if tar and bitumen are random details or intentional breadcrumbs left by the author so we can connect some dots. I wonder what else was built out of tar and bitumen . . .

When God tells Noah to build an ark (that functions as a temple), He instructs him to waterproof the vessel, which makes a ton of sense. Yahweh directs Noah in Genesis 6:14 to "make rooms in the ark, and cover it inside and out *with pitch (kō·per)*" (NRSV).

Waterproof it with pitch. Seems wise. I'm just going to copy and paste the definition for *pitch* here from a Hebrew lexicon:

4109 II. כֹּפֶר (kō·per): n.masc.; ≡ Str 3724; pitch, i.e., a water seal substance for large vessel (Ge 6:14+), note: it is not clear what the organic material was composed of, possibly *tar or some other bituminous material.*[2]

The Babel tower builders were waterproofing their counterfeit temple. They craved the best of both worlds. They wanted to live without God, but they wanted the assurance that comes only with having God in our lives. They desired to live life-styles of *chaos* but still demanded the benefits of *order*.

Jacob falls asleep in Luz and gets a vision for a new way to be human in an individualistic and tribalistic world.

Here's what's wild: Pentecost—the day the church was birthed—was a reversal of Babel.

First, the believers were in an upper room. Elevated space like a tower.

Second, they were gathered in unity. All speaking one language.

Third, they received power to speak in the languages of foreigners.

At Babel, God confused the people's languages as a test.

At Pentecost, God gave people a supernatural gift to understand one another's languages as a test. He wanted to see whether Jesus's disciples would remain in the chaos of tribalism and individualism or embrace the beauty of diversity and bridge building.

There's one final detail that connects Babel to Pentecost.

Why did the builders want to construct a tower reaching to the heavens again? The key phrase is in Genesis 11:4: "Otherwise we will be scattered."

Of course they didn't want to scatter. Safety and security come from settling and building. Building with people who look like us, talk like us, and think like us. Scattering is scary, and settling creates predictability and safety.

The newborn church of Jesus Christ didn't want to scatter either. They almost started building a tower instead of a temple.

But then Acts 8:1 tells us, "On that day a great persecution broke out against the church in Jerusalem, and all except the apostles were scattered throughout Judea and Samaria." Did you notice something about where the church of Jesus was scattered to? *Judea and Samaria.* Those locations sound familiar.

Immediately before Jesus ascended to heaven, He commissioned His followers and told them that they will carry the good news of the gospel to some specific locations. Acts 1:8 records Jesus as saying, "You will receive power when the Holy Spirit comes on you; and you will be my witnesses in Jerusalem, *and in all Judea and Samaria,* and to the ends of the earth." After Jesus said this, "he was taken up before their very eyes, and a cloud hid him from their sight" (verse 9).

The church was commanded to take the gospel message to "all Judea and Samaria," yet Jesus's followers got comfortable in Jerusalem. They got stuck in their ethnocentric comfort zones. They didn't want to scatter into unknown territory and mingle with foreigners. So, God used an unfortunate circumstance to get His children where He had commanded them to go.

Why did God use persecution to scatter them? So they wouldn't get stuck in their tribal, mono-ethnic enclave or Jewish echo chamber but would instead fulfill their call as bridges and ladders and priests.

Here's what this story is asking you to consider:

Would Jacob build another tower or build a temple?
Will we build towers of Babel or temples of the Holy Spirit?
Will we build bridges for God or attempt to build towers to
    reach God?

Each represents a very different way of being human.

Jacob sees a vision of the kind of human God has called him to be. He leaves Luz knowing that he is called to be not a heel grabber but a ladder that Yahweh can use to deliver grace and shalom to humanity.

At this point, Jacob could've turned around and acted like the priest God had called him to be by returning home and reconciling with his brother, since reconciliation and atonement are the main functions of being a priest.

Unfortunately, that's not what happens. It would take Jacob twenty years to finally head home and become the bridge builder God had called him to be. Although Jacob had encountered a ladder in Luz, he would still need to wrestle with a snake named Laban to empathize with his brother, Esau. Which takes us to the next step in Jacob's journey toward shedding his snakeskin and finally being the offspring of Eve.

## Chapter 11

# Limping with Laban

[Nebuchadnezzar] was driven away from
people and ate grass like the ox. His body was
drenched with the dew of heaven until his hair
grew like the feathers of an eagle and his nails
like the claws of a bird.

At the end of that time, I, Nebuchadnezzar,
raised my eyes toward heaven, and my sanity
was restored. Then I praised the Most High; I
honored and glorified him who lives forever.

—DANIEL 4:33–34

Within moments of arriving at Laban's house, Jacob finds
himself smitten with Laban's youngest daughter, Rachel, and
agrees to exchange seven years of indentured service for her
hand in marriage. Jacob works for Laban for seven years, and
the moment he has served his time, Jacob demands a wedding.
This portion of Genesis is hilarious.

Genesis 29:20–21 says, "Jacob served seven years to get Rachel, but they seemed like only a few days to him because of
his love for her. Then Jacob said to Laban, 'Give me my wife.
My time is completed, and I want to make love to her.'"

Pretty straightforward there, Jacob. Not necessarily what I would say to my future father-in-law. But who am I to judge?

Laban calls the entire community together, throws a feast, and gives his daughter to Jacob in marriage. Remember, there's no electricity, and brides at that time wore veils when they got married. The couple consummates their marriage covenant while it's dark outside, and everything goes well.

Until the morning, that is. The light of day reveals that Laban has acted like a snake toward Jacob, and unfortunately, Jacob has married Leah, the less attractive older sister, instead of Rachel, whom he is passionately in love with. This is heartbreaking for everyone involved. Jacob, Leah, and Rachel must all be devastated.

Imagine being Jacob—deceived by a family member who has disguised his older daughter and passed her off as her younger sister. Something about that scenario sounds oddly familiar.

Isaac blesses the wrong brother—Jacob instead of Esau.
Jacob marries the wrong sister—Leah instead of Rachel.

Isaac cannot un-bless Jacob and bless Esau.
And Jacob cannot un-marry Leah and marry Rachel.

These stories are intentional parallels. And Laban has replaced Jacob as the new snake. For the first time in his life, Jacob can empathize with his brother, Esau, and finally understand the pain of being deceived by a trusted family member. Jacob, like Esau, has now experienced irreparable and irreversible betrayal.

God allows Laban to trick Jacob, but not as a form of divine payback. God isn't petty. Godly justice is restorative in nature, so He allows Laban to be a snake in Jacob's life to bring both sobriety and sympathy into Jacob's heart. For the first time, Jacob can see Esau with the eyes of a priest instead of a competitor. Eyes of empathy as opposed to eyes of opportunism.

This situation with Laban also gives Jacob eyes of foresight: When Jacob looks at Laban, he can see his future—a devious, crafty snake of a man despised by his family. Laban is a bridge burner, and his daughters cannot wait to get away from him.

I've learned some interesting facts about snakes. For the most part, they spend their lives in solitude. Except for mating and hibernating, snakes are incredibly solitary. Laban has a family, but his deceptive and manipulative ways force him into loneliness and isolation.

I think Jacob sees this. Jacob finally sees himself not only in Esau but also in Laban.

Jacob's season with Laban leads him to conclude that he's better off taking his chances with a brother who wants to kill him than with an uncle who keeps deceiving him. So, Jacob heads home after twenty long years to attempt to reconnect with Esau.

Why would a snake slither back to face certain death? Because maybe this snake is tired of being a snake. Jacob decides the time has come to confront his brother and reconcile. This is the quintessential decision that marks humans who retain their humanity: a willingness to die to themselves and become sacrifices.

A willingness to face their greatest fears. To walk into situations they can't control or manipulate. To finally be the ladders, the bridge builders. To surrender their lives and be priests instead of beasts.

Once Jacob resolves to surrender himself to the vengeance of his brother and live as a priest, God encounters him again on the exact same path from two decades prior. How do we know these stories are linked? For starters, the angels are back.

When Jacob finally decides to stop running away from the call to be a priest and a bridge and heads back home, Genesis 32:1 tells us that "the angels of God met him." This is not Jacob's first time seeing angels on this exact journey, but last time he was a lot younger and walking in the opposite direction.

Twenty years ago, the angels were in a dream.
This time, the angels meet him and interact with him.

Twenty years ago, Jacob was sent to Paddan Aram by his father.
This time, Jacob is sent to Canaan by the Lord, his heavenly Father.

Twenty years ago, he was completely alone.
This time, he sends his entire family ahead so he can be alone again.

Twenty years ago, Jacob changed the name of a town from Luz to Bethel.
This time, Jacob is the one who'll experience a name change.

The climax of this return to Canaan is an epic wrestling match with a mysterious figure: "Jacob was left alone, and a man wrestled with him till daybreak. When the man saw that he could not overpower him, he touched the socket of Jacob's hip so that his hip was wrenched as he wrestled with the man" (verses 24–25).

Wrestling is an odd way to interact with someone, yet something about it makes so much sense for Jacob's journey of rehabilitation. Through his whole life, Jacob has gone behind people's backs to deceive them. He's not a confronter at all but rather a passive-aggressive backstabber. Except for this wrestling match. Because there's something oddly forthright and innately honest about wrestling. Wrestling requires face-to-face honesty. It requires intimacy and integrity. The encounter forces Jacob out of his default comfort zone.

Verse 31 ends the story by telling us that "the sun rose above him . . . and he was limping because of his hip." The result of this all-night wrestling match is that Jacob is left physically weaker, but it seems like that's the very solution he needed.

For most of his life, Jacob has been too strong, too independent, too self-reliant, and therefore too dependent on his own tricks, craftiness, and cunning mind. Now he is forced to walk in the strength of dependence as opposed to the weakness of independence. Most humans see self-reliance as strength and dependence as weakness. But in God's upside-down kingdom, self-reliance and independence create Chaos.

Jacob is on his way to meet Esau, and instead of approaching his brother in strength, he's forced to do it with a visible limp. There is no way for Jacob to hide this injury. I've watched enough shows on National Geographic to know that the worst thing out in the wild is to have a visible and obvious injury. Animals will either abandon or attack other animals who are bleeding or limping. But God is trying to get Jacob to act like a man, not an animal.

So, Jacob must limp back home to meet Esau. God doesn't allow him to show up in strength but causes him to return limping. Jacob has to trust that God will protect him and that maybe his brother is no longer a beast.

Once Jacob accepts that he's a ladder and a priest,
once he sees his reflection in the face of Laban,
once he sees his own pain in the face of Esau,
once he's learned empathy and been wrestled into honesty,
he must rely on the Lord for every step.

Now the snake has become human. Now Jacob can become Israel. And Israel can limp toward Esau and reconcile.

It's a beautiful moment that required two decades of Yahweh working behind the scenes to gently and intentionally move him toward a less chaotic way of being human.

What has this long journey taught us?

Humans without a vision for themselves and their families tend to act like animals.

Humans without a God-dream typically lack discipline and restraint.

Humans trapped in tribalism build towers, not temples.

Humans who lack empathy act more like predators than priests.

Humans live in communities, while snakes live in isolation.

Humans who are completely reliant on their own cunning schemes don't tend to surrender to God, because they perceive God's way of being human as weak and fragile.

This is how Yahweh brings Jacob back to his true self, defeats the beast, and rescues Jacob. This is how our God turns monsters back into humans.

This is how Yahweh tames the beast in all of *us* and conquers *our* chaos.

The story of Jacob should give all of us hope because it proves that nobody on this side of eternity is beyond healing and restoration. Jacob's story is incredibly similar to King Nebuchadnezzar's story. Daniel 4 teaches that God caused Nebuchadnezzar to devolve into an animal as the fitting consequence for his pride and arrogance, and in true eastern fashion, the Bible shows instead of tells.

His nails became like birds' claws.

He ate grass like an ox.

His hair grew as long as eagles' feathers.

However, the discipline was always designed to bring Nebuchadnezzar to repentance, and Yahweh restores his sanity and his humanity after seven years. Not only can the God of the Bible punish our pride, but the good news is that He restores us when there's humility and surrender. He turns monsters back into men.

This isn't just Jacob's journey.

This isn't just Nebuchadnezzar's journey.

This is our journey as well—or at least it *can be.*

## Chapter 12

# Caged but Not a Beast

> Our struggle is not against flesh and blood,
> but against the rulers, against the authorities,
> against the powers of this dark world and
> against the spiritual forces of evil in the
> heavenly realms.
>
> —EPHESIANS 6:12

In the same way that Jacob deceived Isaac to win his dad's favor, Jacob's sons, who despise their brother Joseph, plot Joseph's demise and deceive their father. Jealousy overtakes them just like it did Cain. They sell their brother as a slave to the Ishmaelites (hint, hint), but they have to come up with a story for their father. The Bible continues showing us who the Serpent's children are.

Genesis 37:31–33 tells us, "Then they got Joseph's robe, slaughtered a goat and dipped the robe in the blood. They took the ornate robe back to their father and said, 'We found this. Examine it to see whether it is your son's robe.' He recognized it and said, 'It is my son's robe! Some ferocious animal has devoured him. Joseph has surely been torn to pieces.'"

A fierce animal has devoured Joseph. A wild animal. A beast of the field. A monster of Chaos.

We know that Joseph wasn't actually devoured, so technically their father is incorrect. But we also know that since the
Bible speaks in the language of looping symbols and repeating
images, Jacob is actually spot on. Joseph has been devoured by
fierce and wild animals—his brothers. Which reveals that his
brothers are the offspring of the Serpent.

Joseph's brothers are beasts. Monsters. Kings of chaos. Which
means that Joseph must be the offspring of Eve and a type of
Christ, right?

Let's look at what the text shows us concerning Joseph:

Joseph is sold for some pieces of silver (Genesis 37:28).
He is sold by his brother Judah (verses 26–27). In Greek,
    that name is Judas.[1]
Joseph is tempted by Potiphar's wife yet is without sin
    (39:6–9).
Although innocent, he is falsely accused and imprisoned
    (verses 19–20).

Sounding familiar yet?

Joseph is condemned with two criminals. One criminal
    will be saved; the other won't (40:1–3, 20–22).
He is stripped of his robe and his cloak (37:23; 39:12).
He is called by God, but his brothers don't believe him
    (37:8).
He is thought to be dead but surprises everyone by being
    alive (37:33–34; 45:3–4).
By the end of the story, every knee bows to Joseph's au-
    thority, including his brothers, who swore they'd never
    bow down to him (42:6).

In this story, Joseph's brothers are the animals. The beasts. The offspring of the Serpent.

Joseph is their prey, but he retains his humanity. Joseph is the offspring of Eve, and his entire life foreshadows the ultimate son of the woman—Jesus.

Patterns. Symbols. Images. Loops.

Welcome to reading Eastern literature with Eastern eyes.

Cain is an animal. Ishmael is a wild animal. Esau and Jacob are both beasts. Joseph's brothers are monsters. All sons of the Serpent. All crushed by Chaos.

This is the dominant theme and lesson of Genesis: It is easy for humans to become animals. Our humanity is delicate and must be guarded with all the wisdom and strength we have.

Sin and Chaos have an agenda—to strip us of our humanity and turn us into monsters. Sin is crouching and desires to attack (Genesis 4:7). But we must rule over the beast because if we don't tame it, we'll become beasts. Jealousy turns us into violent beasts. Lust turns us into animals of instinct. Our unbridled desires turn us into monsters. Ambition and greed intoxicate us until we lose our humanity. Revenge and bitterness exploit our primal natures.

Abel dies at the hands of Cain.

Isaac willingly allows his father to slay him.

Jacob will eventually surrender his life and belongings.

Joseph is a victim of his brothers' jealousy and plotting.

Life seems to not go well for these sons of Eve.

There's a theme here. The lesson of Genesis is that we retain our humanity by being willing to sacrifice our lives. This narrative is offering us a choice: Do we want to be sons and daughters of Eve or offspring of the Beast? Which line of offspring looks like they're winning at life? Do we want to model our lives after the chaos of Cain or the order of Abel? That is the option laid out to every reader of Genesis who understands the pattern.

Death. Surrender. Sacrifice. Turning the other cheek.

Hating your life and saving it.

Or loving your life and losing it.

This is deeply counterintuitive, but it is fundamental for understanding what Genesis is up to and ultimately for understanding the teachings of Jesus.

I remember visiting Robben Island as a young adult, going to Nelson Mandela's prison cell, and reading his thoughts regarding the dehumanization of oppression:

> I knew as well as I knew anything that the oppressor must be liberated just as surely as the oppressed. . . . The oppressed and the oppressor alike are robbed of their humanity. When I walked out of prison, that was my mission, to liberate the oppressed and the oppressor both.[2]

This is what made Nelson Mandela a global hero. He could see what most cannot: that Chaos dehumanizes everyone involved. Mandela avoided the false dichotomy that most modern people fall into and that is deeply entrenched in the psyche of the West—the Marxist divide between the haves and the have-nots, the powerful and the powerless. Mandela was brave enough to see that when Chaos reigns, everyone is a victim and Chaos is the villain, yet everyone is responsible all at the same time.

Maybe the real prison isn't incarceration. Maybe it is victimhood and bitterness.

Racism robs everyone of their humanity—the racist and
the victim.

Pornography robs everyone of their humanity—the viewer
and the performer.

Sex outside God's design robs everyone of their
humanity—all involved parties.

Greed robs everyone of their humanity—the wealthy and
the poor.

I think young people go through roughly three phases pertaining to their parents. Initially, we idolize them. Our parents can do no wrong. We want to emulate them as best we can. Next, we demonize them. They become the reason for everything that is wrong in our lives. They become our main antagonists, and we end up casting them as the villains in the unfolding drama of our lives. Finally, we humanize our parents. Only then can we ever forgive, have compassion for, and build healthy relationships with them.

Once I humanized my father, I could finally forgive him for taking me to a crack house when I was five, forgetting to pick me up from school, and neglecting our family. Humanizing him meant that I could no longer see him as the antagonist in my story. Instead, the Dragon of Chaos became the villain that was against my father and my entire family.

Paul understood that it can be difficult to see the real enemy. This is why he says in Ephesians 6:12 that "our struggle is not against flesh and blood, but against the rulers, against the authorities, against the powers of this dark world and against the spiritual forces of evil in the heavenly realms."

My father was never the real enemy. The demonic spirit of

addiction that was crouching and constantly attacking him was the real beast. Dad needed my love, empathy, prayers, and forgiveness. And all the hate and anger I felt in my heart needed to be directed toward the Dragon that had deceived my dad.

Nelson Mandela was able to see the real enemy, which wasn't the oppressor, because even oppressors are oppressed. The real enemy is always the Chaos monster who seeks to devour both the oppressor and the oppressed. Mandela was wrongfully imprisoned but refused to be victimized. He understood the secret—that every time I villainize another human, I victimize myself.

In the same way, Joseph, Jesus, and Paul were all wrongfully imprisoned but chose not to play the victim card.

Joseph said in Genesis 50:20, "You intended to harm me, but God intended it for good to accomplish what is now being done, the saving of many lives." This kind of perspective can only be the product of a well-ordered, well-gardened soul. Joseph's emotions did not rule him; rather, he chose to interpret life with wisdom.

Instead of playing the role of a victim, Jesus actively chose to lay down His life, declaring, "I lay down my life—only to take it up again. No one takes it from me, but I lay it down of my own accord" (John 10:17–18). Jesus, the Gardener, clearly did a lot of work to tend to the garden of His soul. Which is probably why He's so incredibly effective at tending to the gardens of *our* souls.

This is the secret to preserving our humanity—by retaining our power and authority. The Dragon's agenda is to divide and conquer, so I'm playing right into his hands when I villainize and demonize those who have hurt me. The reason I forgave my father is that I was tired of him having more power over me than I had over myself. I was tired of the Beast using my father to control me.

We're not powerless victims. We're humans made in the image of almighty God, and we're full of power.

## Chapter 13

# Pierced Ears and Empty Stomachs

> Many live as enemies of the cross of Christ.
> Their destiny is destruction, their god is their
> stomach.
>
> —PHILIPPIANS 3:18–19

> If God speaks to you primarily through passion
> and instinct; if all you need to do is examine your
> desires to find out what God wants of you; if your
> essential self is easily and naturally identified
> with your passions—well, you are an animal.
>
> —RABBI DAVID FOHRMAN,
>
> *THE BEAST THAT CROUCHES AT THE DOOR*

Genesis tells us that everything is good. Except one thing—Adam is alone. Not so great. Even God admits that this isn't good. But God doesn't immediately create Eve. This is where the text gets a bit odd and begins offering some clues surrounding the motives of the Serpent. Here's what the Bible says God decides to do in Genesis 2:18–20:

> The LORD God said, "It is not good for the man to be alone. I will make a helper suitable for him."

Now the LORD God had formed out of the ground all the wild animals and all the birds in the sky. He brought them to the man to see what he would name them; and whatever the man called each living creature, that was its name. So the man gave names to all the livestock, the birds in the sky and all the wild animals.

But for Adam no suitable helper was found.

Before Adam is put to sleep so God can pull out his rib to create Eve, we get this weird account of Adam naming animals. Why not make Eve right away? Why parade the wild animals in front of Adam so everyone could conclude that among them no suitable helper was found? This seems misplaced. Why does the Bible start telling us about the animals in the middle of dealing with Adam's relationship issues?

Scripture is teaching us, in a very subtle and Eastern way, that humans and beasts are not designed to be partners. Adam is designed to rule over them, not partner with them. Adam belongs in the garden. The beasts of the field belong in the wild. God and Adam therefore reject all beasts as suitable partners for humanity. Humans are humans; beasts are beasts. They are categorically different in every way, and Adam has been set apart from the beasts of the field.

However, one beast is craftier than the others and refuses to take no for an answer. One of the beasts decides to take another crack at partnering with humanity. One beast is cunning enough to challenge the boundary God established between beasts and humans. This is the motive of the Serpent: to prove that beasts can indeed partner with humans. The Beast proves that he has very human qualities. After all, he can talk and reason. So why doesn't he receive the same privileges as humans? Moreover, the Serpent will ultimately prove that humans have a lot of beast-like qualities, so why exactly do they get special treatment?

Can you see what the Beast is doing? Can you hear the Serpent's arguments?

"We're not that different."

"We're both made from the soil."

"We have lots of similarities."

"We should be partners."

The Serpent wants to exploit the inner beast in every human, and when Chaos has done its job, we're all left a little less human and a bit more monstrous. Make no mistake—the Dragon wants to create a spectrum where God has placed a solid boundary. The Dragon wants to blur the lines because Chaos will always seek to destroy definitions and boundaries.

The fundamental questions that Genesis is begging the reader to wrestle with are deeply philosophical and theological. Questions like these:

What does it mean to be truly human?

What is the purpose and nature of humanity?

What makes a human, human?

When do we know that a person has lost their humanity?

Remember, the Serpent is asking the exact same questions but with a far more cynical tone. Like a lawyer building a case, the accuser asks, "What makes them so special exactly? What is the difference between us? I can talk and reason just like them. They act like animals! We should all be treated with the same measure of justice because there's nothing unique or special about these humans."

When the Serpent recruits Adam and Eve to be his partners in Chaos, he actually makes some interesting claims regarding the nature of humanity. His question to the couple went like this: "Did God say, 'You shall not eat from any tree in the garden'?" (Genesis 3:1, NRSV).

The most impactful teaching I've ever heard on this has come from Rabbi David Fohrman, a Hebrew scholar who says the phrasing in this section of the Torah is very unusual. He suggests that a better translation of this verse would be this: "Even if God said, 'You shall not eat from any tree in the garden,' so what?"[1]

What is the Dragon getting at exactly? He's suggesting that God speaks in more than one way. Yes, God spoke to Adam and Eve audibly and told them not to eat. But doesn't God also speak to us through our desires and instincts? Isn't there a voice inside us? Isn't that voice God speaking to us as well?

Here's a helpful question from Rabbi Fohrman that made this idea click for me: "How does God speak to animals?" Well, He speaks through their natures. God doesn't give them commands; they simply obey and are led by their instincts and urges.[2]

Rabbi Fohrman's content has been so insightful on this. Summarizing won't do it justice, so here's what he writes:

The Almighty doesn't instruct animals intellectually, doesn't speak to them in words. There is no Bible, no Torah, revealed atop a mountain for snakes, birds, and lizards . . . [however,] animals follow the Divine Will quite faithfully. The voice of God beats palpably *inside* of them. God speaks to animals through the passions, desires, and instincts they find within themselves. Every time a grizzly bear goes salmon hunting in an Alaskan river, every time worker bees chase the drones out of a hive—every time an animal acts "naturally," obeying the voice of instinct or desire within itself, the animal follows the Will of its Creator.[3]

Unlike animals, who are naturally chaotic because they are taken from the soil of the wilderness outside Eden, we don't act naturally. On the contrary, we act intentionally.

Yet the Serpent is suggesting that beasts and humans aren't that different, that humans hear the voice of God through their desires just like animals do. God said not to eat from the tree, but that's not the only way God speaks. Adam and Eve eat from the tree because the Serpent convinces them that God is speaking to them the same way He speaks to animals—not through spoken commandments but through feelings, instincts, urges, and desires. That's the deception. And that's how they lose their humanity—by trying to hear God the same way animals do.

If God primarily speaks through urges,
through desires,
through instincts,
through feelings,
then all these things begin to function as our gods.

And that is exactly what has happened. Urges, desires, instincts, and feelings have become gods. Since these are now our authorities, we feel we can disobey the commands God actually put into place because the gods that speak to us from the inside hold more weight.

Countless believers have sat in my office and told me that they know the Scriptures say not to date non-Christians but they've decided to compromise because they just can't shake some feeling they have. They swear God is talking to them through mystical feelings as opposed to the clarity of His written Word.

The specific issues might get swapped around. But the tug-of-war between what the Bible says and what these believers' personal feelings communicate remains the same.

Forgiveness. Same-sex attraction.
Tithing. Premarital sex.
Church attendance and church engagement.
The list goes on and on.

They know what the Bible says. But there's a feeling or an urge they cannot shake. So, they compromise and obey their instincts, and to avoid feeling guilt and shame, they inevitably begin reinterpreting and then misinterpreting Scripture to align with how "God" spoke to them through their feelings.

What happens when humans *think* they hear God through their urges and instincts? You guessed it—Chaos. What happens when humans hear God through His commands laid out in Scripture? You guessed it—Order.

You and I have an opportunity to assert our humanity by listening to God's commands instead of our natural urges and desires. Paul says he's giving the Corinthian church instruction "in order that Satan might not outwit us. For we are not unaware of his schemes" (2 Corinthians 2:11).

This is the scheme of the Serpent: to get Adam and Eve to act like animals so that he can prove there's nothing all that special about us. To get us to hear God the way animals hear Him, thus rendering us unable to rule over the animals. This is the deception.

Don't let the Dragon outwit you. For we are aware of his schemes. Paul tells the church in Philippi that "many live as enemies of the cross of Christ. Their destiny is destruction, their god is their stomach" (Philippians 3:18–19).

Their god is their stomach. Their desires. Their natural urges. Their instincts. Their wants.

But not so with us. We don't follow our stomachs; we follow the commands of God. We assert our humanity by surrendering to the Order of Eden. Resisting the urge to let your feelings and desires control you makes you more human, not less.

Rabbi Fohrman expresses this brilliantly, writing, "If you are able to stand outside your passions and *examine them critically;* if desire is something you *have,* not something you *are;* if God addresses Himself to your mind and asks you to rise above your desires, or to channel them constructively—well, *then* you are a human."[4]

It is imperative that humans can define what it means to be truly human, or else we are doomed to act as beasts. And when humans act like beasts, we multiply chaos. A clear mark of humanity is the ability to examine our passions critically. This makes us uniquely human, and by this we crush chaos.

Exodus 21 instructs masters to set their slaves free after six years. But if an enslaved man didn't want the offered freedom and declared, "I love my master and my wife and children and do not want to go free" (verse 5), the Torah teaches that the master had to respond in a specific way. Verse 6 says, "His master must take him before the judges. He shall take him to the door or the doorpost and pierce his ear with an awl. Then he will be his servant for life."

The master had to pierce the servant's ear in the doorway. But why the ear? And why on the doorpost? It was the ear because hearing the master and obeying their voice was the mark of true devotion and servitude. The pierced ear was a sign of allegiance to the master's voice as opposed to the desires of the stomach. And doorways represent singularity and exclusivity in the Bible. For those who chose a lifetime of servanthood, their ears were the exclusive way they were to hear their masters.

This explains why Paul could be content in the midst of unjust imprisonment. There's a clear reason why he has singularity of focus, why his chief end is to glorify God, and why for him "to live is Christ and to die is gain" (Philippians 1:21). It's because Paul is a slave to the Lord Jesus Christ.

Paul uses the Greek word *doulos* (δοῦλος) to describe himself multiple times throughout his letters. Many English translations opt to translate this word as "servant" or "bondservant," but that removes the intended shock value of the word.

Paul didn't mean "servant." He meant "slave." My favorite Greek-English lexicon teaches that *doulos* is derived from "δέω to tie, bind" and means "a slave, bondman, man of servile condition . . . one who gives himself up wholly to another's will."[5] Another lexicon defines it as "subservient to, slavish, servile."[6] I'm afraid that modern English translations have opted for a softer word based on the shameful and triggering history of American chattel slavery. But there's a different word for "servant" in the Greek language: *diakonos* (διάκονος).[7]

Simply put, Paul said what he said.

Paul doesn't call himself a servant.

He calls himself a slave.

Because Paul knows the secret path to peace is the path of dying to self and submitting to the rule and reign of God. Many of us don't realize that anxiety and loneliness are the price we pay to pursue independent and autonomous lives. If you and I were to see ourselves as slaves to Christ, we'd have so much more peace and much less anxiety.

Years ago, I got invited to speak at a large, prominent Christian conference, and eventually the excitement turned into fear and anxiety around speaking in front of such a huge audience. My thoughts were sabotaging me. My mind was chaotic. I kept thinking, *What if I stutter and trip over my words? What if I don't get invited back? What if nobody is impressed with what I have to say? This opportunity could lead to even greater opportunities, so I'd better not mess this up.*

The more I thought about it, the more anxious I got, and the more I could feel myself drowning in chaos. I remember the Holy Spirit asking me a pivotal question: "Do you want to know why you're so nervous?" I contended that I was nervous because of the grandeur of the opportunity. I argued that I was rightfully anxious given the nature of the speaking engagement. The Holy Spirit kindly said, "No, you're anxious because you're consumed with thoughts that are centered on yourself. Your anxiety is rooted in your selfishness."

Almost immediately I repented before the Lord. And instead of thinking about *my* sermon, *my* reputation, *my* ministry career, and *my* future opportunities, I refocused my thoughts. I started thinking about the couple who'd be in the room whose marriage was on the brink of divorce. I started thinking about the single mom, the discouraged pastor, the burned-out leader, and the teenager battling with pornography addiction. I started thinking about God and how He wanted me to serve these people with His Word.

As my focus shifted from myself to the people that God had called me to minister to, the anxiety subsided, and it was replaced by compassion, love, and righteous indignation. My priorities had been out of order, which created chaos in my soul, and once I brought my thoughts into proper alignment and order, the anxiety inevitably calmed down. The Holy Spirit didn't speak peace over me; He spoke a word of correction so I could reorder my thoughts.

This is why Paul calls himself a slave—not just unto Christ but also unto others. Paul tells the church in Corinth that "I have made myself a slave to everyone, to win as many as possible" (1 Corinthians 9:19). That was the key to crushing my chaos. I had to make myself a slave to the people that God had called me to serve by preaching His Word. I had to die to myself and prioritize their needs above my own concerns.

We live in a world that says we belong to ourselves. It's a world of self-care, self-acceptance, self-love, and self-actualization. Not to mention self-identification and self-awareness and self-expression. We live in a culture that is obsessed with self. This is out of order. It goes against our design. We are lost at sea, in a chaotic storm of selfishness. No wonder anxiety and loneliness are cultural epidemics. They are simply symptoms of a culture of chaos and expressive individualism.

This is an invitation to dethrone the god of self. To give your life away in service and love to the people of God. This is your opportunity to leave independence and selfishness behind—to reject rampant individualism, to lose your life so you can find it. It's your invitation to be truly human. To step into the metaphorical doorway and allow the Master of the universe to pierce your ear and mark you as His and His alone, and to hear His voice through your ears and yours alone.

This is your invitation to reorder your life and crush the Chaos.

# COME
# HELL
# OR
# HIGH
# WATER

SECTION

3

## Chapter 14

# When God Leaves the Group Chat

> Were it not for the Creator's power, by which
> the firmament was created and the sea
> assigned its boundaries, the earth would be
> engulfed by the flowing together of the waters
> and would return to primeval chaos (cf.
> Gen. 7:11; 8:2). No language could express
> more forcefully *the utter dependence* of the
> world upon the Creator.
>
> —BERNHARD W. ANDERSON, *FROM CREATION TO NEW
> CREATION,* EMPHASIS ADDED

My pastor gave a brilliant example in church one Sunday. Pastor Robert Madu and his wife, Taylor, have three young children. Like any good parents, they provide structure, rules, and boundaries for their family. Like most kids, their children don't always love the order they have provided and might say things like "I wish you and Mom would just leave us home by ourselves so we could do whatever we want."

After setting this as the context, Pastor Robert asked our congregation a provocative question: "Suppose Pastor Taylor and I honored our kids' request and left them at home by themselves. How long would it take before they turned our home into a living hell? Without the order that we bring, how fast would that home become a dangerous environment for my children?"

Any parent knows that those kids couldn't survive a single day without the order their parents provide. God forbid if they attempted to cook, took showers, burned themselves, or climbed something and fell. Even though they hate the parental order, it is the very thing keeping them alive. If the children were allowed to govern themselves, they would inevitably turn their home into their hell.

If Pastor Robert and Taylor honored their children's freewill desires and vacated the premises, total chaos would ensue. Leaving humanity to its own chaos is God's common form of punishment and judgment throughout the biblical story, and I think the Flood narrative follows the same pattern.

The Flood account isn't a story of God destroying the earth. Rather it is a story of how we turned our ordered home into a hell of Chaos, and it only took seven chapters of the biblical story for us to do it. Humans desired a world without God, and when God removed Himself, creation simply reverted to its original state—chaos.

This is why the opening lines of Genesis are so important. If creation began as nothingness, and then God flooded the creation, that implicates the character of God. However, if creation's original state was a deep, raging watery abyss of Chaos, then the Flood is simply a story of reversal—where the creation reverts to its original *tehom*.

Genesis 7:11 reads, "In the six hundredth year of Noah's life, on the seventeenth day of the second month—on that day all the springs of the great deep (*tehom*) burst forth, and the floodgates of the heavens were opened."

We know all about this *tehom* that burst forth. It's where Leviathan lives. It's from the second verse of the Bible. It's the *tehom* that Revelation 21:1 says will eventually disappear.

Why is the great deep mentioned in the second verse of the Bible? Because Scripture is making it abundantly clear that God isn't responsible for plunging the earth back into Chaos; humans are. God is good. God doesn't ruthlessly kill humans or desire to destroy humanity. Humans kill humans, and humans make decisions that destroy humanity.

Yahweh wasn't responsible for the fountains of the great *tehom* bursting forth. Leviathan wasn't the culprit who plunged creation back into Chaos. Humans alone had the power to turn our home into our hell. We caused creation to fold in on itself and collapse.

If order invites divine rest, chaos drives God away. And we made it clear—we wanted a world without God, a world of independence and autonomy. We wanted a world ruled by humans, as opposed to one ruled by God through humans. We wanted a world free of God's controlling and overbearing rules.

So, God left us alone. Because fortunately, God honors our freewill choices. He'll never force us into His presence. If God didn't honor our free will, He'd be the monster. And if God is a monster, the rest of the Bible ain't worth reading.

Genesis is drilling these ideas into the psyche of its audience because God's character is on the line. If God is a monster, then obeying Him will create just as much chaos. So, Genesis is painting a picture of God that humanity can trust. Because we must trust His character before we can embrace His Order.

What happened when God left His temple? It returned to

its original state: *tohu va-vohu* and *tehom*. A dark, chaotic abyss unfit for human life. Creation folded in on itself and was pulled back into the Chaos that had engulfed it at the beginning of Genesis. Which means the Flood narrative isn't about God's active wrath but about His passive wrath.

Actually, the passive wrath of God is on display in a lot of places throughout Scripture. Paul describes God as passively wrathful throughout the book of Romans, writing, "God gave them over in the sinful desires of their hearts to sexual impurity for the degrading of their bodies with one another" (1:24).

*God gave them over.* God released them.

God left them to their own devices.

Did God attack them with sinful desire? No. He gave them over to their desires. God consistently gives humans the freedom to pursue what they want, and we create a living hell for ourselves in doing so. He gives us over to the *tehom*. He doesn't cause the fountains of the great deep to burst and drown us; we do. God simply surrenders us to our own self-sabotaging devices.

This complicated dance between the active and passive wrath of God can be found in the life of King Saul as well as in the Flood account. Here's how the Bible describes God's dealings with the wickedness of this king: "Now the Spirit of the LORD had departed from Saul, and an evil spirit from the LORD tormented him" (1 Samuel 16:14).

The Spirit of the Lord certainly departed from Saul—but I would argue that is the extent of God's action. When God's Spirit left Saul, it created a vacuum and an opportunity for an evil spirit to torment the king. I don't think God needed to send the evil spirit. However, it was inevitable that something evil would fill the void that resulted from the removal of God's

Spirit. Saul was left standing in the wake of God's exit, vulnerable to every attack of the Dragon that God had been protecting him from all along.

It's common for humans to blame God for the natural consequences that follow His passive wrath. My interpretation of King Saul's life is that God removed Himself from the group chat and that the fountains of the great *tehom* then burst forth and drowned Saul with chaos and evil. God's wrath was passive. God simply left. He gave Saul over to the natural consequences of the chaos he had chosen.

The Flood narrative could easily paint God as a cosmic killjoy and ruthless judge. Yet it is declaring the exact opposite: Humans are on a path of self-destruction, and God recruits a man named Noah to be a partner in saving humans from total extinction by creating a floating temple amid the chaotic waters.

It's impossible to trust God's Order if we can't trust His character. God doesn't drown people; Chaos does. And we have partnered with Chaos to our own detriment and downfall. All God has to do to punish us is simply get up and walk away. That's it. When God leaves, everything is inevitably plunged back into Chaos.

However, there's hope. God has a plan to save humanity and reestablish Order. The ocean is scary, but the sea won't have the last laugh or the final word. The natural consequences of Chaos will unfold, and the fabric of reality will certainly unravel. God will intervene, but not by preventing the Flood. Instead, He will warn a righteous man named Noah of impending doom.

Noah. Who exercises authority over wild animals.

A man of the soil, says Genesis 9:20.

A man who's naked in his vineyard.

Haven't we seen naked humans who were made from the soil and had authority over animals in the Genesis narrative already? Yes—yes, we have. Their names were Adam and Eve.

So, God will interfere not by preventing the natural consequences of human chaos but by inserting a new Adam into the narrative—a seed of the woman, a man of the soil. And hopefully this second Adam will be able to crush the head of the Dragon.

We'll find out as we keep following the narrative.

## Chapter 15

# The Context of Chaos

The LORD said, "My Spirit will not contend with humans forever, for they are mortal; their days will be a hundred and twenty years."
—GENESIS 6:3

As the biblical story shows, human beings do have the terrible power to pollute the earth with their lifestyle. They do have *the capacity for violence* to the degree that the earth is threatened with a return to chaos.
—BERNHARD W. ANDERSON, *FROM CREATION TO NEW CREATION,* EMPHASIS ADDED

The flood serves to undo the work of creation in Genesis 1.
—GORDON J. WENHAM, *EERDMANS COMMENTARY ON THE BIBLE*

I'll never forget the tears rolling down my wife's face as she expressed the legitimate frustration of being misunderstood. We had gotten into an disagreement that evolved into an argument. Two hours into the conversation, she realized that everything we were discussing was based on a total failure in communication. The emotions of it hit her like a wave, and she broke down. My wife had the purest motives and the most selfless intentions, but I misinterpreted her. I can say with empathy that there's almost nothing more frustrating than that. After ten years of marriage, I can genuinely admit that communication is hard. It requires focus and work.

Tone. Body language. Distractions.
Nuance. Mood. Timing.
Context.

Communication is a challenge, even when we know one another well, speak the same language, and ask follow-up questions. My wife and I aren't separated by language, history, culture, or proximity, and there are still moments when we completely miss the mark. I've realized I need to slow down, assume less, assume the best, give the benefit of the doubt often, stay humble, and stop looking at my phone while my wife is talking. Seriously.

Few things are more demoralizing than being taken out of context. When I was a youth pastor, we did this really extensive sermon series on fear. I taught on the nature of fear for nearly two months. We had altar calls inviting people to address their fears. We rebuked fear. We had small-group discussions and had students memorize Bible verses that focused on fear. We approached fear from every conceivable angle.

At the conclusion of week six of this epic sermon series, a girl came up to me with tears streaming down her face, clearly impacted. She hugged and thanked me and started explaining how this series had changed her life. I'll never forget it. As she wiped away her tears, she said, "Pastor Manny, the Holy Spirit has really used you to set me free from fear these last couple months. My boyfriend's been wanting to have sex for months, but I've been too scared. But not anymore, Pastor Manny. I'm conquering my fear! I'm losing my virginity."

I was in complete disbelief. I was mortified, to be honest.

I would *never* encourage premarital sex between teenagers. Ever. Under any circumstance. And I spent the next twenty minutes talking to her and her small-group leader about the misunderstanding. But this is a classic and albeit hilarious example of the chaos that's possible when people hear *content without context.*

Misinterpretations abound.

I've observed that typically the folks who take the Bible out of context are the kind of people who take other people out of context too. There's a chaos to taking people and God out of context, and it is typically rooted in lots of assumptions, an unwillingness to be flexible, an attachment to ideas that make us comfortable, and a hint of stubbornness.

I have found that the better I get at interpreting Moses, David, and Paul, the better I get at interpreting my wife, my employees, and my friends. Patience, humility, and refusal to jump to conclusions until I know all the details are transferable skills. Conversely, chaos in the realm of interpersonal communication tends to lead to chaos in the realm of theology.

The story of the Flood in Scripture can easily be taken out of context. It's not hard to conclude that God is unfair and unjustly vengeful. But before we jump to that conclusion and create chaos, let's actually place the *content* of Genesis into *context.* We'll look first at the linguistic context since the Bible wasn't written in English and then at the cultural context, which will require us to compare the Flood account in the Bible to the Flood account in *The Epic of Gilgamesh.*

We'll start with translating and interpreting Genesis 6:3—a passage that appears to be easy to understand until we start asking some pretty Eastern questions. In it, we find a prologue where Yahweh divulges His motives for the Flood and His thoughts concerning His creation. Here's what the NIV does with this verse: "The LORD said, 'My Spirit will not contend (*dun*) with humans forever, for they are mortal; their days will be a hundred and twenty years.'"

According to this translation, God is refusing to contend with humans forever. Which is interesting because I would agree that we're a contentious bunch. We don't participate with God easily, and we rarely submit to His will. I can see how that could get tiring. However, I cannot name a time in Scripture where God actually stops contending with us. The entire story of the Bible is God contending with humans. The cross of Christ is God contending with humans—to the point of death!

This translation choice fails to unlock the meaning of the passage and has the potential to paint God as an angry judge instead of the gracious Creator that Genesis portrays. Maybe there's another way to translate this passage that fits cohesively with the rest of Scripture.

The same Hebrew word, *dun,* that could mean "contend" in one context could also mean "abide, dwell, reside, or stay" in a different context. Therefore, other Bible versions choose to part ways with the NIV and translate the word a bit differently.

One of my favorite Hebrew lexicons argues that "abide in, dwell" is the best wording for Genesis 6:3, claiming that "*My spirit will not abide in man forever* . . . best suits the context."[1]

Another resource, *A Dictionary of Biblical Languages with*

*Semantic Domains,* states that *dun* means "remain, abide, i.e., dwell in a certain location (Ge 6:3)."[2] Genesis 6:3 is literally one of the examples this dictionary uses for a prime context where *abide* is a far more fitting translation than *contend.*

If God is stating that He will not continue living among humans who act sinfully and violently, then everything that follows this announcement makes perfect sense—the cosmos completely collapses because God has no choice but to leave the group chat.

One word can make all the difference. And it's so easy to read that verse with no linguistic context and come to really awful and inaccurate conclusions about the character of God. Not only is it easy; it's common. Yet humility acknowledges that communication is difficult and that reading the Bible is more complex than many of us were led to believe in our Sunday school classes.

Most people interpret God's words in the second half of Genesis 6:3 to mean that He now limits human lifespans to 120 years, which is what I grew up believing. However, Abraham lived to be 175 years old, and his son Isaac lived to be 180, and they were alive long after the time of the Flood. Also, if you glance at Shem's genealogy that follows the Flood narrative, you'll see that several people on the list lived past 400 years of age, and all but one lived at least 200 years (Genesis 11:10–32). So maybe something else is going on.

The Dead Sea Scrolls were produced by a community known as Qumran. (Some scholars believe that John the Baptist may have been a part of this sect based on his clothing, preaching, and passion for baptizing folks.) The Qumran sect diligently produced not only copies upon copies of the Hebrew Bible but also commentaries on the Scriptures. In scroll

4Q252, they include a compelling interpretation for Genesis 6:3. Here's an excerpt:

> [In the] four hundred and eightieth year of Noah's life, he came to the end of them and God said, "My spirit shall not dwell with man forever, their days shall be determined to be one hundred and twenty years until the waters of the flood come." And the waters of the flood came upon the earth in the six hundredth year of Noah's life.[3]

The Bible doesn't tell us how old Noah was when God told him to build the ark, so the Qumran community fills in the gaps, writing in their commentary that Noah was 480 years of age at the time. Why would Noah's age when God told him about the Flood matter?

Well, Genesis 7:11 reads, "In *the six hundredth year* of Noah's life . . . all the springs of the great deep (*tehom*) burst forth, and the floodgates of the heavens were opened." So Noah was 600 when the Flood began, and according to the Bible nerds living out in the caves near the Dead Sea, he was 480 at the time of God's announcement. By claiming this, the Qumran community, who had a far better understanding of the Hebrew Bible than many of us do, was subtly arguing that it took 120 years to build the ark. They're offering an interpretation.

This Jewish community didn't believe that God was limiting lifespans to 120 years. Rather, they believed God was giving Noah 120 years to build a house for His presence because He was scheduling His departure from the land.

So, let's put all the puzzle pieces together. In Genesis 6:3, I think God is saying, "My Spirit will not dwell with humans forever. You have a hundred and twenty years until I will no longer dwell here with you." Is it possible that we've been reading these verses in English incorrectly?

The English translators of Genesis have made another fascinating decision that I think paints Yahweh in a light that is inconsistent with the testimony of the Scriptures. The NIV and many other translations render Genesis 6:11–12 this way: "Now the earth was corrupt in God's sight and was full of violence. God saw how corrupt the earth had become, for all the people on earth had corrupted their ways."

According to all the Hebrew lexicons I could find, the Hebrew word here for "corrupt" (*sahat*) has another meaning that's actually more common and more often used. About half the time when the Bible uses this word, translators choose to render it as *ruin*.[4] So, this Hebrew word can mean "corrupt," but it can also mean "ruin, destroy, or damage irreparably."[5] Context always determines which meaning the word will take.

Let's just experiment with some different options to see if they fit the context of this passage.[6] It could be communicating, "Now the earth was ruined, destroyed, and irreparably damaged in God's sight and was full of violence. God saw how ruined, destroyed, and irreparably damaged the earth had become, for all the people on earth had ruined, destroyed, and irreparably damaged their ways."

What if God *saw* that the land was irreparably damaged?

What if God didn't ruin the earth by flooding it with water?

What if *humans* ruined the earth by flooding it with violence and evil?

What if God saw that the land was destroyed and therefore chose to give humanity over to their own chaos and destruction?

Once God sees the destruction of the land, He tells Noah

His solution for this human-induced destruction. Hopefully we have learned at this point not to assume we understand the text and not to take Scripture at face value.

Let's turn our attention to Genesis 6:13. The NIV translates it very differently than the NASB1995, and I think it makes a massive difference in the picture the text paints concerning God's character. Here's what the NIV translators chose to do with this verse: "God said to Noah, 'I am going to put an end to all people, for the earth is filled with violence because of them. I am surely going to destroy both them and the earth.'" This sounds a lot like the active wrath of God. In an effort to make the language more readable, the NIV has painted God with a brushstroke that I don't think the original author intended.

The NASB1995 offers a more accurate translation of verse 13: "God said to Noah, 'The end of all flesh has come before Me; for the earth is filled with violence because of them; and behold, I am about to destroy them with the earth.'"

The NIV wording—"I am going to put an end to all people"—promotes the active wrath of God.

The NASB1995 wording—"The end of all flesh has come before Me"—portrays the passive wrath of God.

Those phrases are worlds apart. The original Hebrew suggests that God has seen how the scenario will play out. He's already observed the destruction humans have brought on the land, and now the destruction of the humans themselves is before God's eyes. God is simply saying that He has seen the end—how humans will ultimately self-destruct—and He's chosen not to intervene but to allow their chaos to overtake and drown them.

We create chaos when we assume we know what the text *means* just because we've heard what it *says*. There's often a sizable gap between what is said and what is meant. And the words of God are too important for us to jump to conclusions or cling to interpretations that disregard context.

Historically, the church has multiplied chaos by holding to interpretations for the sake of tradition versus historical context. In June 1633, Galileo was condemned as a heretic for daring to believe that Earth orbited the sun, because this claim was understood as being contrary to Scripture. The Roman Inquisition found his ideas to be untenable and "sentenced him to house arrest where he remained until his death in 1642."[7] Those who condemned Galileo upheld a literal interpretation of Scripture without regard for linguistic or cultural context, and they forever changed the relationship between science and religion. Talk about chaos.

When the Christian judges overseeing Galileo's case condemned him, they based part of their argument on Psalm 93:1, which says:

> The LORD is king, he is robed in majesty;
>     the LORD is robed, he is girded with strength.
> He has established the world; *it shall never be moved.*
> (NRSV)

The Roman Catholic Church couldn't reconcile what Galileo had discovered through his telescope with "clear" teaching from the Bible that stated the world shall never be moved. A literal interpretation of that last line and other passages had one of history's greatest minds locked away on house arrest for almost a decade. That's chaos. That's fundamentalism. The inquisitors understood what that psalm *said* but completely missed what it *meant.* By opting for the simplest, most straightforward reading of the passage, they failed to appreciate the beauty and complexity of God's Word.

For those who think literal interpretations of Scripture are a thing of the past, just wait until you meet a flat-earther and they quote Psalm 104:5 to you.

On May 10, 1845, white Baptists in the southern United States "withdrew fellowship from their northern counterparts" based on their biblical interpretations regarding the practice of slavery.[8] Abolitionist groups argued for context and appealed to the narrative arc of Scripture. However, pro-slavery southern Baptists argued for the "*plain meaning of Scripture,*"[9] and Richard Furman, president of the South Carolina State Baptist Convention, had previously written that "the right of holding slaves is *clearly* established in the Holy Scriptures, both by precept and example."[10]

Clearly established. *Clearly.* The confidence in which this statement was made blows me away.

Enslaving large groups of people is already wicked enough, but justifying it with God's Word and out-of-context interpretations has created more chaos in this nation than we can measure. Humans have been mishandling Scripture and ignoring context for a long time.

Handling Scripture this way has caused lots of people to leave Jesus's church because they couldn't distinguish between the baby and the bathwater—what God said versus how He was interpreted. So, they jumped ship and now they're drowning in the chaos of secularism.

Along my journey as a pastor, I've observed that the folks who want to argue for a flat earth, who are really argumentative about the letter of the law, and who take the Bible extremely literally and get nervous about learning context and history and language—those folks aren't typically the best at relating to their kids, navigating nuanced topics, or sharing Christ. Those Christians aren't the ones winning their co-workers over to the faith. It's very hard to compartmentalize broken communication habits. Here's the irony: They're so scared of the chaos of uncertainty and mystery that they end up creating the chaos of control and fear-based religiosity. Sometimes by trying to avoid chaos, we create chaos. Because fundamentalism is a chaos that typically breeds the chaos of unhealthy deconstruction in the next generation.

If you favor a more literal approach to Scripture, I understand your fears. You mean well. You're scared that if we interpret the Bible using symbols, context, and history, we'll be able to make the Bible say all kinds of things. I understand the fear, but it isn't new, and it creates chaos. So I'm inviting you to explore the beautiful complexity of the Bible within the safe confines of orthodox confessional Christianity.

If you've escaped the chaos of fundamentalism but now you're lost and wandering in the wilderness of an endless and toxic deconstruction journey, I understand your fears. You trusted leaders, and you trusted what they told you. And they betrayed that trust by giving you their *interpretations* of the Bible and telling you those interpretations were authoritative. So now you don't know whom or what to trust. I understand, and I'm inviting you to fall in love with the Scriptures again and encounter them afresh. God's Order doesn't look like the fundamentalism you escaped. Your fears are legitimate, but they don't give you a lifetime pass to run away from God.

Whether you're stuck in the chaos of literalism or the chaos of secularism and deconstruction, the invitation is the same. I'm inviting you to behold the beauty of the Scriptures based on their cultural, historical, and linguistic context and discover for yourself what God has *said*—and, more importantly, what He *means* by what He's said.

There's one final piece of context, because the Babylonians had their own version of the Flood story. It makes a lot of sense to study the story that the biblical narrative may be responding to.

The Flood account in *The Epic of Gilgamesh* is very similar to the story we have in Genesis. Utnapishtim is essentially the Babylonian version of Noah. Both Noah and Utnapishtim build very large boats to save humanity, gather animals of all species to load onto their arks, use birds to find land after the flood, find their arks coming to rest on mountains as the flood subsides, offer sacrifices upon exiting their arks, and are promised that this will never happen again.[11]

Don't ignore the similarities. I'm convinced that the writers of the Bible knew that the biblical texts would make the most sense when readers understood the cultural contexts that surrounded the Scriptures. However, although the similarities are there to capture our attention, they're not the focus. The *differences* are the focus, and they are striking.

In *The Epic of Gilgamesh*, the reason the ark is built is slightly sneaky and scandalous. It's built behind the back of the main god who wants to flood the humans—Enlil. Utnapishtim builds the ark, and then at the end of the story, Enlil finds out that his plans to kill humans have been foiled.

In the biblical story, God reveals His plan to Noah. Noah doesn't have to go around God's back to save humans. Nobody wants to save humans more than God, and since He loves humanity, He gives Noah a 120-year heads-up on His plan.

In *The Epic of Gilgamesh,* the gods decide to flood the earth because humans are loud and disturb the gods' peace and rest. These gods have nothing to say about morality or sin or evil. The moral fiber of human beings isn't even on their radar.

In the biblical story, God isn't petty. He doesn't care whether humans are loud. He cares about morality, character, and evil. The God of the Bible cares about keeping Chaos at bay and about humans' ability and willingness to participate with Him in creating beauty and Order.

These conclusions can be made only when Genesis is placed in context and comparison with its contemporaries. And I think these are the conclusions that the writer of Genesis wanted his audience to make. Because Genesis is designed to set the record straight and reveal the loving, patient character of God. Genesis is designed for careful meditation. It makes the most sense when placed in context. Sometimes when we read the Bible, there's a gap between what is *said* and what is *meant*. That's not a design flaw; it's a design feature. Because these texts were designed not for casual or careless reading but for faithful and diligent disciples who value what these texts mean as much as what they say.

So, the chaos of humanity has caused God to depart from His creation, which will inevitably unravel the Order and unleash the Chaos of Genesis 1:2. Will Noah do something to bring the presence of God back into the creation? Will Noah be able to get the divine presence to rest on the earth again? Will God provide a way for us to create a new temple so we can house His presence and have Order restored?

If I were reading this for the first time, these would be the questions in my mind. So, let's see what the Bible tells us about the boat Noah builds.

## Chapter 16

# Noah's Temple

> The biblical writers saw both the tabernacle
> and [Noah's] ark as serving the preservation of
> humanity.
>
> —GORDON J. WENHAM, *EERDMANS COMMENTARY ON
> THE BIBLE*

> The information on the structure of the ark and
> the chronology of the deluge (flood) . . .
> confirms the *homology* with [the Jewish]
> temple and [temple] worship.
>
> —JOSEPH BLENKINSOPP, *CREATION, UN-CREATION,
> RE-CREATION: A DISCURSIVE COMMENTARY ON
> GENESIS 1–11,* **EMPHASIS ADDED**

The opening words of the Bible insinuate that creation was a chaotic, untamed mess and that the Spirit of the Lord was brooding over the surface of this raging and wild sea. Again, a pretty epic visual, if you ask me. God takes the chaos and does something profound that often goes overlooked—God doesn't bring peace; He brings order to the chaos of the unformed and barren creation.

God brings order to chaos by creating temple spaces. Out of

the chaos of creation, God planted a temple garden. And out of the chaos of the Flood, God had Noah construct a floating temple that sustained human life amid the chaotic floodwaters. However, the Bible doesn't *tell* us that Noah's ark was a temple. It *shows* us.

Why is it crucial to build a temple? Well, because the entire Flood is a result of God refusing to dwell with His people. Therefore, a temple is necessary so that the presence of God can return to its central place of importance.

The text gives us a bunch of clues that this ark is no regular boat but an ordered, sacred temple space enabling God to dwell with Noah's family. Let's examine these clues, starting with the instructions that God gives Noah for building the ark:

> Make yourself an ark of cypress wood; make rooms in it
> and coat it with pitch inside and out. This is how you
> are to build it: The ark is to be three hundred cubits
> long, fifty cubits wide and thirty cubits high. Make a
> roof for it, leaving below the roof an opening one cubit
> high all around. Put a door in the side of the ark and
> make lower, middle and upper decks. (Genesis 6:14–16)

First, anyone notice that there are some nonnegotiable items missing from this boat? No rudder, keel, bow, mast, or stern. Interesting boat.

Second, the boat is to be built with three distinct sections: upper deck, middle deck, and lower deck. God commands Noah to build the ark according to a three-in-one ratio. Kind of like an outer court, inner court, and holy of holies maybe?

Third, the word *cubits* sounds a bit familiar. Let's compare what we have here in Genesis to the construction of the temple.

In Genesis 6:15, God tells Noah to make the ark

three hundred cubits in length,
fifty cubits in width, and
thirty cubits in height.

In 1 Kings 6:2, the Bible says the house that King Solomon built for Yahweh was

sixty cubits in length,
twenty cubits in width, and
thirty cubits in height.

We get cubit measurements for length, width, and height for both the ark and the temple. Maybe the Bible is trying to show us that Noah built a temple? Gordon J. Wenham, in *Eerdmans Commentary on the Bible,* comments that "Noah's ark is recognizably boat-shaped, each deck of which was the same height as the tabernacle and three times the area of the tabernacle court." Wenham, a respected scholar, doesn't find these dimensions to be coincidental and neither should we.[1]

What's more, we also see cubits used as the unit of measure for the ark of the covenant (Exodus 25:10; 37:1), the table in the tabernacle (Exodus 25:23; 37:10), the alter for burnt offerings (Exodus 27:1; 38:1), the altar of incense (Exodus 30:1–2; 37:25), portable stands in the temple (1 Kings 7:27), the bronze altar in the temple (2 Chronicles 4:1), and a bronze platform in the outer court (2 Chronicles 6:13). All of these relate to a temple or house of God's presence in some sense and demonstrate a correlation between the ark and the temple.

Fourth, although we get no details concerning a rudder or keel for this boat, the door is clearly important. What other building places a massive importance on its door?

Hmm. Oh yeah. The temple.

Who's the ultimate fulfillment of its door? In John 10:9 Jesus indicates that the image of the temple door was simply a type or a shadow pointing to the truth of His reality: "I am the door. If anyone enters by Me, he will be saved, and will go in and out and find pasture" (NKJV).

Were there multiple doors to board the ark? No.

Were there multiple doors into the holy places at the temple? No.

Are there multiple ways to God? No.

John 10:9 declares that Jesus is the only door to salvation.

Fifth, the term *ark* is a very interesting choice. In Hebrew, the word is *tevah*, and it's a loaner from another culture— Egypt. Most languages, including English, have these loaner words. For example, the English word *baptize* is a loaner from the Greek language, where that term is passive. But instead of creating an English equivalent, we just adopted the entire Greek word into the English language.

The same thing happened with the Egyptian word *tevah*,[2] which the Hebrews incorporated into their own language. In Hebrew, it means "basket" or "box" and is what baby Moses's mom prepared and placed him in so he wouldn't drown in the Nile.[3] In its original Egyptian context, though, a *tevah* was more than merely a box or basket; it could refer to a chest, holy shrine, or coffin that contained images and idols of the Egyptian gods and that was used in a temple for the purpose of worship.[4] According to scholar Abraham Yahuda, in certain festivals these arks (*tevahs*) that contained images of the gods "were carried on the Nile, from one temple-town to another."[5]

The original audience of Genesis are freed slaves steeped in Egyptian culture—they are familiar with the Egyptian version of the *tevah* and have seen these idol-filled shrines floating down the Nile. In the Genesis author's retelling of this story, why would God have Noah build a boat with the same name as an Egyptian dwelling place for gods and idols? Maybe God wants to fill His *tevah* with creatures made in His image. Maybe this is more than a boat. Maybe Noah is constructing a temple that will be carried on the raging waters of the Flood.

Sixth, God commands Noah to bring food into the ark with him. In Genesis 6:21, God says, "You are to take every kind of food that is to be eaten and store it away as food for you and for them."

Now let's look at God's instruction to Moses concerning food for the tabernacle. In Exodus 16:32, He commands Moses to keep some manna "for the generations to come." So, Moses told Aaron to "take a jar and put an omer of manna in it. Then place it before the LORD" (verse 33). Later, the jar of manna was put in the ark of the covenant, which was housed in the tabernacle (Hebrews 9:2–4).

The word *place* in Exodus 16:33 is a fascinating Hebrew term that actually should be interpreted as "rest."[6] Why is this important? Because Noah's name (נֹחַ, *Noach*) . . . yeah, it means "rest."[7] It's almost like the people who wrote this had help from the Holy Spirit or something. It's too good.

Seventh, Noah performs one of the largest burnt offerings

recorded in Scripture (Genesis 8:20). Who performs whole burnt offerings? Priests. What is Noah functioning as? A priest managing a temple.

I think seven correlations between the construction of Noah's ark and the construction of the temple is enough to make anyone consider that the Bible is trying to show us something. But for good measure, here's an eighth. Once Noah is done building the ark, here's what Scripture tells us in Genesis 6:22: "Noah did everything just as God commanded him." Once Moses is done building the tabernacle, here's what Scripture tells us in Exodus 40:16: "Moses did everything just as the LORD commanded him."

And if anyone needs a ninth correlation, the ark comes to rest on top of a mountain. Where is Abraham commanded to sacrifice Isaac? A mountain. What does that exact location become? The Temple Mount where Solomon builds a dwelling place for God.

Maybe the ark is more than a boat. Perhaps it is a dwelling place for God. It could be that the world needed ordered sacred space so we could dwell with God again.

Maybe you feel like God is offering you a temple when your circumstances suggest you need a boat. Maybe you need to restore order to your chaotic life and don't see how a temple is relevant to your problems. Allow me to help. God's Order precedes His presence, and His presence always leads us into more order.

I promise you, if you build a dwelling place for God's presence, you'll look up and realize that the temple you've built can keep you safe through the flood. No wonder the writer of Psalm 46:1–3 testifies:

> God is our refuge and strength,
>> an ever-present help in trouble.
> Therefore we will not fear, though the earth give way
>> and the mountains fall into the heart of the sea,
> though its waters roar and foam
>> and the mountains quake with their surging.

Can you read between the lines of this psalm? The writer is essentially saying, "Though there's a flood of Chaos around us, though the waters roar and the sea swallows up creation, we won't be afraid of the flood. Why? Because God is our refuge. Our hope isn't in a boat; it's in a God who's an ever-present help when there's trouble."

I think this writer was reflecting on the Flood story when he penned these words. Noah built a dwelling place for the divine presence; it just so happens that the temple he built was a boat. Genesis emphasized this vessel as a temple, but that's visible only with Eastern eyes.

I have a hunch that if we were to diligently present ourselves as temples of the divine presence, God would take up residence within us and His wisdom would begin to bring order to our chaos. And together, we could bring order to the cosmos, and the earth would be full of the glory of God again.

## Chapter 17

# Passive Wrath and Active Grace

> You've had so many reasons to leave
> But You're still here with me
> Oh God I'm grateful
>
> —LYRICS FROM "YOU REMAIN," PERFORMED BY TODD
> GALBERTH AND WRITTEN BY CHANDLER MOORE

I think we should ask whether the interpretation of the Flood I'm presenting fits with the picture the rest of Scripture paints concerning God's character. Already in the Bible, we've seen God punish Adam, Eve, and Cain, so there's a track record to check.

God made the consequences associated with eating from the tree of the knowledge of good and evil really clear in Genesis 2:17: "When you eat from it you will certainly die." No confusion there.

Once Adam and Eve ate from the tree, did God kill them? No—no, He didn't.

Zero acts of immediate capital punishment.

Zero executions performed at the crime scene.

Zero heads rolled.

What did God do instead? He removed them from His presence and revoked their access to the tree of life. Active wrath would have required their immediate deaths, based on the consequences God clearly outlined. Yet He simply removed them from the Garden, and since they couldn't eat from the tree of life, they were forced to confront the reality of their eventual expiration. In the garden, Adam and Eve encountered God's passive wrath as opposed to His active wrath. God chose grace instead of judgment. There's a monumental difference between actively killing them and simply removing them from a source of life they were never entitled to in the first place.

God's very first act of judgment provides a pattern. God opts for passive wrath over active wrath. He blends a healthy amount of mercy with His justice.

How does God then handle the murder of Abel? According to the law of Moses, Cain should have been executed. Is Cain met with the consequence of capital punishment? No. Instead, Cain is exiled from God's presence. This is the same consequence God had given Adam and Eve. This is the passive wrath of God again. Exile as opposed to death.

Throughout the biblical narrative so far, God has yet to display His active wrath, and despite what you might think, I would maintain that the Flood story is no different. God follows the pattern He's set in motion. Instead of killing humans, God simply leaves the group chat. The Flood is a form of exile—only instead of humanity being exiled, God exiles Himself, and humanity has to deal with the consequences of their chaos. Passive wrath.

The notion that the Old Testament is legalistic as opposed to the New Testament that centers on grace is unfounded. The grace of Yahweh is on full display through the entire Hebrew Bible if you have eyes to see and ears to hear. When God departs from His creation or removes Himself from our lives, everything inevitably folds in on itself and sinks back into Chaos. That's how the passive wrath of God works. But we must acknowledge the flip side of the coin—active grace.

One of the many reasons I love God with all my heart is that there have been so many moments where He could've left— but He didn't. So many seasons where my sin should've driven Him away. So many moments when I defiled His temple with chaos and He had every right to abandon me. But instead, He stayed.

He remained. Held it all together. He didn't let everything cave in and crumble.

So many times, like David in Psalm 51:11, I've prayed the following prayer: "Do not cast me from your presence or take your Holy Spirit from me." David's prayer is essentially saying, "Don't evict me from Your garden, and don't evict Yourself from my life."

Maybe David understands the stories of Adam, Eve, and Noah. Maybe David understands that God's presence and God's Order are one and the same. David is known throughout history as a leader and king who prioritizes the worship and the presence of God. He has zeal for God's house and wants to build a dwelling place for the divine presence. He's a new Noah, laying the groundwork for building the house of God and for prioritizing the presence of God in Israel.

This explains David's response when his wife Michal thinks he is acting in a manner unfit for a king by publicly worshipping with passion and exuberance. Michal's perspective is that the king of Israel should act in a reserved and respectable fashion. But David has placed a priority on the divine presence and responds to his wife's critique by saying, "I will celebrate before the LORD. I will become even more undignified than this, and I will be humiliated in my own eyes" (2 Samuel 6:21–22). These words are spoken from the heart of a true worshipper. For David, Yahweh's presence is the main nonnegotiable element in life.

True worship has a way of cutting through the Chaos. A true prioritization of God's presence begins to recalibrate our lives and restore Order. When we build and centralize a temple for God to dwell in, the Chaos fails to overtake us.

Sometimes we get the passive wrath of God—where He departs and all hell breaks out in the wake of His absence. But other times we get the active grace of God—where He stays, even though He could depart, and He wins us back to Himself with His grace, patience, and loving-kindness.

One thing that unequivocally links David to Noah is that Yahweh makes covenant with both men. There are only four moments in the entire Hebrew Bible where Yahweh chooses to establish and strengthen His covenant with His people. To be honest, if someone could remember only four names and stories from the entire Hebrew Bible, these would probably be the ones:

Noah
Abraham
Moses
David

The Mount Rushmore of the Old Testament.

When Yahweh makes a covenant with Noah in Genesis 9:12–16, this is what He says:

This is the sign of the covenant I am making between me and you and every living creature with you, a covenant for all generations to come: I have set my rainbow in the clouds, and it will be the sign of the covenant between me and the earth. Whenever I bring clouds over the earth and the rainbow appears in the clouds, I will remember my covenant between me and you and all living creatures of every kind. Never again will the waters become a flood to destroy all life. Whenever the rainbow appears in the clouds, I will see it and remember the everlasting covenant between God and all living creatures of every kind on the earth.

Can you notice any repeated words in God's speech to Noah? In these five short verses, the word *rainbow* is either repeated explicitly or alluded to at least five times. Which means it must be really important. However, there is no word for "rainbow" in Hebrew. Let that sink in.

The Hebrew word used in this passage is *qeset*,[1] but it doesn't translate as "rainbow." Yet that's what the NIV translation says. So, what's going on?

Here's how the NRSV translates verses 13–15: "I have set my bow in the clouds, and it shall be a sign of the covenant between me and the earth. When I bring clouds over the earth and the bow is seen in the clouds, I will remember my covenant that is between me and you and every living creature of all flesh; and the waters shall never again become a flood to destroy all flesh."

"I have set my *bow* (*qeset*) in the clouds." *Qeset* simply means "bow."[2] And the image Yahweh is meaning to evoke is of an archer's bow. "The word *qeset* denotes the hunter's . . . and warrior's . . . weapon by which arrows are shot."[3]

Here's a moment where the NIV translators meant well by

making the text easier to understand, but good intentions can sometimes remove the set of images that the original audience would have had in their minds.

An archer's bow is a weapon, and Yahweh is using this image to communicate something important concerning His character and His covenant. If you imagine a rainbow as an archer's weapon in the clouds, one thing becomes very clear— the arrow is pointing away from the earth and toward the heavens.

If you've ever had a weapon pointed in your direction, then you understand the intense and immediate anxiety that comes with being face-to-face with a lethal threat. Back when I was an immature youth pastor and working in one of the southern states of the US, I used a shotgun for a sermon illustration. There were absolutely zero bullets in this weapon, but I pointed it at the audience to demonstrate a point, and the chaos of panic immediately overtook the room. Instant fear. Instant anxiety.

It was very memorable and probably also traumatic. But thank God there's no video evidence of this. And thank God my senior pastor didn't fire me. I'm wiser now, I promise.

We could've done without the live demonstration and the possible trauma it caused, but the illustration was potent. Because most of us live under the crippling fear and anxiety of God's bow pointing directly at us. We navigate life as if we're in God's crosshairs, and this subconscious fear of wrath and punishment creates a collective culture of anxiety. Most of us feel like we're staring down the barrel of heaven's shotgun, just waiting for the other shoe to drop. You may not realize that the chaos of your anxiety is fueled by your latent and subconscious fear of God's disapproval and wrath. But the truth is that the peace *of* God typically can't materialize until you accept that you're at peace *with* God—and, maybe more importantly, that God is at peace with you.

For some of us, this is the announcement we didn't even know we needed, but please hear me: God put His bow away long ago.

The national holiday known as Juneteenth is a public acknowledgment and symbol of the fact that there's often a gap between the truth and our lived experience and reality. Abraham Lincoln announced the Emancipation Proclamation on January 1, 1863. Robert E. Lee surrendered to the Union Army on April 9, 1865, and the Confederate military department covering Texas disbanded on May 26, 1865.

However, it wasn't until June 19, 1865—nine hundred days after the Emancipation Proclamation went into effect and two months after the end of the war—that Major General Gordon Granger brought the news of freedom to enslaved Americans in Texas.[4] These men and women were free, but the news simply hadn't reached them. The war was over, they were free, but they didn't know it yet.

God's bow isn't aimed at you. God hung up His bow a long time ago. He poured out all His wrath on His Son a long time ago, but maybe the good news is just now reaching you.

God is at peace with you. He desires to walk in covenant with you. And the chaos of anxiety surrounding your status with God can finally be calmed.

Scholars have often wondered how it's possible that so many cultures across the ancient world have recorded stories regarding a catastrophic flood. People groups from all over the globe have these prehistoric flood stories in common. Which points to some kind of traumatic memory in the collective human psyche. Humankind as a whole has always known anxiety and fear in the aftermath of the Flood. This is why God has displayed His bow in the clouds for all people to see and be consistently reminded of the good news of our peace treaty with God.

Yahweh is saying to Noah and to all humanity, "Next time I flood the earth with water, it will be because the arrow pierced Me, not y'all." The proof that humanity and Yahweh are in covenant is the fact that He's willing to be on the receiving end of the archer's arrow rather than make us pay the penalty of our sin. His covenant with Noah is essentially Yahweh saying, "This is going to hurt Me more than it's going to hurt you"— and actually meaning it.

The archer's bow that God has set in the clouds is positioned so that the arrow pierces Him as opposed to humanity. Which is exactly what's happening on the cross. Jesus is elevated above the earth, and John 19:34 tells us that "one of the soldiers pierced Jesus' side with a spear, bringing a sudden flow of blood and water."

The arrow of the archer's bow was finally released as Jesus hung on Calvary's cross. And as the arrow pierced Divinity, a flood of water and blood poured out to cleanse the land and forgive humanity. That is active grace.

There's not much active wrath in the biblical text. And there's not much passive grace. When there's wrath, it's passive. When there's grace, it's active. Whether we're studying a flood of rain in the Old Testament or a flood of water and blood pouring from a pierced Savior on Calvary's hill, we see passive wrath and active grace.

## Chapter 18

# Moses and His Dragon

Thus says the Lord GOD:

> I am against you,
>   Pharaoh king of Egypt,
> *the great dragon* sprawling
>   in the midst of its channels,
> saying, "My Nile is my own;
>   I made it for myself."

—EZEKIEL 29:2–3, NRSV, EMPHASIS ADDED

My whole life, I believed that Beren*stein* Bears was the correct spelling for the book series I read and enjoyed as a kid. You can probably imagine my confusion and utter shock when I found out that's never been the spelling. According to every single internet search that anyone can find—and the official website[1]—it's always been Beren*stain* Bears.

I'm ashamed to admit that my initial reaction was to assume there was some kind of conspiracy theory. Someone must have gotten rid of all the copies with the original spelling from my childhood and replaced them with this new weird one. I'm not alone, by the way. Millions of people incorrectly remember the spelling of this book series. I know because we've all found each other on the internet.

There's a term for this phenomenon—where a significant portion of the population incorrectly remembers an event or shares a memory of an event that did not actually occur. It's called the Mandela effect.

> Did the Fruit of the Loom logo ever have a cornucopia
> with fruit pouring out?
> Does Pikachu's tail have a black tip?
> Does Mr. Monopoly wear a monocle?

If you said yes to any of those, you're probably under the influence of the Mandela effect.[2] Because the correct answer to all those questions is no. However, millions of people remember the Fruit of the Loom logo having a cornucopia, Pikachu having a black-tipped tail, and Mr. Monopoly sporting a monocle. These are all very popular examples of communal false memories.

Most people think Darth Vader said, "Luke, I am your father" in *The Empire Strikes Back,* but the actual line is "No, I am your father." The quote "If you build it, they will come" said to be from *Field of Dreams* is actually "If you build it, he will come." And many people remember the Evil Queen from *Snow White and the Seven Dwarfs* saying, "Mirror, mirror on the wall," but she actually says, "Magic mirror on the wall."[3]

All of these are popular examples of the Mandela effect. However, this phenomenon extends beyond pop culture. For myriad reasons, many Christians have communal false memories of biblical stories and events. Like Moses throwing down his staff before Pharaoh and it becoming a snake. That's a communal false memory. And everything from Charlton Heston's portrayal of Moses to *The Prince of Egypt* reinforces this. So, what actually happened?

Exodus 7:10 records that "Moses and Aaron went to Pharaoh and did just as the LORD commanded. Aaron threw his staff down in front of Pharaoh and his officials, and it became a [*tannin*]."

A *tannin*. A dragon.

A Chaos dragon.

A sea monster.

Talk about a plot twist.

Moses and Aaron throw down a staff, and it becomes a dragon. That single detail changes this story in the best way imaginable—a breadcrumb that alters how we interpret the character of Moses and the entire story of Exodus.

The Exodus story begins with a wicked, paranoid, and unnamed Pharaoh who enslaves the people of Israel and decrees that all infant Hebrew boys be thrown into the Nile and drowned. But one mom decides to defy Pharaoh and hides her son for three months. Finally, when she can no longer hide the baby boy, she makes an ark for her son. Instead of tossing him into the chaos to drown, she places him within the ark and then puts the ark in the water.

As fate would have it, Pharaoh's daughter is the woman to find this baby mysteriously and safely in the reeds along the Nile. The Bible tells us in Exodus 2:10 that Pharaoh's daughter names him Moses, saying, "I drew him out of the water," and Moses ends up in the very home of the man who ordered his death. Talk about irony.

Let's recap.

We've got a famous river prominently featured, an ark used

as a means of salvation through water, a boy who's named after his association with the water, and eventually a staff that can turn into a dragon. We're only a few pages into the Exodus story, and already we have enough breadcrumbs to begin piecing this puzzle together—because something tells me that the Exodus story may be about Chaos and Order.

We've seen all the images and symbols that have signified Chaos throughout the biblical story thus far. Water. Dragons. Floods. Arks. All the usual suspects are present in Exodus. And now that we have the tools to interpret ancient patterns and Eastern symbols, it's time to let go of our false communal memories and replace them with artifacts from the ancient path.

Again, Exodus begins with a new Pharaoh who is intimidated by the growth and strength of the Israelites. He decides to enslave and oppress God's people by making their lives bitter with harsh labor and forcing them to work "in every kind of field labor" (Exodus 1:14, NRSV).

Genesis has already equipped us to interpret what Exodus is describing. Genesis told us that Adam and Eve were deceived by a beast of the field and that Cain took Abel out into the field and acted like a violent beast toward his brother. Genesis described Esau as a man of the field.

The Serpent. Then Cain. Then Esau. Inhabitants of the field and thus beasts and agents of Chaos. A very clear and recognizable pattern. Pharaoh has brought the people of Israel out to the field—the exact same way Cain brought his brother out to the field. Pharaoh isn't just a king; he's a king of Chaos.

Remember how the Serpent was the craftiest of the beasts? That word *crafty* in Hebrew is *arum*[4] and means "wise," "cunning," or "shrewd."[5] Well, as Pharaoh is debating a solution for the growing population of Israelites, he says in Exodus 1:10, "Come, let us deal shrewdly with them" (NRSV).

Shrewd. Just like the Serpent.

There's an obscure character in the Bible named Nimrod. He's buried within a genealogy and rarely ever talked about, but he's oddly very important. Genesis 10:8 tells us that Nimrod is "the first on earth to become a mighty warrior" (NRSV). Verses 10–12 show that he's out in the wilderness, moving east of Eden, building cities in the land of Shinar. He builds Babel. He builds Nineveh. And the text says that's "the beginning of his kingdom" (verse 10). Fascinating character yet relatively unknown and unpopular.

When we get to the story of Babel, we learn that Nimrod and his crew are using brick and mortar to build their city. Brick and mortar. We don't see these words often throughout the Torah. In fact, we will see them only one other time.

Exodus 1:11–14 says that Pharaoh oppressed the Israelites and that "the Egyptians came to dread [them] and worked them ruthlessly. They made their lives bitter with harsh labor in brick and mortar." The Israelites "built Pithom and Rameses as store cities for Pharaoh."

Brick. Mortar. City building. Hmm. Sounds like Pharaoh is a new Nimrod.

Pharaoh is the new Serpent. The new Cain. The new Nimrod. Pharaoh is a shrewd beast, a cold-blooded murderer, and an empire builder. Pharaoh is the Chaos trifecta. Pharaoh is a king of Chaos, a Chaos dragon.

The writer of Exodus hints at this, but the prophets Ezekiel and Isaiah state it very plainly. Yahweh commands Ezekiel to prophesy against Pharaoh, saying, "Set your face against Pharaoh king of Egypt, and prophesy against him and against all

Egypt; speak, and say, Thus says the Lord GOD: I am against you, Pharaoh king of Egypt, the great dragon sprawling in the midst of its channels, saying, 'My Nile is my own; I made it for myself'" (Ezekiel 29:2–3, NRSV).

Wait a second. Did Yahweh just call Pharaoh a great dragon?

Yes. That is precisely what happened.

Pharaoh has unleashed a level of chaos that we have yet to see in the biblical narrative. The writer of Exodus links him to the patterns of Chaos we've already seen, while highlighting that something unprecedented is also happening in the story. We've never seen an international superpower enslave an entire ethnic group, countless baby boys drowned in the Nile by a tyrant, or a world leader who claims to be the incarnation of a god.

We've seen Chaos, but not like this.

When God splits the Red Sea and Pharaoh follows behind to recapture the Israelites as slaves, God causes their chariot wheels to get stuck, which allows time for Israel to completely pass through the Red Sea safely. Then Exodus 14:28–29 says that "the waters returned and covered the chariots and the chariot drivers, the entire army of Pharaoh that had followed them into the sea; not one of them remained" (NRSV).

In Isaiah 51, the prophet is meditating on this exact moment. He is reflecting on how Yahweh delivered His people from Egypt when they were stuck between the armies of Pharaoh and the sea. Here's what Isaiah writes:

> Was it not you who dried up the sea,
>      the waters of the great deep;
> who made the depths of the sea a way
>      for the redeemed to cross over? (verse 10, NRSV)

The prophet Isaiah is clearly recounting a specific moment in history—the people of Israel miraculously crossing the Red Sea on dry ground—and it's quite fascinating to see what he writes in verse 9:

> Awake, awake, put on strength,
>     O arm of the Lord!
> Awake, as in days of old,
>     the generations of long ago!
> Was it not you who cut Rahab in pieces,
>     who pierced the dragon? (NRSV)

Isaiah says that God, through the Red Sea judgment, "cut Rahab in pieces" and "pierced the dragon."

Rahab was a famous Chaos dragon known by name throughout the ancient world,[6] but here Isaiah uses this name as a substitute for Pharaoh. Isaiah sees Pharaoh through the lens of an ancient worldview, and now we can as well.

The biblical authors see Pharaoh as a dragon. Moses. Ezekiel. Isaiah. They all view Pharaoh this way.

So, what does Yahweh equip Moses with as he goes to confront the most powerful human leader on the planet? You guessed it. A staff that can turn into a dragon. Because Pharaoh will be consumed by the very Chaos he's created.

## Chapter 19

# Plagues of Chaos

> The order God introduced to chaos in Genesis 1
> is now yielding, as far as the Egyptians are
> concerned, to chaos once again. In fact, the
> plagues and the Red Sea incident are nothing
> less than a series of creation reversals.
>
> —PETER ENNS, *EXODUS*, THE NIV APPLICATION
> COMMENTARY

It could easily seem as though Yahweh is being unjust, extreme, and unreasonably cruel as the plagues pull Egypt back into Chaos. But we must unearth the context beneath the surface before we jump to conclusions. The Flood narrative has already established that Yahweh is loving, gracious, kind, and merciful, and this account of the plagues cannot erase or undermine that.

So, we must ask an important question: Who was Pharaoh according to the Egyptian religious pantheon?

Pharaoh proclaimed himself to be the incarnation of the Egyptian god Horus, and he was believed to be the son of Ra, the sun god. He represented the entire pantheon of gods to the Egyptian people. Simply put, Pharaoh was a god.

This detail changes everything. Because Yahweh is going to engage with this self-proclaimed god as if he's actually a god. And by the end of the narrative, Pharaoh will know that he is neither the incarnation of Horus nor the son of Ra but a mere mortal whose arrogance has provoked the wrath of the one true God.

Since a deity should be able to keep their creation from falling into chaos, Yahweh will prove to Pharaoh that he is a mere human by sending plagues of de-creation and Chaos on the land of Egypt. Yahweh's response to Pharaoh is layered, brilliant, and designed to demonstrate that Pharaoh is utterly dependent on the only God who can pull creation out of Chaos and sustain Order.

Remember, creation is the process whereby Yahweh brought Order out of Chaos. The plagues are simply a reversal of that process.

In creation, water is gathered together. Genesis 1:9–10 records that "God said, 'Let the water under the sky be *gathered* to one place, and let dry ground appear.' And it was so. God called the dry ground 'land,' and *the gathered waters* he called 'seas.'" In the plagues, Aaron and Moses hold the staff over all of Egypt's "pools [or *gatherings*] of water," and they become blood (Exodus 7:19–20, NRSV). The Hebrew word used here to describe the gatherings or pools of water is *miqweh*, which is the exact same word from the opening chapter of Genesis when God creates the seas.[1] Coincidence? I don't think so.

In creation, Yahweh brings Order by creating a clear boundary between the water and the land, separating these two realms from each other. In the plagues, that boundary is erased as frogs overrun the land. Frogs dwell on both land and water and represent the undoing of Yahweh's clear boundary from Genesis.

In creation, Yahweh brings forth humanity from the dust of the ground. In the plagues, that dust becomes an infestation of gnats covering every living thing in the dust of their own mortality. (I hope you're seeing a pattern emerge.)

In creation, God brings forth plant life on the third day. Genesis 1:11 records, "God said, 'Let the land produce vegetation.' . . . And it was so." In the plagues of hail and locusts, all vegetation in Egypt is destroyed.

In creation, Yahweh brings forth light. In the plagues, Egypt is covered in thick darkness.

The plagues are a reversal of creation. By the end of them, the Order of creation has been completely undone and Egypt is plunged back into the Chaos of *tohu va-vohu*. Pharaoh is powerless to either prevent this from happening or pull Egypt out of the Chaos. The plagues are the measured consequence for a human daring to believe that he is divine and worthy of worship.

Instead of "Let's talk about this man-to-man," Yahweh essentially says to this mere mortal who has exalted himself to the place of god, "Let's handle this God to god." Yahweh isn't treating Pharaoh like a human but judging him according to his self-proclaimed status.

The majority of us aren't slave-holding, genocidal tyrants propping ourselves up as deities. However, all of us battle with arrogance, self-reliance, idolatry, and narcissistic tendencies. The Exodus story makes it clear that those qualities create chaos, because despite what we tell ourselves, we as humans don't have the power to sustain order in our own strength. We were designed to be dependent on the one true God that creates and sustains Order and holds back the Chaos.

There's a small Pharaoh in all of us. We all desire to be exalted—even at the expense of others. And we've all experienced order unraveling and chaos unfolding. We've all experienced a plague of Chaos at some point. Chaos that brings us to our knees and urges us to humbly repent and acknowledge our utter and desperate dependence on the Creator of life and Order.

There are two clues that lead us to believe we are supposed to see Pharaoh not as an individual but as a representative of the entire office.

The first is that we never get a name for this Pharaoh. Clearly Moses knew this man's name. Which means the omission of this information is intentional on the author's part. Around 170 Pharaohs ruled throughout Egypt's history. Yahweh is judging the idolatry of every Pharaoh who ever dared exalt himself to the status of a god, not simply the actions of the individual ruler standing before Moses and Aaron.

Our second clue is found in Exodus 12:12, which declares Yahweh's purpose for the plagues: "I will pass through the land of Egypt that night, and I will strike down every firstborn in the land of Egypt, both human beings and animals; on all the gods of Egypt I will execute judgments: I am the LORD" (NRSV).

Numbers 33:3–4 testifies to the same fact: "On the day after the passover the Israelites went out boldly in the sight of all the Egyptians, while the Egyptians were burying all their firstborn, whom the LORD had struck down among them. The LORD executed judgments even against their gods" (NRSV).

Yahweh is sending the plagues as judgment for idolatry—judgment on all the gods of Egypt, including Pharaoh. Simply put, idolatry will always result in Chaos.

Why is Yahweh judging these gods? Does Yahweh take these gods and false deities seriously? The simple answer is yes.

Yahweh takes them seriously because the Bible doesn't operate from a monotheistic perspective. If you grew up learning that Judaism, Christianity, and Islam are all monotheistic religions, this may come as a shock and cause some confusion. Quite frankly, the biblical authors never promote monotheism or espouse a monotheistic worldview. (Stay with me.) Monotheism is the *belief* in one god. Instead, the biblical authors promote and espouse monolatry or a monolatrous worldview.

And what is monalatry? The exclusive *worship* of one God.

Yahweh takes the gods of Egypt seriously because they are real. We are foolish if we don't believe that there are fallen angels, demonic forces, powers, principalities, and powerful regional beings of wickedness that receive worship as gods.

Hathor.
Isis.
Osiris.
Heket.
Hapi.
Horus.
Pharaoh.

These beings are real. These beings have power. They are fallen and corrupt spiritual powers—not a figment of human imagination. They have truly appeared to humans, impressed humans with their supernatural power, and led humans astray.

The apostle Paul takes these beings seriously when he gives the Corinthian church instructions to help bring order into their chaotic lives. This church is full of chaos. One guy is sleeping with his father's wife. There are frivolous lawsuits and divisive factions. People are getting drunk during communion, and folks are fighting one another and competing to give prophetic words during the worship service.

This church in Corinth is a mess. So, Paul writes to help

establish some much-needed order. And much of that order is rooted in the Corinthians turning away from idols and giving their exclusive allegiance and devotion to Jesus. This is what Paul says in 1 Corinthians 10:20–21:

> The sacrifices of pagans are offered to demons, not to God, and I do not want you to be participants with demons. You cannot drink the cup of the Lord and the cup of demons too; you cannot have a part in both the Lord's table and the table of demons.

Paul doesn't downplay the severity of idolatry but calls it out for what it is—the worship of demons. He has a monolatrous worldview and understands that rebellious and fallen angels are actively recruiting human adherents.

Zeus.
Aphrodite.
Poseidon.
Real beings with real power.

Chaos finds a doorway into our lives through demonic forces who appeal to the appetites of our flesh. Aphrodite knows that to have loyal and devoted followers, she must have thousands of temple prostitutes wandering the streets of Corinth. The prostitutes are simply bait to get humans to worship demons.

Most people are looking for sexual pleasure, not a religious experience, so the demonic being the Greeks called Aphrodite cloaks and camouflages the religious devotion under the veneer of sexual ecstasy. It's a brilliant strategy.

When I think of the postmodern world and the rampant

sexuality of our age, it is clear that countless people have invited Chaos into their lives through the doorway of sexual indulgence and expression. I call this the Trojan horse effect. Chaos enters through the gate of our souls undetected because it never appears as an army of soldiers armed to annihilate. Chaos always masquerades as a gift—but once that gift is safely behind the walls of our souls, Chaos breaks out of the horse and we realize we've been duped.

Paul wants the Corinthian Christians to be on alert. What may seem like an innocent dinner party with some meat that's been sacrificed to Athena or Hermes could actually invoke the manifest presence of demonic powers that will inevitably trigger a plague of Chaos.

An innocent Tinder hookup can easily lead to a soul tie that brings unimaginable chaos into your life because while our bodies are intoxicated with pleasure, our souls mingle. I've counseled countless adults who mysteriously started struggling with depression and couldn't trace the origin for that form of Chaos until we started to examine the entry point of sexual experiences in their lives.

Our culture is full of demonic access points that usher in Chaos:

Carefree and commitment-free sex.
Chakra stones that you can buy at Urban Outfitters.
Music from artists who experiment with the occult.
Regular, unrestrained viewing of pornography.
Smudging and sage-burning rituals.

The list is endless.
All forms of idolatry that ultimately bring a plague of Chaos.

As the people of Israel leave Egypt, God is aware that they desperately need Order to be restored to their lives. They've lived as slaves in a culture of immorality, injustice, and idolatry for centuries. So, once they've passed through the Red Sea and experienced the salvation and deliverance of Yahweh, it's time for Moses to give them the Law.

This isn't legalism or opposed to grace. Legalism is placing obedience before salvation. Had Yahweh given the Ten Commandments on stone tablets as the people stood in front of the Red Sea and made them agree while under duress—that would be legalism. But Yahweh doesn't do that. Yahweh saves and delivers them from bondage and *then* gives them the Law and the commandments once He has already removed their chains of slavery.

This is the same pattern that Jesus follows. Jesus sets us free from the bondage of sin and death by His atoning and sacrificial work on the cross. And once we place our faith in this King Jesus, He says in John 14:15, "If you love me, keep my commands."

Yahweh always liberates His people not only from the sin of slavery but also from the slavery of sin—both then and now.

The crossing of the Red Sea isn't the end of the Exodus narrative. What happens for the remaining twenty-six chapters?

After fourteen chapters of Chaos, it's finally time for Order.

The rest of Exodus focuses on the Law that will govern the behavior of this new society and the tabernacle to house the presence of God. Because without law and presence, we don't stand a chance of conquering the Chaos or creating Order. Let's keep tracking the story and crushing Chaos.

## Chapter 20

# A Portal Back to Eden

The precise and perfect dimensions of the tabernacle indicate a sense of order amid chaos.

—PETER ENNS, *EXODUS*, THE NIV APPLICATION COMMENTARY

To think of the tabernacle as an act of cosmic re-creation is precisely what the building of the tabernacle originally intended to convey. . . .

In the midst of a fallen world, in exile from the Garden of Eden—the original "heaven on earth"—God undertakes another act of creation, a building project that is nothing less than a return to pre-Fall splendor.

—PETER ENNS, *EXODUS*, THE NIV APPLICATION COMMENTARY

The biblical writer wishes the reader to view the construction of the tabernacle as an act of creation.

—PETER ENNS, *EXODUS*, THE NIV APPLICATION COMMENTARY

Once God leads His people through the chaos of the Red Sea, it's time to bring order to their lives. It's time to take them back to the garden—an ordered and sanctified space where God can dwell among them. So, God instructs them to build a tent for His presence—a tabernacle designed to restore cohabitation between God and humanity.

When you get to Exodus 25 and start reading the instructions for this tent, it's easy to get bogged down by the details. Outer coverings of ram and goatskins. Linen curtains woven with blue, purple, and red designs. A floor-mounted golden candelabra with seven lamps. A large bronze altar made from an acacia wood frame with horns on the corners.

Actually, there are so many details that it should lead the curious reader to wonder whether more is going on here than the mere construction of a tent. First, God speaks seven times in Exodus[1] to give Moses the instructions for the tabernacle. Can you think of another time when the construction of something was split into a seven-part process? Yeah, the creation account in Genesis. Peter Enns points out in his groundbreaking commentary on Exodus that, "Commentators for centuries have noticed that the phrase 'the Lord said to Moses' occurs *seven* times. . . . It seems clear that the purpose of this arrangement is to aid the reader in making the connection between the building of the tabernacle and the seven days of creation, both of which involve six creative acts culminating in a seventh-day rest."[2]

For the ancient audience, the seven-part instruction found in Exodus clearly correlates to the Creation account, yet for modern readers, this connection is most likely unclear and that's because we're so removed from this overall style of communication.

Second, a lampstand in the inner court of this tent has six

branches (Exodus 25:32–35). But why branches? Maybe because the lampstand should make us think of a tree. Why a tree? Can you think of a time in Genesis when a tree was the centerpiece of the story? Yeah, the Garden of Eden.

Third, this lampstand also gives light. In fact, it has seven lamps attached to those six branches and the center post (verse 37). Let's think. When was light a crucial part of a story that revolved around the number seven? The creation account in Genesis.

Fourth, the tabernacle has a large bronze water basin in the outer court (30:18). Because we can't talk about creation without talking about water.

Fifth, the designers of this tent are filled with wisdom, which is fascinating. Here's what God says to Moses in Exodus 31:3–5 concerning Bezalel, who'll build God's ordered dwelling place and sanctuary: "I have filled him with the Spirit of God, with wisdom, with understanding, with knowledge and with all kinds of skills—to make artistic designs for work in gold, silver and bronze, to cut and set stones, to work in wood, and to engage in all kinds of crafts."

Why exactly would Bezalel need wisdom? Well, Wisdom actually has a speech in Proverbs where she shares her perspective from the days of creation. Proverbs 8:22–24 records:

> The LORD created me at the beginning of his work,
>      the first of his acts of long ago.
> Ages ago I was set up,
>      at the first, before the beginning of the earth.
> When there were no depths, I was brought forth,
>      when there were no springs abounding with
>      water. (NRSV)

Why do the tabernacle builders need the wisdom God had when He created the world, specifically the Garden of Eden? Maybe the tabernacle is a return to Eden. In the same way God pulled creation out of Chaos and created a refuge where His presence could dwell with humans, maybe the tabernacle is supposed to be a sanctuary from the chaos of the wilderness.

Sixth, when the construction of the tabernacle is completed in Exodus, the language mirrors the completion of creation in Genesis. The human author of these texts wants us to see something. This is how the Bible teaches us theology—by forcing us to dig for treasure, staring at texts until we notice the parallels. In Exodus, Moses sees the work of the tabernacle and pronounces a blessing; in Genesis, God sees the work of creation and pronounces a blessing.

Here's a diagram to see how the passages mirror each other:

| Tabernacle | Creation |
|---|---|
| "Moses saw all the work, and behold . . . as the LORD had commanded, so had they done it. Then Moses blessed them" (Exodus 39:43, ESV). | "God saw all that He had made, and behold, it was very good" (Genesis 1:31, NASB1995). "God blessed them" (verse 28). |
| "Moses finished the work" (Exodus 40:33). | "The heavens and the earth were finished. . . . And on the seventh day God finished the work that he had done" (Genesis 2:1–2, NRSV). |

Lastly, God told Moses to weave cherubim into the curtains of the tabernacle and to place two cherubim on top of the ark of the covenant.

We've seen cherubim before, haven't we? Where? In the Garden of Eden. Here's what Genesis 3:24 says: "After [God] drove the man out, he placed on the east side of the Garden of Eden cherubim and a flaming sword flashing back and forth to guard the way to the tree of life."

Cherubim were placed at the entrance of Eden to guard the tree of life from Adam and Eve. Now the cherubim of the tabernacle are welcoming the sons of Adam and the daughters of Eve back into God's presence with a new tree of life.

As long as the people of God carve out ordered space for the divine presence, it's as if the effects of the Fall are neutralized. God has offered His people a road to experience restored Order.

The construction of the tabernacle isn't about building. It's about new creation, and the same Creator who pulled this world out of Chaos is at work again with a new fledgling nation of freed slaves. The construction of the tabernacle is about Order ruling over Chaos—Sabbath rest and reentry into Eden and God providing refuge for His people amid chaotic waters and ravenous wilderness.

Welcome to the world of Scripture. Where Noah's ark is really about the tabernacle. But then you find out that the tabernacle is really about creation. Which means Noah's ark is about creation too because each loop gives new meaning to the last loops—and there are more loops here than on a roller coaster at Six Flags.

Welcome to the mystery.

Welcome to the lifelong pursuit of wisdom.

Welcome to an Eastern way of engaging with the text.

# THE
# PRINCE
# OF
# PEACE

SECTION

4

## Chapter 21

# Breaking the Cycle of Chaos

> In the gospels . . . Jesus is presented as a
> creator figure who confronts the powers of
> *chaos.*
>
> —DOMINIC RUDMAN, "THE CRUCIFIXION AS CHAOS-
> KAMPF," EMPHASIS ADDED

The second verse of the Bible is packed with intentional imagery. In this one short verse, we get the Chaos of *tohu va-vohu,* followed by the deep waters of the *tehom,* and ending with the wind of God hovering over the surface of the Chaos waters.

Chaos. Water. Wind.

*Tohu va-vohu. Tehom. Ruach.* In that specific order. We're two verses into the biblical text, and we're already halfway into a pattern that will persist and permeate through the entire narrative of the Bible.

In the next verse, God speaks, and the authority of His spoken word moves creation from Chaos to Order. For the next several days of creation, God will impose His divine Order on creation as the Chaos bows and submits to the will and wisdom of the Creator.

Order never happens by accident or chance. Order requires intentionality.

So far, then, we have Chaos, water, wind, word, and Order. We're five steps into our six-step pattern, and the pattern will always end with a test.

Because boundaries aren't boundaries until they're tested. God will test Adam and Eve to see whether they will partner with Him to extend the boundaries of divine Order or choose to partner with the Dragon and become agents of Chaos.

Spoiler alert: They fail the test, and creation is plunged back into Chaos. Five steps forward. Six steps back. And the cycle starts over.

This six-step pattern will appear over and over again:

Chaos.
Deep waters.
Wind or Spirit of God.
The voice of Yahweh.
Divine Order.
A failed test.
Repeat.

This is the precise pattern of the Flood account in Genesis. At the beginning of the Flood narrative, society has descended into Chaos. Genesis 6:5 describes the moral and cultural Chaos as follows:

The LORD saw how great the wickedness of the human race had become on the earth, and that every inclination of the thoughts of the human heart was only evil all the time.

When there's smoke, there's fire. And when there's Chaos, there's water. So, what happens right after the text describes the moral and cultural Chaos of the cosmos? The fountains of the great deep burst forth. Floodwaters. Followed by the Spirit of God hovering above the Chaotic waters.

Here's how Genesis 8:8 describes it: "Then he sent out a dove to see if the water had receded from the surface of the ground." Remember, the text shows us using images and symbols. It rarely tells us. But if we have eyes to see, we'll know exactly what the dove represents.

So far we have Chaos, deep waters, Spirit of God. We now know the pattern, so we know what to expect.

Like clockwork, the voice of Yahweh commands Noah to come out of the ark (Genesis 8:15–16). And again, Yahweh moves the creation from Chaos to Order, creating a world that is safe and inhabitable for Noah and his family.

Yet the cycle isn't complete without a test. This testing of Noah and his family is in a vineyard as opposed to a garden, but unfortunately that doesn't change the results.

They fail the test. And again, we've taken five steps forward and six steps back.

Noah and his family cannot sustain the Order of God in the cosmos, and humanity continues to spiral into more and more Chaos.

As you read the text, it is natural to begin to feel trapped in this never-ending loop of Chaos—where we get close to breaking free of the gravitational pull Chaos exerts on the human race but ultimately fail the final test that would grant us lasting Order and permanent peace.

But the Bible isn't even close to being done with this pattern. So next up, we have the people of Israel enslaved by a narcissistic and paranoid Pharaoh. This is unprecedented Chaos. And then there's even more Chaos as Yahweh brings a series of plagues that completely unravel the Order of creation.

So naturally, God leads His people to the Red Sea. Because deep waters are always the second step in this loop that humanity can't seem to break free from.

Here's a nerdy fact before we observe our third step in the Chaos cycle: The Hebrew word for "Spirit," *ruach*, also means "wind" and "breath." Wind. Breath. Spirit. Same exact word.[1]

Now let's read what happens next. Exodus 14:21 tells us:

> Then Moses stretched out his hand over the sea, and all
> that night the LORD drove the sea back with a strong
> east wind (*ruach*) and turned it into dry land.

Of course there was wind. We have a pattern to maintain, and the biblical authors take these patterns very seriously. This is the same word from the second verse of Genesis where the wind of God hovered over the surface of the deep. So far in this story, we've got Chaos, deep waters, and then the ruach of God.

Like clockwork, God then speaks, and the waters return to their original position.

Which then triggers the next step in the sequence: Order.

The Law. Commands. The Mosaic covenant at Sinai.
Leviticus. Deuteronomy. The Ten Commandments.
Instructions for building a tabernacle.
Law codes. Governmental structure.
Bureaucracy. Judges.
Divine Order. All in the wilderness.

And then we have multiple failed tests in the wilderness.

The bitter waters of Marah. The golden calf.
The refusal to trust the good report of Joshua and Caleb.
Korah's rebellion. The endless grumbling.
The desire for the food they ate in Egypt.

The list goes on and on.

Yahweh says in Numbers 14:22–23 that Israel not only failed multiple tests while they were in the wilderness but also actually turned the tables on Yahweh and tested Him ten times. He tells Moses:

> Not one of those who saw my glory and the signs I per-formed in Egypt and in the wilderness but who disobeyed me and tested me ten times—not one of them will ever see the land I promised on oath to their ancestors.

Yahweh tested the generation who came out of Egypt and commanded them to invade the land of Canaan, but only Joshua and Caleb trusted that Yahweh would deliver the Canaanites into their hands. Only Joshua and Caleb had faith. So, the entire generation of freed slaves failed God's test, and they died in the wilderness.

Let's recap:

Utter Chaos.
Deep waters.
Wind of God.
The voice of Yahweh.
Divine Order.

Testing. Failure.

Repeat.

This is not a coincidence. This is a six-part template, and the entire Bible follows it. Let's study one more example.

The land of Canaan has descended into moral and cultural Chaos. So, God leads Israel to the Jordan River while it's at flood stage. Deep waters. Joshua 3:15–17 says:

> Now the Jordan is at flood stage all during harvest. Yet as soon as the priests who carried the ark reached the Jordan and their feet touched the water's edge, the water from upstream stopped flowing. It piled up in a heap a great distance away. . . . So the people crossed over opposite Jericho. The priests who carried the ark of the covenant of the LORD stopped in the middle of the Jordan and stood on dry ground, while all Israel passed by until the whole nation had completed the crossing on dry ground.

Did you notice that detail about the Jordan River being at flood stage? Very intentional. The author wants us to link this narrative with every other flood story in the Scriptures because they don't want us to miss the pattern.

Also, what does the ark of the covenant represent exactly? The presence of the living God. And as long as the priests are carrying the ark, the presence of Yahweh is hovering over the floodwaters of the Jordan. Coincidence? Absolutely not. The authors of the Bible are following a pattern.

What typically follows the spirit or presence of Yahweh? His word. So, what happens next? Joshua 4:1 records, "When the whole nation had finished crossing the Jordan, the LORD said to Joshua . . ." Yahweh speaks to Joshua, and things begin to fall into order.

The people of Israel conquer Jericho in an ordered fashion. They follow the commands of Yahweh concerning the rhythm and pattern of when and how to march around the city's walls. They place the priests in the proper position. As a unit, they're silent when they're required to be and shout when commanded. And together in one organized accord, they overtake Jericho. Talk about Order.

So far in this story, we have Chaos, deep waters, Spirit of God, voice of God, and divine Order. Which means a test is coming next. And like clockwork, a man named Achan takes for himself what he is not authorized to. The Order is short lived because the narrative in Joshua 7:1 immediately following the battle of Jericho tells us that "the Israelites were unfaithful in regard to the devoted things; Achan . . . of the tribe of Judah, took some of them. So, the LORD's anger burned against Israel."

They had just experienced the unity of divine Order. Marching in unison. Obeying the command of God through Joshua. Shouting in unison on the final day. And then one rogue soldier wanted to steal some of the spoils of war. This is the Chaos of rampant individualism. Even though Eastern worldviews are more group oriented, there was still a temptation toward selfishness and self-focus.

Notice how the Bible tells us that Israel (*plural*) sinned against Yahweh. But then tells us that a man named Achan (*singular*) was the one who sinned.

To the modern Western reader, this naturally appears as a contradiction. But to the ancient Eastern reader, this made complete sense. The entire army suffers the consequences of

Achan's sin because we truly are bound together in a mysterious and slightly unexplainable way. The Bible is warning against the chaos that ensues when we live in ways that are selfish and self-centered.

The Israelites not only fail this test at the city of Ai, but they also fail to take full possession of the full breadth of the Promised Land. Joshua 13:1–2 tells us, "When Joshua had grown old, the LORD said to him, 'You are now very old, and there are still very large areas of land to be taken over. This is the land that remains.'"

And not only do the people of Israel fail to take full possession of their promised inheritance, but Judges 2:7–11 tells us that Joshua's generation also failed to pass along the baton of faith to the next generation:

> The people served the LORD throughout the lifetime of Joshua. . . . Joshua son of Nun, the servant of the LORD, died at the age of a hundred and ten. . . . After that whole generation had been gathered to their ancestors, another generation grew up who knew neither the LORD nor what he had done for Israel. Then the Israelites did evil in the eyes of the LORD and served the Baals.

Talk about one failed test after another. Judges is the sad and depressing story of how Chaos gets a foothold in the nation of Israel and how that foothold turns into a stronghold. By the end of Judges, Chaos has overtaken the land, and this process will repeat again and again:

> Chaos → Deep waters → *Ruach* or the Spirit hovering → Yahweh speaking → Divine Order → A failed test.

Five steps forward. Six steps back. Caught in an endless cycle of Chaos.

This exact copy-and-paste Chaos cycle can be found throughout the entire Old Testament. I could give more examples, but you get the point. If there's something that the Old Testament hammers home, it's this six-part Chaos cycle.

Put yourself in the shoes of Matthew's original audience. Matthew is writing to Jews who are very familiar with the Hebrew Scriptures and undoubtedly aware of this Chaos cycle.

Imagine what they think as they hear and read that Jesus goes into the deep waters of the Jordan to be baptized by John. That the Spirit of almighty God descends on Jesus in the form of a dove, hovering above the deep waters. That a voice from heaven begins to speak as Jesus is in the Chaos waters, with the Spirit brooding over the deep. Imagine their thoughts when they learn that Jesus is getting baptized not to be cleansed of sin but to do what is proper—to establish Order and to fulfill all righteousness.[2]

And lastly, imagine them listening with bated breath as Jesus is immediately led out into the wilderness to be tested. This is where things always go wrong. This is the point where we always take six steps back after five solid steps forward.

The state of the entire human race is complete Chaos. Jesus enters the same deep waters as Israel when conquering Canaan. Then the same dove from Noah's narrative begins hovering. The same voice that commanded creation to come into Order speaks. Jesus is obedient to a baptism He doesn't need so that things can be done properly and in Order. And then Jesus is led into the same wilderness where Yahweh tested Israel.

And the only element missing in this iteration of the pattern is a human who fails God's test. This moment with Jesus is the only one where we have this Chaos cycle but we don't have a failed test that triggers the system to start from the beginning. Finally. Six. Steps. Forward.

Chaos → Deep waters → Spirit of God → Voice of God → Divine Order → Test complete.

For the very first time in human history, we've gotten to the end of this six-part Chaos cycle and there's actually hope. What would Matthew's audience have taken from this story? That Jesus has come to put a final end to Chaos and to provide a path so you and I can finally partner with God to bring sustained Order into the cosmos.

The original audience would have felt the weight of Chaos and hopelessness immediately lifting from their shoulders. Wandering around in an endless cycle is draining and depressing. Feeling as though you are doomed to be dragged underwater by the undertow of Chaos is daunting. Feeling the shame of failing over and over again is overwhelming.

Matthew's audience would've heard this story and known that their Messiah had finally arrived. The same God who made the Chaos bow in Genesis 1 was now here in the flesh and had accomplished what we were all powerless to do, and He had now empowered us to follow in His footsteps. And this is exactly what Matthew wants. Matthew's gospel has an emphasis on discipleship—Jesus is not only to be worshipped as God but also copied as Man.

This story from Matthew's gospel is a reminder: The cycle has been broken, and we are not hopelessly trapped by Chaos or confusion. We have an invitation to walk in the freedom of God's Order and wisdom.

When most people read the story of Jesus being baptized, we don't immediately see that this is a narrative of Chaos and Order. However, ancient audiences would've recognized the pattern, and this now gives us license to see the rest of Jesus's ministry through the lens of an ancient hermeneutic.

Jesus is on assignment to conquer the Chaos, tame the Beast, and extend the Order of God. That's the mission. The New Testament uses different language than the Old Testament to talk about Chaos and Order, so sometimes it's difficult to discern that Jesus is on mission too.

All the physical healings. All the exorcisms. Jesus's teaching on the Law. His preaching of the kingdom. And all the miracles. These all fit in the paradigm of Chaos and Order.

This account of baptism and wilderness testing is designed to be our first impression of Jesus and His ministry. And when we interpret this first impression according to an ancient hermeneutic, the story begins to color all the other stories of Jesus in the Gospels.

First impressions stick. For better or worse. They affect every subsequent interaction, so it's vital that we understand this first impression of Jesus based on the intent of the author and the cultural context clues at our disposal.

As we turn to other moments in Jesus's life and ministry, let us remember that His entire ministry started by standing in the floodwaters of the Jordan as an agent of God's Order and a Prince of Peace. Everything Jesus does afterward is colored by the inaugural moment of His baptism and His subsequent wilderness testing. Jesus is the Chaos Crusher. Jesus is the Beast-taming, Dragon-conquering, Chaos-crushing Messiah. Born as the offspring of the woman to crush the head of the Dragon. Born to break the cycle of Chaos so that all God's children may be free.

Welcome to the New Testament.

Welcome to the person and ministry of Jesus.

Welcome to partnering with God to build a kingdom of peace and Order.

## Chapter 22

# Plunder the Dragon

By withstanding Satan's temptations, *Jesus bound Satan* . . . and could begin *plundering* Satan's house, freeing people from Satan's dominion. . . . *Orderly cosmos was overcoming chaos.*

—SIDNEY GREIDANUS, *FROM CHAOS TO COSMOS,* EMPHASIS ADDED

A dragon is no idle fancy. Whatever may be his origins, in fact or invention, the dragon in legend is a potent creation of men's imagination, richer in significance than his barrow is in gold.

—J. R. R. TOLKIEN, "BEOWULF: THE MONSTERS AND THE CRITICS"

Whether dragons are *literally* real will have to be a debate for other books, but what I do know for certain is that J. R. R. Tolkien understood their importance. He knew dragons were vital because of what they *represented.*

As a professor at Oxford, Tolkien was brilliant enough to write and publish commentaries and books on theology. However, he opted to place theological ideas and the Christian worldview within narrative-based fantasy because the act of capturing the imagination is the surest way of influencing the mind. His wager was successful.

It seems safe to say that more people have interacted with Tolkien's work than with any theologian's writings I know. Karl Barth and Thomas Aquinas were absolutely brilliant. But I've never personally met anyone who hasn't read or watched *The Lord of the Rings* or *The Hobbit*. I've met dozens of non-Christians who have watched and read the full *The Lord of the Rings* anthology, yet I have never met a non-Christian who's that familiar with G. K. Chesterton, John Calvin, or Martin Luther. Narrative and fantasy don't make things *less* serious— they actually make theology *more* effective.

Tolkien and Lewis knew they couldn't teach theology in a way that was truly biblical without dragons. However, Tolkien's character that we know as Smaug wasn't created ex nihilo but was inspired by the story of Fafnir.

According to Nordic mythology, Fafnir's father comes into possession of a great hoard of gold and a magical ring. Fafnir eventually is filled with so much jealousy and greed that he murders his father to possess the treasure for himself. Over time, as Fafnir becomes consumed with the gold and the ring, he turns into a dragon. Legend says that Fafnir flees into exile with the ring and hoard of gold, sits on it, and becomes a dragon.[1]

Fafnir's brother, Regin, wants revenge for their father's death at Fafnir's hands, so Regin re-forges a sword for the hero Sigurd and convinces him to kill Fafnir. Sigurd agrees and hides in a pit in order to deal a lethal blow to Fafnir's vulnerable underbelly as he passes above Sigurd's hiding spot. As Fafnir is dying, he begins to work his cunning charm on

Sigurd to figure out who's truly behind his death.[2] The conversation between Fafnir and Sigurd is mirrored in the conversations between Bilbo Baggins and Smaug.[3] Both Smaug and Fafnir are witty, poetic, charming, and crafty. Reading the dialogue of these dragons immediately makes me think of the deceptively poetic charm that Lucifer wielded in the garden.

Tolkien's Smaug is described as "devious and clever, vain and greedy, overly confident and proud"[4] by some and "frightening, but surprisingly knowable"[5] and possessing "the most sophisticated intelligence"[6] by other commentators.

The more descriptions of Smaug I read from Tolkien specialists, the more I realized that Tolkien had brought the Dragon from Genesis to life. Tolkien's dragon is crafty.

Fafnir's downfall due to obsessive greed is mirrored in Tolkien's character Gollum. Both are driven to murder out of lust for treasure (in both cases, a magical ring) and flee into the wilderness to protect it. As with Fafnir, the treasure Gollum so covets becomes the source of his downfall. Gollum's obsession becomes his curse. Both characters are seen devolving into wicked, less-than-human creatures, living only for the treasures that have consumed their minds and become their idols, until that which is most valuable to them completely consumes them.[7]

Both Gollum and Fafnir devolve into beasts. They both completely lose their humanity.

This is what Tolkien was able to demonstrate through his literature, and it's exactly what the Bible has been communicating since Genesis.

Cain devolves into a beast. Ishmael is a wild donkey.

Jacob and Esau are both born the offspring of the Beast, the Dragon.

Joseph's brothers are robbed of their humanity by jealousy, envy, and vengeance.

But one of the most dramatic accounts of a human devolving into an animal is the prophet Daniel's description of King Nebuchadnezzar. At this point in our journey, we've developed an ability to interpret what the Bible means by what it's showing us. Daniel 4:33 records, "Immediately what had been said about Nebuchadnezzar was fulfilled. He was driven away from people and *ate grass like the ox.* His body was drenched with the dew of heaven until his hair grew like the *feathers of an eagle* and his nails like the *claws of a bird.*"

Because of Nebuchadnezzar's arrogance, pride, and failure to acknowledge the Lord, he loses his sanity and becomes a wild animal. He becomes a beast. The Bible doesn't *tell* us but *shows* us this using imagery and symbols.

Meanwhile, the character that provides a literary juxtaposition to Nebuchadnezzar is Daniel. Whereas Nebuchadnezzar devolves into a wild beast, Daniel has supernatural authority over wild animals who should be devouring him. Daniel 6:22–23 records Daniel testifying about the deliverance of Yahweh, saying:

"My God sent his angel, and he shut the mouths of the lions. They have not hurt me, because I was found innocent in his sight. Nor have I ever done any wrong before you, Your Majesty."

The king was overjoyed and gave orders to lift Daniel out of the den. And when Daniel was lifted from the den, no wound was found on him, because he had trusted in his God.

Daniel is actually part of a pattern. The Bible doesn't depict many humans as having authority over wild animals, and it presents those same humans as having authority over their own *passions* and *desires* and *instincts*. The external authority over the beasts is designed to reflect the internal authority over the beast that resides in all of us.

When we first meet Daniel, he's exhibiting authority over his physical appetite. Daniel 1:8 says that he "resolved not to defile himself with the royal food and wine, and he asked the chief official for permission not to defile himself this way." Daniel's life demonstrates that taming the hungry lions in the den begins with taming your appetites and wants.

In the Old Testament, only three humans demonstrate an ability to tame and live at peace with wild animals. Adam is the first. The Bible tells us that "the man gave names to all the livestock, the birds in the sky and all the wild animals" (Genesis 2:20). The process of naming these animals assumes that Adam is living at peace with them, exercising God-ordained authority over them. Once Adam rebels against God and obeys his appetite, he is no longer able to tame the wild animals. He loses power over the external beasts because he lost power over the internal beast.

The second human to tame wild animals is Noah. The Bible says that Noah and his family "entered the ark to escape the waters of the flood. Pairs of clean and unclean animals, of birds and of all creatures that move along the ground, male and female, *came to Noah* and entered the ark" (Genesis 7:7–9).

Daniel is the third character in the Old Testament to tame wild beasts and to be safe among them. This is a symbol throughout the Bible. Humans who have tamed their inner monsters have authority to dwell in peace with the beasts of the field.

And that's the context we need in order to appreciate the description of Jesus's temptation narrative found in Mark's gospel. Matthew's and Luke's accounts are full of details regarding the nature of the temptations and the conversations between Jesus and the Dragon. However, in Mark's gospel we get two verses. Mark would rather show than tell. Mark 1:12–13 presents this scene for us: "At once the Spirit sent him out into the wilderness, and he was in the wilderness forty days, being tempted by Satan. *He was with the wild animals,* and angels attended him."

Adam
Noah
Daniel
Jesus

In a world where jealousy, avarice, lust, vengeance, and idolatry have robbed humans of their humanity and turned them into animals, Jesus was in the wilderness taming the wild beasts and demonstrating His ability to tame His own appetite.

Matthew and Luke *tell us* that Jesus was fasting and hungry yet refused to turn the stones into bread so He could feed Himself. Mark *shows us* by placing wild beasts in the narrative that are tamed by the authority of Jesus.

Many of us have attempted to tame lions but have never tamed our lusts. We've attempted to calm storms but have never calmed our souls. We desire control over others, but we lack the best kind of control—self-control. And whenever we become obsessed with controlling externals as opposed to internal matters, we create chaos. So much of our anxiety is rooted in our desire to control things that aren't and will never be in our control.

The legacy of the dragon known as Fafnir lives on in both Smaug and Gollum, who have plunder that they have devoted their lives to protecting. Gold. Jewels. Rings. Wealth.

The entirety of their focus, attention, and devotion is pointed in one direction: protecting the plunder they have worked so hard to accumulate. And in this way, Fafnir, Smaug, and Gollum have a lot in common with our Dragon from Genesis.

Satan also has plunder. He has deceptively plundered the authority given to image bearers and has held humans captive under the power of Chaos and sin. The Dragon from the garden has also escaped into the wilderness to protect his plunder. And as soon as Jesus emerges from the Chaos waters of baptism, He heads into the desert to plunder the ancient Dragon.

Not only does Jesus go out into the desert to demonstrate His authority over His flesh and to tame the wild animals according to the pattern set by Adam, Noah, and Daniel. Jesus also enters the wilderness to confront the Dragon.

Jesus goes off into the desert to tame the beasts, to crush the Chaos, and to plunder the Dragon and rob him of his ill-gotten gains.

Jesus is driven out into the realm of Chaos for the confrontation with the Dragon that we've been anticipating since Genesis 3:15. The Spirit compels Jesus to confront the Dragon on the Dragon's *own turf.*

Jesus is not on the defensive.

Jesus seeks to confront Chaos head-on.

In the very first and foundational section of this book, we established that the desert wilderness was directly associated with Chaos. The desert was the realm of *tohu va-vohu,* so it makes complete sense that the desert would be Jesus's priority. Jesus is crushing Chaos.

One of my favorite scholars, Craig Keener, says, "Many believed that demons were especially attracted to places like pagan temples, graveyards and *deserts.* Readers would thus sense the suspense as Jesus battled with Satan on *Satan's own turf.*"[8] The setting is a clue to Jesus's identity and the nature of His ministry. Scholars agree that "the desert is viewed as a realm of demons and death; . . . its demonic *wildness* resembles the primeval *chaos* of the creation."[9] Jesus is following the outline laid out by the Father—to move the cosmos from Chaos into Order.

This is a matter of primary importance. Jesus makes it clear to His disciples in Mark 3:27 that "no one can enter a strong man's house without first tying him up. Then he can *plunder* the strong man's house." Jesus is essentially attributing the success of His ministry to the successful binding of the Dragon that happened in the desert.

There's this line in *The Hobbit* that I love. Smaug is beginning to have a clear effect on Bilbo, and the passage reads, "That is the effect that *dragon-talk* has on the inexperienced. Bilbo of course ought to have been on his guard; but Smaug had rather an overwhelming personality."[10]

By withstanding the Enemy's dragon-talk, Jesus not only overcomes the temptation but also binds Satan so that He can effectively plunder the Dragon of his most valuable possession—people.

This is the great reversal of the Gospels. Jesus binds Satan to free people. Jesus plunders the plunderer.

There's another detail that connects the chaos language from Genesis to the gospel according to Mark. Genesis 3:24 says, "After he drove the man out, he placed on the east side of the Garden of Eden cherubim and a flaming sword flashing back and forth to guard the way to the tree of life." The detail to pay attention to here is how God expelled the man out of Eden. God *drove* him out.

The image is intentionally physical and aggressive. *Drove out.* Cast out. Expelled—*ekballo* ($\varepsilon\kappa\beta\alpha\lambda\lambda\omega$)[11] in the Septuagint, the Greek translation of the Old Testament.

This detail has minor significance until you read Mark's account of Jesus's life. Mark writes, "The Spirit immediately *drove him out* into the wilderness. He was in the wilderness forty days, tempted by Satan; and he was with the wild beasts; and the angels waited on him" (1:12–13, NRSV).

Same exact description of how Adam and Eve were cast out of Eden. Drove out. Expelled. Same Greek word (*ekballo*) from Genesis 3:24 and a very intentional choice by Mark. Jesus goes through the Chaos waters of baptism and is immediately cast out into the wilderness. Why? So He could subdue the Chaos on our behalf and we could all regain access to the garden.

He who knew no sin was treated as sin so that we might become the righteousness of God (2 Corinthians 5:21). This is the scandalous exchange and great reversal of the gospel: He who was perfect was treated as a sinner so that sinners could be treated as perfect.

Adam and Eve are expelled out of the garden.
Jesus is expelled into the wilderness.

Adam and Eve eat the fruit in the garden.
So, Jesus fasts in the wilderness.

Adam and Eve fail to subdue the animal within the garden.
So, Jesus has to subdue the animal within and without in
    the wilderness.

Jesus was driven out so that we could be brought back in.
The wilderness is not our fate. We're not stuck out in the desert. We can return to the garden—we can enter and find rest
for our souls.

Immediately following the binding of the Dragon in the desert, Jesus begins preaching the good news. The Cross has not yet
happened, but the gospel announcement of freedom and deliverance can go out like a clarion call because the defeat of the
Dragon has begun. Satan has been bound, and now Jesus will
begin setting captives free and thereby plundering the Dragon.

Jesus then calls His first disciples. While they're in Capernaum on the Sabbath, a man who is demon possessed begins
to cry out and question Jesus. Mark 1:25–26 records the response: "'Be quiet!' said Jesus sternly. 'Come out of him!' The
impure spirit shook the man violently and came out of him
with a shriek."

In our English translations, nothing here would arrest our
attention. However, in the original language of Mark's gospel,
something both profound and subtle is happening. When you
consult a Greek lexicon for the phrase Jesus declares, it becomes clear that He does not simply say "Be quiet" to the
demon that is possessing the man. The Greek word used here
is *phimoō* (φιμόω), and it means "*to close the mouth with a
muzzle, to muzzle.*"[12]

Who needs a muzzle? Beasts.

Minions of a plundered Dragon need muzzles. Wild, untamed animals and dragons need muzzles. A *tannin* needs a muzzle. Mark is intentionally using chaos language.

And Mark isn't going to stop here.

Mark is adamant that Jesus be portrayed as the ultimate son of Eve—who muzzles the monsters, plunders the Dragon, tames the Beast within and without, restores the pathway to the Order of Eden, and crushes the Chaos.

Let us keep exploring the Gospels and discovering the person of Jesus.

## Chapter 23

# The Tempter and the Tempest

Jesus can control the primeval forces of *chaos* that reside in the seas.

—GARY M. BURGE AND GENE L. GREEN,
*THE NEW TESTAMENT IN ANTIQUITY,*
EMPHASIS ADDED

Not only did Jesus's success in the wilderness break the Chaos cycle for humanity, but hidden within the narrative are nuggets of wisdom that have the power to break us out of our individual cycles as well. There's a cheat code here, so let's wander into the wilderness of Jesus's temptation so we can march out of our personal chaos and confusion.

Matthew 4:1–11 is a pretty detailed, lengthy account of the face-to-face showdown in the wilderness between Satan the tempter and Jesus the Dragon-slaying, Chaos-conquering Prince of Peace and Order.

I have three observations on this text in Matthew 4, and the first is simple yet profound. I'll lay out the verses that immediately stuck out to me while I was reading. Let's see if you can spot the same observation that popped off the page for me.

Verse 3: "The tempter came to [Jesus] and *said . . .*"

Verse 6: "'If you are the Son of God,' he *said,* 'throw yourself down.'"

Verse 9: "'All this I will give you,' he *said,* 'if you will bow down and worship me.'"

Classic dragon-talk.

This may be incredibly obvious, but it seems that speaking is crucial to the Tempter's ability to tempt Jesus. Without the capacity to engage us in active conversation, it would be impossible for the Tempter to create chaos or confusion in our lives. If only there was a way to silence or muzzle this Tempter, then his power and influence would be utterly neutralized.

The longer we grant the Dragon an audience to talk and converse with us, the more our lives are filled with chaos and confusion. Being able to discern the Dragon's voice and influence is vital for creating and maintaining ordered souls and lives.

Second, this Dragon contorts and distorts the words of God. The Dragon has studied Scripture and knows the words of Yahweh so well that he's able to use them to his advantage. This twisting of the truth is the ultimate and most diabolical form of Chaos. The Dragon is a master of weaving lies together with the truth, and this is insanely dangerous.

I know it's a tall order, but we have to be people of the Word if we're going to establish God's Order in our lives. Eve was deceived because she seemed to not really know the intricacies of what God had actually spoken to Adam. Maybe Adam didn't communicate well. Maybe Eve didn't listen to Adam intently when he relayed the commands God had given him. Either way, half-truths are very hard to detect when you're not an expert at knowing the Truth.

Last, the Beast that Jesus is resisting and overcoming in the wilderness desperately desires worship. The Dragon explicitly requests that Jesus bow down and offer worship in exchange for ruling the kingdoms of earth. Satan kind of shows his hand a bit in this final temptation, and now we know some valuable intel surrounding the motives of this Beast that we didn't know back in Genesis. He desires worship.

Matthew paints a fascinating picture of this Dragon and Tempter: His dominant strategy is conversation. He has an incredible knowledge of the written Scriptures and the spoken words of God. And last but certainly not least, he wants worship.

This same story is recorded in Matthew, Mark, and Luke. Luke's version is almost identical to what we have in Matthew—except for one small addition at the end of the story. Luke 4:13 tells us, "When the devil had finished all this tempting, he left him until an opportune time."

Wait a minute. An opportune time? Am I missing something? I assumed that Jesus's passing these three tests would put an end to the struggle between Him and the Dragon forever. I assumed this was a decisive victory. However, the Bible teaches us one of the most valuable lessons concerning Chaos and its cycle with this detail found in Luke's gospel.

On my own journey to conquering chaos, I've learned that sometimes it's simple to *obtain* order. But it is always difficult to *maintain* order. Because every time you choose order over chaos, the Beast leaves you alone and simply waits for an opportune time. There is no once-and-for-all test that God will give any of us to secure permanent order in our lives.

A moment of weakness. A moment of doubt.

When you're tired. When you're overwhelmed.

Like a skillful hunter stalks its prey, the Beast watches and
waits.

Dr. Luke tells us that Satan leaves the desert with a plan to
tempt Jesus at a later, more opportune time. Yet Luke doesn't
explicitly identify for his audience when this opportune time
arrives. Instead of earmarking it for his readers, Luke simply
leaves it ambiguous and up for debate, like a classic Eastern
storyteller.

So, it is up to us to ponder and meditate. Is the moment in
the Garden of Gethsemane when Jesus is sweating blood and
panicking Satan's opportune time to tempt Him? This moment
of weakness sounds like an opportunity to me.

Maybe Satan shows up while Peter introduces the idea of
being the kind of Messiah that doesn't need to die on a Roman
cross. The Bible tells us that "Jesus turned and said to Peter,
'Get behind me, Satan! You are a stumbling block to me; you
do not have in mind the concerns of God, but merely human
concerns'" (Matthew 16:23). Jesus seems to discern in Peter's
words an influence that goes way beyond Peter.

Perhaps there's a private moment of temptation and testing
that isn't even recorded in Scripture. Or perhaps the opportune time Luke alludes to is incredibly subtle and easy to mistake.

Maybe the moment Satan is waiting for appears during a
ferocious storm while Jesus and His crew are on the Sea of Galilee. All three Synoptics tell the story of Jesus sleeping through
the storm and then waking up and immediately rebuking it,
but Mark provides an extra detail that Matthew and Luke

choose to leave out of their accounts. Mark records the exact words Jesus speaks to the Chaos: "He got up, rebuked the wind and said to the waves, 'Quiet! Be still!' Then the wind died down and it was completely calm" (Mark 4:39).

Jesus speaks to the waves. And Mark records that Jesus says, "Quiet! Be still!"

This is an interesting translation choice. And by interesting, I certainly mean inaccurate. Our English translations are incredibly reliable, but this verse is a missed opportunity in my opinion.

The Greek word here for "be still" is *phimoō* (φιμόω)—a term we encountered at the end of the previous chapter. A simple search reveals some other places where this word shows up in the Bible. In both 1 Timothy 5:18 and 1 Corinthians 9:9, it is used when Paul quotes, "Do not muzzle an ox while it is treading out the grain." So *phimoō* is translated as "muzzle" in these verses but as "be still" in Mark 4:39.

According to Strong's *Concise Dictionary*, this word means "to muzzle."[1]

According to the Liddell and Scott's *Greek-English Lexicon*, it means "to muzzle."[2]

According to every resource on Logos Bible Software, it means "to muzzle."[3]

Therefore, Mark 4:39 should read like this: "Jesus got up, rebuked the wind and said to the waves, 'Quiet! Be muzzled!' Then the wind died down and it was completely calm."

As we noted in the last chapter, beasts, wild animals, and dragons are the ones who need muzzles. *Tannin* need muzzles. Again, Mark is using chaos language on purpose.

Mark is deliberately using the word *phimoō* to conjure a specific image in the minds of his readers. He's depicting Jesus as the great Dragon tamer while simultaneously portraying the storm as a Chaos monster.

Jesus has the kind of authority we haven't seen since Yahweh split the waters to bring forth land on the second day of creation or placed the *tannin* in the open ocean on the fifth day. Jesus commands the sea and the sea monsters, and they both obey His spoken word.

But I think something else is going on right beneath the surface of the text—something that adds a dimension to what we've already laid out. There's another layer to the muzzling of the waves and the wild Chaos. What if by muzzling the tempest, Jesus is actually muzzling the Tempter? What if the stories of the desert and the sea are connected?

When we looked at Jesus's test in the wilderness, we realized that the only thing Satan did throughout the entire narrative was talk. That's it. Talking is the only effective thing we've ever seen Satan do. In that way, Satan is a lot like Goliath.

Think about it: Goliath didn't go out to the center of the battlefield every day and spar with some other Philistine warriors. Nope, Goliath just talked a big game. He never displayed or demonstrated an ounce of brutal or barbaric behavior. All Goliath had was words, but with words alone he struck fear into the heart of a whole nation.

Satan is no different. Satan has one superpower: words. That's how he creates confusion and Chaos and gets his ideas lodged in our minds. That's how he could unravel God's Order and usurp Adam and Eve's authority in the garden—with words. The Dragon didn't perform miracles for Adam and Eve or impress them with his power and might. He just talked them out of Order and straight into Chaos.

The Tempter has one card to play. He's low-key a one-trick

pony. Only one tool in his toolkit. Only one weapon in his arsenal: words.

So yes, beasts need muzzles. And yes, dragons need muzzles. But a tempter who skillfully wields the power of words also needs a muzzle. And a tempter who may be hiding behind the camouflage of a raging tempest definitely needs a muzzle.

If your opponent's primary weapon of waging war against you is their words, then muzzling them seems to be a great strategy. So, what does Jesus do? He muzzles the talking Tempter and the raging tempests.

Maybe this is the opportune time Luke was referring to at the end of the temptation narrative. However, if this storm was the opportunity Satan was looking for, then it backfired terribly. Because this story looks more like an opportunity for Jesus to finally muzzle the Beast than a chance for the Beast to overpower Jesus with temptation.

We need to tie up one loose end before we move on, and it has to do with the Dragon inviting Jesus to bow down and worship him. That moment in the wilderness is odd and fascinating. Moreover, I think this seemingly insignificant detail may be the missing link connecting the story of Satan tempting Jesus to the story of Jesus calming the storm. (By the way, there are no insignificant details when studying the biblical text. Only keys to unlock mysteries that camouflage themselves as insignificant details.)

Let's start by looking at these verses:

Mark 4:39 says Jesus "got up, rebuked the wind and said to the waves, 'Quiet! Be still!' Then the wind died down and it was completely calm."

Luke 8:24 says Jesus "got up and rebuked the wind and the raging waters; the storm subsided, and all was calm."

Matthew 8:26 says Jesus "got up and rebuked the winds and the waves, and it was completely calm."

There are slight differences, but one fact that is unchanging and constant across all three accounts is that Jesus rebukes the storm. And that is just flat-out weird. Because the storm is only doing what storms are supposed to do—be a storm. Last time I checked, winds and waves have been programmed to blow and toss. Nature isn't doing anything unnatural here, so it's odd that Jesus rebukes the storm for simply behaving like one.

All great parents are keenly aware that ignorance and nature can't be rebuked or disciplined. Only rebellion can be rebuked. Ignorance requires instruction. I can't justifiably rebuke my children if they're not aware that they're even doing something wrong. I'm personally not in the habit of rebuking my two-year-old for simply acting two years old.

Therefore, if Jesus is rebuking the winds and the waves, something else is going on, and I have a hunch of what it is. In the Old Testament, Israel is constantly drawn to worship a false god, an idol, named Baal. And interestingly enough, Baal is the Canaanite storm god. He is typically depicted as riding on the clouds with the power to control the winds and the rain.

This is the main idol that draws Israel away from Yahweh. Many of us may want to judge the Israelites for worshipping the Canaanite storm god instead of Yahweh, but we should be careful before we throw stones at others. We may want to ask whether we've sinned in the same way. Because I would contend that when Satan wants worship from us, he doesn't ring our doorbells holding a pitchfork and with horns protruding from his forehead.

Nope. I think when Satan wants worship, he does exactly what he did in the Old Testament. He wraps himself in the proverbial winds and waves and storms of life, and just like the disciples in the boat with Jesus, we are utterly convinced that those storms have ultimate power over our lives.

Storms of sickness. Unemployment.
Political upheaval. Social unrest.
Prodigal sons and daughters.
Infertility and miscarriages.
Anxiety and depression.
Storms of Chaos.

Those storms speak. And we can also often hear the Tempter's voice through the tempests that rage out of control in our personal lives. Honestly, we're the most vulnerable and most susceptible to his voice during seasons where storms are raging around us. Something about a storm creates uncertainty within us.

There's a popular book series that a bunch of my friends have been pressuring me to read for years. Thank the Lord it got adapted for television, because there was no way I was ever going to read *The Wheel of Time.* But I absolutely love the TV series on Amazon Prime.

In one scene, all the main protagonists are walking through an ancient magical pathway, and they get attacked by an entity known as Machin Shin (Black Wind). It's a swarm of insect-like flying creatures that whisper dark lies to each character in their mind. Even though everyone is standing together, the swarm says something unique to each individual, and nobody can hear what the Black Wind is saying to the person standing next to them.

I imagine the storm on the Sea of Galilee—and all storms—to be a lot like the Black Wind in *The Wheel of Time*. My wife and I went through the Covid-19 pandemic together, but what the tempest whispered to her was different from what it whispered to me. And the same goes for every storm we've ever faced together.

The reality is that storms speak. But the good news is that Jesus has muzzled both the Tempter and the tempest, which means you have the power to mute the Dragon when the chaos gets unbearable. Instead of entertaining lies, use the power at your disposal, and put the muzzle back on the Dragon of deception.

The Dragon has been muzzled. So, if you're hearing his voice, you have somehow unmuzzled him, and the truth is that his words will only exacerbate the chaos in your life. You cannot always control the chaos, but you can muzzle the voice of the one who wants to rob you of your peace and joy in the midst of it.

Life is full of storms, and I would argue that behind every tempest is the voice of the Tempter. A tempter whose words can be heard through the winds and the waves. A tempter telling us that our God is powerless to rescue us or, even worse, that He is powerful but doesn't care enough to rescue us.

This is why Jesus rebukes the storm. Because the storm is claiming for itself glory that belongs to God alone. Because the storm is seeking to elicit worship and allegiance from you and me.

This is why storms need muzzles.

When Luke recounts this story, he includes Jesus asking a

very pivotal and piercing question to His disciples: "Where is your faith?" (Luke 8:25). Jesus isn't saying they don't have faith. He is acknowledging that they indeed have a whole lot of faith—but it is fueling the wrong vehicle.

The issue is not their measure of faith but the misplacement of it.

Where is their faith? It's obvious, actually. Examine their words: "Master, Master, we're going to drown!" (verse 24). They believe in the power of the storm more than they believe in Jesus.

Their faith is in the storm. Their faith is in the new, rebranded Baal, the storm god.

Because the storm can never get your worship without first getting your faith. And the storm can't get your faith without getting your attention and your focus.

Where should their faith be? In the words spoken by Jesus. Before the storm comes, Jesus makes sure to speak to the disciples, and that should be the anchor to their faith. Jesus says in verse 22, "Let us go over to the other side of the lake." Those aren't simply directions. Embedded in them is a promise.

Jesus says that the destination is the other side of the lake— which means the storm is lying when it tells me that my journey will end at the bottom of the sea.

The Tempter is a master of knowing precisely what God has said. He's a Bible nerd.

Which means the words of God must be my anchor when the winds and waves tell me that I should believe the whispers of fear, doubt, and anxiety.

I think this storm is the opportune moment. Because Satan knows that if he can get to Jesus's disciples, then the movement will never outlive Jesus. The test in the wilderness was to tempt

Jesus. But I think this moment on the Sea of Galilee is a war over the hearts and minds of the men who have pledged their allegiance to Jesus yet don't know how to face the winds and waves of Chaos.

And this story proves that Jesus will never abandon us to face the Chaos alone. He shows up to muzzle the Tempter and the tempest so that "in fear and amazement" we, like the disciples, can say, "Who is this? He commands even the winds and the water, and they obey him" (Luke 8:25).

## Chapter 24

# One Small Step for Man

> By *walking* on the sea Jesus overcomes the powers of chaos.
>
> —W. D. DAVIES AND DALE ALLISON, *MATTHEW 8–18,*
> INTERNATIONAL CRITICAL COMMENTARY, EMPHASIS
> ADDED

> The surging sea represents the powers of chaos, evil, and death. . . . Jesus' walking on the sea symbolizes divine omnipotence over the powers of chaos, evil, and death.
>
> —ROBERT H. GUNDRY, *COMMENTARY ON THE NEW*
> *TESTAMENT*

Prior to 1954, the entire world "was convinced that the human body could not physically run a mile in under four minutes. Scientists, physicians, and even athletes believed the human heart might explode" if someone pushed their body to run at such a strong pace.[1]

The world's smartest and most experienced professionals agreed that running a mile in under four minutes was impossible. They had data. Facts. Graphs and charts that outlined the amount of energy your muscles would need versus the capacity of the human lungs and heart.

The verdict was decided: A four-minute mile was impossible. Nobody in recorded history had ever done it, so the proof was in the pudding.

Until May 6, 1954, when Roger Bannister ran a mile in 3 minutes, 59.4 seconds—proving that this was never a physical barrier but a psychological one.[2]

Forty-six days after Bannister broke this world record, it was broken again, by an Australian named John Landy. Once Bannister became the first human in recorded history to run a mile in under four minutes, there was immediately a second. Then, in 1955, "three runners broke the four-minute barrier *in a single race.*"[3]

What was believed to be physically impossible according to scientists, medical professionals, and athletes all over the world was becoming common. Before the close of the twentieth century, almost a thousand runners had broken the previously elusive four-minute barrier. And as of June 2022, it had been broken by 1,755 athletes.[4]

There is a plethora of lessons to glean from this, but let's consider a couple of them. First, the psychological barrier was much stronger than the perceived physical barrier.

Second, once a single human proved that running a mile in under four minutes could be done, it immediately broke the hypnotic effect of the psychological barrier. For hundreds of years, this feat was thought to be impossible. Then all of a sudden, Roger Bannister does it, and it takes only forty-six days for another human to achieve the same accomplishment. Because humans are inspired by other humans.

In an unexplainable way, humans have a phenomenally strong impact on one another. The moment Bannister broke the four-minute barrier, it was as if every human on the planet received access to that iOS update. We're oddly interconnected and interdependent in that way.

Which explains how Peter can conquer the Chaos and walk on the Sea of Galilee, as Matthew's gospel details. Peter sees Jesus do it and therefore knows it is possible. Here's the account in Matthew 14:25–29:

> Shortly before dawn Jesus went out to them, walking on the lake. When the disciples saw him walking on the lake, they were terrified. . . .
>
> "Lord, if it's you," Peter replied, "tell me to come to you on the water."
>
> "Come," he said.
>
> Then Peter got down out of the boat, walked on the water and came toward Jesus.

Had Peter seen God the Father or the Holy Spirit walking on the water, he would've probably just stayed put in the boat. However, Peter sees a human being out there on the sea.

Peter sees a Man walking on the water. A Man who gets hungry and thirsty and tired. A Man who is like Peter yet unlike him in so many ways. But He isn't walking just on water. Because everything we've learned so far should clue us in to the exact image Peter perceives as he looks out on the waves.

Peter sees a Man walking triumphantly on the Chaos—the same Chaos that humans had been drowning in since the fall of Adam. And if Jesus, fully Man, can walk victoriously on the

Chaos, then so can Peter. This is the only interpretation that makes Peter's response make any sense.

Mark's version of this story intentionally uses chaos language and hides a subtle clue in the text. Mark tells us that Jesus is about to walk right past His own disciples. Such an odd and seemingly insignificant detail. Mark 6:48 records, "He saw the disciples straining at the oars, because the wind was against them. Shortly before dawn he went out to them, walking on the lake. He was about to pass by them." What? About to pass by? Why? Doesn't He walk out on the water to help them? This is beyond confusing.

Well, it's baffling until you read Job 9, where Job is talking about the awesome wonder of Yahweh. In this passage, Job says all kinds of things that demonstrate the nature of God's divinity: Yahweh moves mountains and shakes the earth. Yahweh controls the sun and the stars. He is "the Maker of the Bear and Orion, the Pleiades and the constellations of the south" (verse 9).

Most of this chapter in Job is about the wonder and power of the Creator of the universe. It's humbling and awe-inspiring content to read. The entire list proves the divinity of Yahweh, for He's the only being in the universe who can perform such wonders. And in the list of all the nature-defying things Yahweh has the power to do, we find this:

> He alone stretches out the heavens
> > and treads on the waves of the sea. . . .
> When he passes me, I cannot see him;
> > When he goes by, I cannot perceive him.
> > (verses 8, 11)

This is classic chaos language. Yahweh alone walks on the waves of the *tehom*. So, since Jesus is walking on the waves in the pages of the Gospels, both Matthew and Mark are telling us Jesus is God without telling us Jesus is God. Like good storytellers, they are portraying Jesus as divine.

But we have an odd and interesting twist in Job 9. Yahweh treads on the *tehom*, yet He walks right past Job, and Job is unable to perceive Him. Yahweh is not only all powerful and awesome but also holy, slightly unapproachable, and definitely unrelatable. The entire Old Testament points to the truth that Yahweh is nothing like His creation. He is holy because He is indeed wholly other.

Mark alludes to this passage in Job with the subtlety of an artist. However, Jesus doesn't walk past the disciples. Instead, the disciples cry out to Him, and Mark says He immediately responds and climbs into the boat and the wind dies down.

Yahweh walks on Chaos, and so does Jesus.
This is Jesus's divinity on display.

Yahweh walks past, but Jesus doesn't.
This is Jesus's humanity on display.

Fully God. Fully man.
Both displayed in the same story for those with eyes to see.

Maybe the image of Jesus overcoming the Chaos doesn't move you or inspire you. I can understand that point of view. And honestly, I'd say we're in the same boat. (Get it? I couldn't resist.) Jesus walking on the water has never been my favorite part of the story. Jesus walking on the water is incredible and highlights His divinity for me in a special way. But it's hard to see Jesus the way Peter saw Him.

Peter and all the disciples engaged Jesus as a human and needed a revelation of His divinity. Even when they realized He was the Jewish Messiah, that wasn't a divine category for them. The disciples didn't fully realize Jesus was divine until after the Resurrection.

However, most of us have engaged with Jesus as a divine being for all our Christian lives. We sing worship songs to Jesus. We pray to Him. We know Jesus as God, and therefore, we need the exact opposite revelation as the disciples did. Many of us desperately need a revelation of Jesus's humanity that will cause us to behold Jesus the Man, follow in His footsteps, and finally walk on our Chaos.

Maybe instead of focusing on Jesus when you read this story, focus on Peter. Matthew, Mark, and John all include this story in their gospel narratives, but only Matthew adds the detail that Peter walked on the water too. And to be honest, it's my favorite part of the story. I may not be able to follow in Jesus's footsteps, but I for sure think I could walk in Peter's. Because Peter isn't divine at all. Much like Roger Bannister, Peter is the proof of what humans are capable of when they redefine what it means to be human and offer themselves to the Spirit of the living God.

Peter is just as human as you and I are, and he walked on the Chaos. And if Peter can conquer the Chaos, you can definitely conquer the chaos that exists in your life, whatever it is. It doesn't have the final word or the last laugh.

One last curveball.

Matthew's account lets us know that Peter successfully makes it to Jesus. This is clear in the text because when Peter starts sinking, Jesus is right there to save him:

When he saw the wind, he was afraid and, beginning to sink, cried out, "Lord, save me!"

Immediately Jesus reached out his hand and caught him. "You of little faith," he said, "why did you doubt?"

And *when they climbed into the boat,* the wind died down. Then those who were in the boat worshiped him, saying, "Truly you are the Son of God." (Matthew 14:30–33)

When they climbed into the boat? Wait a minute. Let's read between the lines here.

How do they get back to the boat exactly? Does Jesus carry Peter? Does Peter get a piggyback ride? Do the other disciples come pick Jesus and Peter up?

I don't think so. I think Peter has to conquer the Chaos . . . *again.* I would argue that Peter walks on the water twice. Not just once.

Getting out of a boat and walking on water are very difficult. But there's a blind optimism that comes with leaving the boat. Sometimes when we're full of faith, we feel invincible. However, getting over our failures to walk on the water a second time is even more difficult. Knowing that the worst-case scenario is actually possible but still choosing to take a risk—that's real faith.

I remember when my wife and I had built up enough faith to try in vitro fertilization (IVF) for the first time. We had been walking through the chaos of infertility for five years at that point. We emptied our savings account to try this really expensive procedure, and we miraculously got pregnant. It felt like we were walking on water. The day my wife told me we were expecting a baby was one of the happiest moments of my entire life.

And then we sank. When we went in for our first ultrasound, the nurse uttered words I'll never forget. With a pale face and a trembling voice, she said, "There's no heartbeat."

And with those words I was at the bottom of the sea. I sank into depression, into fear, into doubt. And I was drowning in anger. Namely, I was angry with God, but it spilled over onto everything and everyone.

Months went by. My wife had done a way better job of processing her emotions and muzzling the Dragon than I had. I remember the day she told me she wanted to try IVF again, and from a place of trauma and fear I responded, "Never again."

I refused to make myself that vulnerable and to get my hopes that high ever again. I simply refused. It seemed safer to just accept defeat.

And that's where so many of us are. Life has happened, you've encountered a storm, and the tempest and the Tempter have your ear. You are standing next to Jesus as He's telling you to walk with Him back to the boat, and you are paralyzed. You've overcome the chaos of fear once before, but now the chaos of trauma has you stuck.

I know exactly how you feel. And so does Peter.

After more months of stubbornness, I finally became more scared of never having children than of losing another baby, so we conquered the Chaos *again* and tried IVF one more time. We walked back to the boat, and I'll never regret it because it proved to the Dragon that Chaos could not keep the Arangos in a cycle forever.

Today my son is three years old. His name is Theophilus, and he's tangible proof that Chaos isn't in control.

God will never place more on us than we can handle. And if the God of the universe is whispering in your ear to take a step and start walking back to the boat, then you must muzzle the

Dragon, acknowledge your emotions, subdue and rule over them, and—with all the courage you've got—conquer the Chaos again.

I've done it.

Peter has done it.

You can do it.

On July 20, 1969, as Neil Armstrong took his first steps on the moon, he made an iconic statement that immediately resonated with millions of people. The phrase was heard on TV and then made headlines in newspapers around the world in dozens of languages. Neil Armstrong realized that his steps on the surface of the moon represented something for all of humanity. This wasn't just a moment of personal achievement but a moment that held significance for the entire human race. He had a fitting response to the moment and commented, "That's one small step for [a] man, one giant leap for mankind," as he walked on the surface of the moon.

In many ways, Neil Armstrong and Roger Bannister share a lot in common. Their stories reveal the deeply communal and interconnected nature of the human experience. Their moments of individual achievement unlocked new possibilities for all of us.

As I meditate on Jesus and Peter walking on the surface of the water, I can hear Neil Armstrong's words in my mind. Jesus and Peter took small steps out there on the water, but those small steps moved the human race forward by leaps and bounds. As you meditate on the humanity of Jesus and the boldness of Peter, I pray that their steps would inspire a giant leap in your personal life. Getting out of the boat and walking on the waves was one small step for Peter, but it has the potential to be a giant leap forward for you.

## Chapter 25

# Pregnant with a Prophet

> In the case of the Son of Man, "the heart of
> the earth" takes the place of "the belly of the
> sea monster". Both represent liminal states
> connected with death.
>
> —JOHN NOLLAND, *THE GOSPEL OF MATTHEW,* NEW
> INTERNATIONAL GREEK TESTAMENT COMMENTARY

While most of my friends from school were lost in the mythical worlds of Harry Potter, I was becoming obsessed with Greek mythology.

Spoiler alert: My friends and I were all nerds—private-Christian-school, Hacky-Sack-in-the-hallway nerds. My seventh-grade AP Western Civilization teacher absolutely loved us, probably because we were the only people on the planet who thought this poor man's Sheldon Cooper was cool. I remember the day he introduced us to Greek mythology. I was hooked. Gods and goddesses. Demigods and villains. Epic heroes and fanciful monsters.

That same year, *Gladiator* came out, and I remember my parents taking me to watch it on its release day, May 5, 2000.

I also read Homer's *The Iliad* and *The Odyssey* that year. A world of wonder opened up to me: Icarus. Achilles. Prometheus. Pandora's box. Poseidon. Zeus. Hermes. Apollo.

The world of Greek mythology was also full of a rich diversity of sea monsters: Scylla and Charybdis. The Lernean Hydra. The Sirens. But none more important than Cetus (κῆτος or *Kētos* in Greek).

Cetus makes an appearance in the famous myth of Perseus and Andromeda. Andromeda was the beautiful daughter of the king and queen of Aethiopia, and her mother made the mistake of invoking the wrath of Poseidon, putting their entire nation at risk of being destroyed and devoured by Cetus the sea monster. To avoid total annihilation, an oracle instructed the king and queen to sacrifice their daughter to Cetus by tying her to a rock close to the shore.

So that's exactly what Andromeda's parents did. But before the sea monster could devour her, a hero named Perseus saved the day. Perseus had just returned from defeating the famous Medusa and learned of Andromeda's peril just in time.

One version of this famous myth says that Perseus slayed the sea monster Cetus with a sword lent to him by the god Hermes. Another version says Perseus used the decapitated head of Medusa to turn Cetus to stone. Either way, Perseus saved Andromeda, the damsel in distress, from imminent demise as only a Greek hero can.

This story was legendary in the Greco-Roman world and has continued to make its way into famous works of visual arts and literature. The Roman poet Ovid recounts the myth of Perseus, Andromeda, and Cetus the Sea Monster in his classic work *Metamorphoses*. The world-famous painter Rembrandt depicted this myth in his 1630 oil-on-panel masterpiece titled *Andromeda Chained to the Rocks*. In the 1851 novel *Moby-*

*Dick,* Herman Melville discusses the Perseus, Andromeda, and Cetus myth in two different chapters of his classic work.

But perhaps the most shocking place that I've seen this myth appear is on the lips of Jesus of Nazareth as He's debating some Pharisees in Matthew's gospel. Matthew 12:39–40 records the following words:

> [Jesus] answered, "A wicked and adulterous generation asks for a sign! But none will be given it except the sign of the prophet Jonah. For as Jonah was three days and three nights in the belly of a huge [Cetus or κῆτος (Cetus) in Greek], so the Son of Man will be three days and three nights in the heart of the earth."

Jesus used the Greek word *kētos* (or *κῆτος*)[1] to describe whatever swallowed Jonah. Why most English translations use the word "fish" here is mind-boggling to me. Because *kētos* ("latinized as cetus")[2] ain't a fish. Not even close.

Here's how the NRSV chooses to translate these exact same verses from Matthew:

> He answered them, "An evil and adulterous generation asks for a sign, but no sign will be given to it except the sign of the prophet Jonah. For just as Jonah was three days and three nights in *the belly of the sea monster,* so for three days and three nights the Son of Man will be in the heart of the earth."

A plethora of words in the Greek language mean "fish"— words that are used throughout the New Testament to identify fish.[3]

*Kētos* doesn't mean "fish."

Jesus clearly articulates that Jonah was in the belly of a sea monster or Chaos dragon. Which means the story of Jonah is way more interesting than most of us have ever imagined. The Old Testament never explicitly calls the beast that swallowed Jonah a *tannin*. It simply says in Jonah 1:17 that "the LORD provided a huge fish to swallow Jonah, and Jonah was in the belly of the fish three days and three nights."

Huge fish. Not a dragon. Not a sea monster. Not a *tannin* or a κῆτος. So why does Jesus call this same fish a cetus? Why do we find the word κῆτος on the lips of Jesus?

When Western readers find inconsistencies like this, it typically triggers us to doubt the validity of the biblical text. Eastern readers are triggered by these wrinkles in the text as well—but triggered to solve the text's mysteries. Eastern (and ancient) readers believe that inconsistencies lead us from shallow water into the depths of wisdom, mystery, and paradox.

Proverbs 25:2 teaches us, "It is the glory of God to conceal a matter; to search out a matter is the glory of kings." This proverb is the epitome of Eastern culture and an Eastern worldview.

With that, we turn to our runaway prophet, Jonah. First, the sea is featured as a prominent part of this story. And not only do we have the open sea, but there's also a storm. Sounds chaotic to me.

Jonah 1:4–5 says:

The LORD sent a *great wind on the sea,* and such a *violent storm* arose that the ship threatened to break up. All the sailors were afraid and each cried out to his own god. And they *threw the cargo into the sea* to lighten the ship.

Great wind on the sea. Violent storm. Cargo into the sea. I think maybe the author wants us to notice the sea and the chaos that Jonah has created with his disobedience.

In the next portion of Scripture, notice which word is repeated over and over for emphasis. Verses 11–13 read as follows:

> The sea was getting *rougher and rougher.* So they asked him, "What should we do to you to make the sea calm down for us?"
>
> "Pick me up and throw me into the sea," he replied, "and it will become calm. I know that it is my fault that *this great storm* has come upon you."
>
> Instead, the men did their best to row back to land. But they could not, *for the sea grew even wilder* than before.

The sea got rougher and rougher. The sailors wanted to make the sea calm down.

"Throw me into the sea," Jonah said. A great storm. The sea grew wilder.

This is chaos language.

Second, Jonah prays from within the belly of this great fish and uses some fascinating language. Jonah 2:5–6 records the poetic prayer that came from the mouth of this runaway prophet inside the fish:

> The engulfing waters threatened me,
>     the deep surrounded me. . . .
> But you, Lord my God,
>     brought my life up from the pit.

The deep, the *tehom,* surrounded me. More chaos language.

Third, sea monsters are common mascots for the violent and evil empires of the ancient world. Egypt. Babylon. Assyria. These human kingdoms and their kings are all depicted as dragons in the writings of the Prophets because they wreak havoc, destruction, and chaos on the world. Where exactly is Jonah supposed to be going? Nineveh. The capital city of Assyria.

Assyria is the dragon. Nineveh is the belly of that dragon.

The figurative belly of the Beast is where Jonah should be headed. But instead, he runs. And winds up in the literal belly of the beast. I think Jonah gets the irony—that either way the belly of the beast is inevitable, so he may as well obey and surrender to Yahweh's will.

Everything about this story has classic images and symbols of Chaos. But then we get a curveball. In place of the obvious sea monster, we get a fish. The ancient audience would've seen a *tannin* in their imaginations even though the text doesn't use that exact word. We know this because Jesus interpreted the story that way; Jesus put the puzzle pieces together like an ancient reader.

So, back to Jesus in Matthew 12. What exactly is He saying?

Jesus is saying that His God-given assignment is to surrender Himself to the belly of the Beast—a rich and multilayered symbol to say the least. The belly of the Beast represents the Dragon who stood before Adam and Eve, the Satan. Jesus declares in this passage that He plans to surrender Himself to this rebel archangel and embrace death at the hands of His eternal enemy. The belly of the Beast represents every human agent of Chaos who Jesus would sacrifice His life for—so that they could have God's Order. But the belly of the Beast also represents the Dragon's earthly physical expression of violence and power known as the empires and kingdoms of humanity.

In the same way Jonah entered the heart of the Assyrian Empire, Jesus would die on a Roman cross so that the gospel could infiltrate the most powerful and beast-like empire the world had ever seen. Maybe Jesus foresaw Paul traveling on Roman roads to plant seeds of the gospel deep within a broken and corrupt empire.

Jesus was saying not only that He would surrender Himself to the belly of the Beast but also that death wouldn't get the last laugh. There's one more layer of meaning concealed in the text of Jonah. Jonah 2:2 says, "From deep in the realm of the dead I called for help, and you listened to my cry." Jonah equated the belly of the beast with the realm of the dead. Fascinating detail. Jonah experienced a resurrection of sorts.

We must address one last wrinkle in the text. This is impossible to notice when reading an English translation but very obvious when reading these texts in Hebrew. When the "fish" swallows Jonah, it is male. Then something fascinating happens. When it vomits Jonah out, it's female. The biblical authors are begging us to see this inconsistency. But what's the significance?

We have a female fish with something living in her belly. Yup. The authors want us to see that the fish is pregnant. Pregnant with a prophet. Jonah sinks to the bottom of the *tehom*. Is swallowed up by Chaos. Calls the belly of the beast the realm of the dead—aka his tomb. But then the belly of the beast is revealed to be a womb instead of a tomb.

And thus, Jonah is reborn.

This is what Jesus saw. This is what Matthew 12 is about.

Which is why He used this story to predict that His tomb would also be a womb—and that from His resurrection, new-creation life would enter the world.

## Chapter 26

# The Genesis of Jesus

> "In the beginning"—no Bible reader could see
> that phrase and not think at once of the start of
> Genesis, the first book in the Old Testament:
> "In the beginning God created the heavens and
> the earth."
>
> —N. T. WRIGHT, *JOHN FOR EVERYONE, PART 1*

John starts his gospel account with some iconic words: "In the beginning" (1:1).[1]

In. The. Beginning. Talk about bold.

John is making it very clear right away that he is writing a new Genesis.

I think it's difficult for us to comprehend how daring it was for John to begin his account with these three words. It was unheard of for a Jewish author to attempt to appropriate the venerated opening words of the Torah. John's got some serious chutzpah, and he sees in the person of Jesus the same creative power that formed the universe.

Using the words "in the beginning" would be equivalent to a current United States president starting a speech with "Four score and seven years ago." Anyone who's aware of the context would immediately begin drawing lines between our modern issues and those during the US Civil War when Abraham Lincoln originally penned the words. Or it'd be like writing a speech titled "I Have a Dream." Everyone would know that it was in reference to the original speech by Dr. Martin Luther King, Jr. Yes, a reference. But also a reinterpretation.

I officially knew I was old when I referenced the song "Through the Fire" by Chaka Khan and someone almost twenty years younger than I am corrected me, saying, "Do you mean 'Through the Wire' by Kanye West?"

It took me a moment to figure out which of the infinite number of questions in my mind I'd ask first. I went with "Are you aware that Kanye sampled Chaka Khan's music for his song?" They were not. And because they weren't familiar with the original, it was impossible to fully appreciate the remix.

We've studied Genesis heavily in this book so we can truly appreciate the depth and nuances of the remix: the new creation story that John gives us in his gospel account.

The sample is not only a reference to the original music but also a reinterpretation. John is referencing Genesis, but he's also reinterpreting it through the lens of Jesus. And I desperately want to know the Jesus that John knew—the God-man who emanates Order and subdues Chaos in all its forms on a daily basis.

Genesis is a story of God conquering Chaos and creating Order in the cosmos.

Which means the new Genesis is probably about Chaos and Order as well.

I would contend that John believes everything about Jesus: His teaching and His miracles. His birth. His life. His death. His resurrection. Everything. That it has all brought new creation into this broken cosmos.

For John, Jesus of Nazareth is working on the exact same project that Yahweh was working on in the creation account of Genesis—pulling the world out of Chaos and imposing Order so that abundant life could spring up and flourish.

Anytime I played video games with my friends as a kid and was losing too badly, I had this obnoxious tendency of hitting the restart button. I look back at my younger self and shake my head in embarrassment, but I can't deny that if my friends were beating me and I knew a comeback was impossible, I would just hit that restart button and the entire screen would go black. I was a menace.

John is boldly claiming that the life, death, and resurrection of Jesus was a restart button for the entire creation. That Jesus represents a new beginning for the human race and the entire cosmos. Adam is no longer the chaotic mold that new humans get poured into and formed from; the Order of Jesus becomes the new mold for the model of life we follow.

Jesus offers every human an opportunity to be made new. Like Yahweh in the creation account, Jesus has an Order that He wills to impose on the soil of creation and of our souls. When we surrender to Jesus's lordship, we are truly cut from a different cloth than our forefather Adam, made from a radically different mold, and can now live according to the new creation Order.

If we observe the texts of Genesis and John, we'll spot the moment when the restart button gets hit. All throughout John's gospel, the Pharisees are frustrated that Jesus doesn't follow their particular brand of Sabbath rules. But something deeply profound and cosmic is happening as it pertains to the Sabbath.

Jesus sees His ministry as the work of new creation. Yahweh

didn't rest until the work of the original creation was complete; therefore, in John's gospel, Jesus doesn't rest until the work of new creation is finished.

Genesis 2:1–2 tells us that after six days of God's ordering, organizing, speaking, and shaping, "the heavens and the earth were *finished*" and then reiterates that "on the seventh day God *finished* the work that he had done" (NRSV).

The key word to notice here is *finished*. John will show us that Jesus is up to the same thing as Yahweh. In John 19:30, he wrote that Jesus said, "'It is *finished*.' Then he bowed his head and gave up his spirit" (NRSV).

It. Is. *Finished.* That's a loaded phrase.

Just like Yahweh finished the work of creation, Jesus has finished the work of new creation. And just as the Father had finished pulling the cosmos out of Chaos, Jesus has finished pulling the new creation out of Chaos. Jesus has finished the work of crushing Chaos.

If you're reading the gospel of John in isolation, you may think this statement from Jesus merely pertains to His atoning work on the cross. However, if you know the song John has sampled, then you're aware that he is referencing the finished work of creation in Genesis.

So yes, the atoning work of the Cross is finished. But also, the work of new creation is finished. And the second would be impossible without the first. Once Jesus dies, the old creation of Chaos and death dies along with Him. This is the moment the restart button gets hit. However, the thing that separates a restart button from a simple power button is its ability to cause the reappearance and reanimation of energy and life.

In John 20:1, we get the understatement of a lifetime: "Early on the first day of the *week,* while it was still dark, Mary Magdalene came to the tomb and saw that the stone had been removed from the tomb" (NRSV). The first day of the week. John is telling us not only which day it is but also much more. This is his way of saying that it's the first day of new creation and that this Resurrection Sunday provides just as clean of a slate as Adam had on his very first day of the week. So yes, it is the first day of the week—Sunday. But it is also the first day in the new world Order that Jesus has inaugurated.

In Genesis, Yahweh conquered Chaos and established Order in one week. The word *week* is found here during the Resurrection story to demonstrate that Chaos has been conquered again and that now we can face the tests that so many before us have faced and failed.

Remember, the six-part pattern we've outlined always ends with testing. Adam and Eve failed. Noah failed. Moses failed. Joshua failed. Multiple generations of the Israelites failed. But none of them had the secret weapon that Jesus procured for us—the Holy Spirit.

Paul says in his letter to the Romans that "the Spirit of him who raised Jesus from the dead is living in you" (8:11). The Resurrection proves that the animating power of the Holy Spirit can accomplish what is absolutely impossible with mere human power and means. The Resurrection proves that a new day has dawned and that humanity has crossed into a new creation world where the Holy Spirit is available in a new way.

And now that the Holy Spirit dwells in us, we can finally get to the sixth and final stage of the Chaos cycle and demonstrate to the Lord that we can be tested and trusted. The resurrection of Jesus means the rules on the playing field have permanently changed.

Neither Adam nor Eve failed in the Garden of Eden because they were human.

They failed because they didn't have the Holy Spirit living in them.

But in the new creation, we have a secret weapon. A secret weapon that made its appearance on the first day of the week as Mary went to a garden to anoint the body of Jesus. A secret weapon that raised the literal body of Christ and empowers the figurative body of Christ to

conquer the Chaos,
survive the waters,
receive the Spirit,
obey God's voice,
embrace the Order,
and pass the test.

This was the Jesus that John knew. The Jesus who brings new creation. The Jesus who conquers Chaos. The Jesus who cleanses us with His blood so we can receive the infilling of the Holy Spirit. The Jesus who gives us a new beginning, breaks cycles, and teaches us to pass tests so we can sustain the Order that He's created.

## Chapter 27

# The Jesus That John Knew

John thinks he is writing a new Genesis.
—N. T. WRIGHT, "WHAT JOHN REALLY MEANT:
THE GOSPEL OF THE NEW TEMPLE"

As the gospel of John unfolds, it becomes undeniable that John is not only looking at Jesus through the lens of Genesis but also rereading Genesis through the lens of Jesus's life and ministry.

The first clue that jumps off the pages is the overwhelming presence of water in John's gospel. There's water everywhere—which should immediately cause our internal alarms to go off because water is our primary symbol for Chaos and creation. Picking up exactly where Genesis leaves off, water takes center stage in John's gospel as a powerful and intentional symbol.

In John 2, we have six stone water jars used for ceremonial cleansing.

In John 3, Jesus tells Nicodemus he must be born of water and the Spirit.

In John 4, Jesus offers a Samaritan woman living water when He meets her at a well.

In John 5, we're at the Pool of Bethesda where angels periodically trouble the waters.

In John 6, Jesus walks on the water in the middle of a storm.

In John 7, Jesus says that rivers of living water will flow from those who believe in Him.

In John 9, we have blindness healed by Jesus's saliva and a visit to the Pool of Siloam.

In John 19, Jesus's side is pierced, bringing a sudden flow of blood and water.

John is proclaiming something profound through these symbols and images: The God from Genesis who made the sea, gave the oceans their boundaries, set the *tannin* within them, and split the waters so dry land could emerge has come from heaven in the form of Jesus to reestablish Order and to subdue the Chaos once again.

John is begging us to see that new creation Order has broken into this world and is taking root in the soil of the old-world system.

Yet John doesn't stop his barrage of symbols with water. We learned in the beginning of this section that if we've got water, we're probably going to get the *ruach* (breath) of God somewhere. John's gospel doesn't close without the *ruach* of God making an appearance.

When Jesus appears to His disciples after the Resurrection, He desperately wants to deliver the gift of the Holy Spirit to them. John 20:21–22 records Him saying, "'As the Father has sent me, I am sending you.' And with that he *breathed* on them and said, 'Receive the Holy Spirit.'" Jesus breathed on them, and they received the Holy Spirit. This moment is supposed to spark John's audience to meditate and remember the last time they've seen God breathe on someone. Yeah, it was Genesis.

In Genesis 2:7, we have this incredible moment where Yahweh breathes His *ruach* into the mouth of Adam. The text says that Yahweh formed Adam from the dust but that Adam needed the animating breath of life. Therefore, God "breathed into his nostrils the breath of life, and the man became a living being."

Why does Jesus breathe on the disciples in John's gospel? Because He is the author of the new creation. Also, John is emphasizing the importance of the Holy Spirit in every believer's life. The presence of the Holy Spirit for the disciples is given the same level of importance as the very breath of God that brought life into Adam's body.

Without the wisdom, guidance, and discernment of the Holy Spirit, the believer's life will inevitably descend into Chaos. Without the fruit and the gifts of the Holy Spirit, churches will descend into Chaos. The Holy Spirit is the animating breath in the life of every Christian, and we must be aware of our daily and desperate need for the renewing power of the Spirit of God.

Remember the pattern: If we have water and the breath of God, we probably have the voice of God. Which is exactly why John includes a story of Jesus bringing Order through the power of His spoken words. John 4:46–53 tells us about a royal official who begs Jesus to come heal his son. Jesus and the official are in Cana, and the boy is in Capernaum.

> The royal official said, "Sir, come down before my child dies."
>
> "Go," Jesus replied, "your son will live."

The man took Jesus at his word and departed. While he was still on the way, his servants met him with the news that his boy was living. (verses 49–51)

Death had to obey the spoken words of Jesus. Disobedience wasn't an option for the death that wanted to claim this boy as its own. Let that sink in. Death had to obey Jesus, but you and I exercise the freedom to walk in disobedience daily.

The voice of God—the teaching and instruction of Jesus— has the power to bring Order. Jesus's words absolutely have the power and potential to bring Order into our lives, but only when we unconditionally obey Him and apply His instructions appropriately.

I've learned that wherever there's disobedience, there's also a lack of trust. When we disobey, it's typically because we trust ourselves more than the methods, timing, or way of Jesus. But can we be real? Trusting yourself has only led you to chaos. I don't know any people who've created order in their lives by trusting themselves.

To trust in the words and instructions of an invisible God may feel like chaos at first, but it always brings order. Trusting in ourselves gives us an illusion of control, but that's not true order. Following your instincts will inevitably lead to chaos unless you have submitted your will to the authority of the Holy Spirit.

John is making his point very clear here with Jesus's ability to rescue the royal official's son from the jaws of death. The same God who spoke to the Chaos and brought Order to it with His spoken words in the beginning has arrived in the flesh. The Word has truly become flesh and made His dwelling among us.

So, let's recap. Humanity has descended into Chaos. And John shows us water—lots of water. We also have ruach. Jesus breathes on the disciples, and they receive the Holy Spirit. And we have the divine Word: Jesus speaks and death obeys. Which means we should see Order being displayed in John's gospel.

Oh, we definitely have Order. John orders everything around the number seven. Can you remember where we've seen that number before? Yeah, in creation. Genesis 1.

There are seven miracles that John calls signs.

There are seven strategically placed discourses of teaching.

Jesus attends seven festivals throughout this account.

Jesus reveals His identity seven times, and each is marked by the words "I am."

And the book actually follows a seven-day structure.

Talk about intricate and ordered.

The Synoptic Gospels include countless miracles that Jesus performed. But not John. John's gospel has only seven. For John, the miracles are accomplishing the exact same thing as the original seven days of creation. The miracles symbolize new creation and the dominion of Order over Chaos. The miracles point to Jesus's identity as the one who comes to plant the seeds of the new creation in the soil of this world.

John includes seven blocks of teaching or discourses in his gospel. Because for John, Jesus's teaching accomplishes the exact same thing as the original seven days of creation—Jesus's wisdom and understanding establish Order and eliminate chaotic mindsets and systems of thinking. We can literally order our lives around the teachings of Jesus and build on the solid foundation of His truth.

John includes seven festivals in his account to meticulously detail how Jesus is the fulfillment of Passover, Hanukkah, and the Feast of Tabernacles. Because for John, the entirety of the Old Testament is incomplete without Jesus. Moreover, times and seasons are nonnegotiable elements of Order throughout the canon of Scripture. In the creation account, God orders time. Throughout the Law, God orders time using the festivals. And Jesus orders His life around these rhythms and then fulfills them.

In a very real way, you'll never begin to bring Order to your life without ordering the way you spend your time. The way you structure your days. The rhythms of your schedule. Anniversaries. Holidays. The flow of your months and years. I remember being a new youth pastor in a new city at a new church and desperately needing to bring order to the lives of my volunteers, parents, and teenagers. So, my wife and I sat down with the county's public school calendar and mapped out an entire year of sermons, events, and programming before Thanksgiving of the next year. We exerted influence over the culture of the youth ministry by simply ordering our days, weeks, months, and years around wise planning.

If you don't control your schedule, it will control you. Since Yahweh knows this, He dedicated an entire day of creation to ordering time. And Jesus followed an order and a structure for His days and years.

Lastly, John includes seven "I am" statements of Jesus in his gospel. For John, Jesus's identity can be fully appreciated only when we understand the identity of Yahweh in the account of Genesis. Without identity, there can never be Order. Without an awareness of Jesus's true identity, there can never be true Order. And without an understanding of our own identity, there will always be Chaos.

According to John, the life and ministry of Jesus marks the

beginning of a brand-new creation. Another moment in history where Order will subdue the Chaos. And the question you and I need to answer is this: "Which creation do I want to be a part of?"

The fallen creation ruled by Chaos?

Or the ordered new creation ruled by Jesus?

The gospel of John forces its readers to acknowledge that we are currently occupying two realms of reality simultaneously. John intentionally portrays Jesus in a way that forces his audience to realize that a new creation is now at work within this old creation and that we have to choose to engage in the creation we discern spiritually as well as the one we experience with our physical senses.

But John's gospel doesn't have a temptation narrative where Jesus and Satan face off in the desert. John omits that entire part of Jesus's life.

So, where's the moment of testing? My hunch is that John would place this moment of truth within a garden. But to find the answer, we'll have to do a bit of digging and dot connecting, which we'll turn our attention to next.

## Chapter 28

# The Jesus Judas Thought He Knew

> Then Satan entered Judas, called Iscariot, one
> of the Twelve.
> —LUKE 22:3

> As soon as Judas took the bread, Satan
> *entered* into him.
> —JOHN 13:27

As we search for a moment of testing in John's gospel, let's remember that John is obsessed with Genesis and tries to focus our attention there. So, including a story of Jesus being tested in the wilderness doesn't fit with John's agenda. Since the wilderness imagery is a call back to the story of Exodus, the omission makes thematic sense.

If John were to place a story in his gospel to demonstrate Jesus passing the test of a lifetime, where would that test take place? Probably a garden, right? Well, we certainly have a garden story in John's gospel. John 18:3 tells us:

> Judas came to the garden, guiding a detachment of soldiers
> and some officials from the chief priests and the Pharisees.
> They were carrying torches, lanterns and weapons.

In the same way that Satan, in the form of a Dragon, entered into the Garden of Eden to tempt Adam and Eve, I would contend that Satan, in the form of Judas, entered into the Garden of Gethsemane to tempt Jesus Christ of Nazareth. Had Judas and Satan been successful, it would've thrown the new creation project into absolute chaos—which would've been a repeat from Genesis. Unfortunately, most Christians probably don't see this moment with Judas as a temptation, but I would argue that Judas's role has been slightly misunderstood. So let me present an alternative view.

What if Judas thought he was helping? (Stick with me.) What if Judas thought he could force Jesus's hand by setting up a scenario where Jesus would have to react in violence? What if Judas thought he could manipulate Jesus into being the kind of Messiah that everyone (including Judas) expected Him to be? What if Judas believed what all the rest of the disciples believed—that Jesus was going to lead an armed rebellion to finally free Israel from Roman military occupation?

Peter and the rest of the gang were utterly confused by the idea of Jesus suffering and sacrificing His life on a Roman cross. Absolutely befuddled and bewildered. The idea of a suffering and dead Messiah was so incomprehensible that the Gospels emphasize over and over just how helplessly confused all the disciples were whenever Jesus brought up the topic.

The disciples had absolutely no idea what Jesus was talking about when He started talking about the Crucifixion. Matthew, Mark, and Luke include multiple stories of Jesus telling His disciples that He would suffer and die and then rise again, and each time, His disciples just didn't get it.[1] They were angry even. I wish I could walk you through each story, but I'll just mention once more the one where Peter rebuked

Jesus for claiming that He must suffer and die and Jesus responded by saying, "Get behind me, Satan!" (Matthew 16:23; Mark 8:33).

Try to understand the worldview of Jesus's disciples. They weren't stupid. Most of these boys had more Scripture committed to memory than anyone you or I will ever know. But they could not wrap their minds around a suffering or crucified Messiah. Peter had walked on water but could not fathom a Messiah dying on a cross. These boys had cast out demons yet could not understand what Jesus was talking about when He said He was going to suffer and die. Let that sink in.

These men were smart. But they were stuck in their cultural definition of the word *Messiah*. They believed the Messiah would lead an army into Jerusalem and use violence and force to heroically liberate the people of Israel from the Romans. And get this—they not only were anticipating a war with the Romans but also believed that Jesus would be victorious. James and John even said to Him, "Let one of us sit at your right and the other at your left in your glory." To which Jesus replied, "You don't know what you are asking" (Mark 10:37–38).

These guys were down for a violent revolution and thought Jesus would win. This single question from James and John encapsulated the disciples' cultural worldview and understanding (or lack thereof). And Jesus's response says it all: He had zero plans of leading an armed rebellion against the Roman government. Zero.

The disciples all believed that Jesus would call Israel to arms, organize an army, and lead a military campaign. Nothing demonstrates this more than Peter's response to Judas leading armed men to come arrest Jesus.

John 18:10 tells us, "Then Simon Peter, who had a sword,

drew it and struck the high priest's servant, cutting off his right ear." Peter had a sword—a sword he was clearly very good at handling—and he came to Jerusalem ready to use it. Why? Because the disciples all believed that Jesus was going to be a military commander. I know that sounds laughable, but when they pictured the Messiah, they envisioned all the military leaders throughout Israel's history who God had raised up and anointed for military combat.

Joshua. Saul.
David. Gideon.
Samson. Judas Maccabeus.
All military leaders.

The word *Messiah* simply means "anointed one,"[2] and most of the anointed ones in the Old Testament were kings or leaders who led armies and fought battles against Israel's enemies. So, it's not completely foreign that Judas, Peter, and all the other disciples understood the role of the Messiah according to political and militaristic terms.

Maybe Judas was manipulating the situation to get Jesus to react based on who he wanted Jesus to be, as opposed to who Jesus was called to be. Maybe Judas had an agenda. And regardless of what Jesus had said, Judas simply could not let go of his agenda in exchange for the mission Jesus called them to follow.

In this way, there's a Judas in each of us. A part of us that would rather be loyal to our agenda than the mission God has called us to. Consider how Judas responded when his plan didn't work and Jesus was actually arrested. Judas was remorseful to the point of suicide:

When Judas, who had betrayed him, saw that Jesus was condemned, he was seized with remorse and returned the thirty pieces of silver to the chief priests and the elders. "I have sinned," he said, "for I have betrayed innocent blood."

"What is that to us?" they replied. "That's your responsibility."

So Judas threw the money into the temple and left.

Then he went away and hanged himself. (Matthew 27:3–5)

I get choked up when I try to read those verses aloud. Because I think they demonstrate the layered complexity of the human experience. I think they show that Judas didn't have completely evil intentions. I don't think he betrayed Jesus thinking it would turn out the way it did. I think Judas just wanted to provoke Jesus to action.

Judas could not forgive himself for this miscalculation. He was beyond broken and resorted to suicide. Which means Judas misunderstood Jesus twice.

Judas was wrong not only about the culture and ethos of Jesus's lordship and kingdom but also about the grace and forgiveness of Jesus as Savior. I don't think he just wanted thirty pieces of silver, a petty sum for the magnitude of his actions. I think Judas had a plan that backfired. I think Judas had a vision for who he wanted Jesus to be and that agenda became an idol. People do chaotic things when idolatry is involved.

Judas is an easy character to villainize. However, once someone has become a villain in our eyes, it's hard for us to learn anything from them and their mistakes. Humanizing Judas doesn't justify his sin or legitimize his failure, but it allows us to see how we've all acted just like Judas in some area of our lives.

When we cannot let go of our agendas, when we see Jesus as a means to a political end, we create Chaos. When we attempt to control situations that are out of our control, when we think we can manipulate God, when we refuse to trust the plan God has laid out, we create Chaos.

Some biblical scholars who are way smarter than I am think Judas's last name, Iscariot, is really more of a title—a clue to his political affiliations. The Sicarii were a group of Jewish vigilantes who were known for assassinating Jewish noblemen in crowded areas by using short daggers hidden under their cloaks. The name Sicarii comes from the Latin word *sicarius,* which is translated as "dagger man."[3]

So, Judas Iscariot may actually be Judas the *Sicarius,* which would make him an extreme Zealot to say the least. And if any group in Israel was known for their bent toward extremism, it was the Zealots. I can see Judas the Dagger Man picturing a dormant warrior hidden within this rabbi and healer named Jesus and creating a scenario to wake the sleeping giant, arouse the wrath of the Messiah, and call Israel to arms in the Garden of Gethsemane.

The temptation in Genesis, in the Garden of Eden, was centered on identity. This moment in the Gospels, in the Garden of Gethsemane, is about identity as well.

In Eden, the Dragon promised that Adam and Eve would be like God once they ate the fruit, but the reality is that they were already like God. They had been made in His image. In Gethsemane, the Dragon tries to convince Jesus that He can rescue Israel another way, without the excruciating pain of the Cross. Judas's way is a viable option. But this temptation fails. Jesus knows exactly who He is, and the river of behavior always flows from the lake of identity.

In Eden, the Dragon made Adam and Eve doubt the goodness and the character of God the Father, so they turned to trust themselves and the Dragon. In Gethsemane, Jesus stands firm on the truth that the Father isn't killing Him. Jesus is willingly sacrificing His life because He trusts the will and way of God the Father.

In Eden, the Dragon convinced Adam and Eve that humans can hear God not only through Yahweh's spoken words but also through their desires and instincts. In Gethsemane, the Dragon wants Jesus to consider whether God the Father may be talking through Judas or Peter. However, Jesus has disciplined Himself to hear God within the boundaries God has set, and He has circumcised ears to hear God well.

In John's gospel, this is the test. This is the key moment of temptation. Everything was lost in Eden, but everything is recovered in Gethsemane. And because Jesus passed this test, we have a model to help us pass as well.

There's a Judas in each of us that will lead us to Chaos. I pray this chapter encourages you to search your heart and expose the inner Judas who sees Jesus as a means to an end. I gently invite you to repent and place your agenda and your desire for control on the altar of sacrifice.

There's also a lot of Jesus in each of us, and His Spirit lives in these temples we call bodies (1 Corinthians 6:19). I pray that this chapter inspires you to find your garden and to pass your test so you can be an agent of divine Order in this world of Chaos we presently occupy.

## Chapter 29

# The Chaos Crusher

> When *darkness,* earthquake, and the tearing of
> the veil accompanied the *death* of Jesus, Jews
> of his day would have feared the end of the
> world—*the victory of chaos.* The signs three
> days later would have alerted them that a new
> age was at hand.
>
> —MICHAEL HEISER, *THE BIBLE UNFILTERED,*
> EMPHASIS ADDED

> The *death* of this creator figure on the cross is,
> in a sense, the ultimate *victory of Chaos* over
> creation.
>
> —DOMINIC RUDMAN, "THE CRUCIFIXION AS CHAOS-
> KAMPF," EMPHASIS ADDED

After three years of successfully confronting the chaos of the Dragon throughout the Gospels, Jesus had only one form of chaos left to defeat. One final step in this epic journey to crush the Chaos and establish divine Order for the new creation.

Jesus has conquered the desert wilderness, overcome the temptation of the Beast, muzzled the Dragon, and tamed the raging storm. Jesus and Peter have both tread on the surface of the deep.

However, Chaos has not been fully crushed.

The Beast and the desert have been crushed. The flood and the storm, the *tannin* and *tehom*, the wilderness and darkness—all crushed by Jesus.

Jesus has confronted and conquered almost every single symbol of Chaos that existed in the ancient world. Jesus is undefeated. Chaos has never gotten the best of Him. The Dragon has failed at every turn to tempt, overpower, or outwit Jesus. The odds are stacked in Jesus's favor as we approach the climax of the Gospels.

I was born and raised in Boston, Massachusetts, so naturally I'm a Boston sports fan, and I will never forget the 2007 NFL season for the New England Patriots. I religiously and enthusiastically watched every single game that season.

The Patriots went undefeated in the regular season that year—only the fourth team in NFL history to do so and the first since the 1972 Miami Dolphins. Tom Brady threw a then record fifty passing touchdowns. Randy Moss caught an NFL-record twenty-three receiving touchdowns. The Patriots went into Super Bowl weekend undefeated and heavily favored.

Nobody would've predicted what happened next. The Patriots lost the Super Bowl. One of the most precise and gifted football teams ever assembled lost in the final game.

I stared at the television speechless.

Every single piece of evidence pointed to the fact that the Patriots would win. I can remember the disorienting cloud of depression and anger that descended on the city of Boston over the following days and months.

In the same way, Jesus was undefeated against Chaos in the Gospels. Every single piece of evidence pointed to the fact that Jesus of Nazareth would continue an undefeated streak of crushing Chaos, but then the chaos of death defeated Jesus on the cross.

His followers were utterly dumbfounded. Depressed. Disoriented. Confused. Scared. Reeling with the reality of loss and defeat.

So often when we read the Bible, it's as if we're watching a movie and we've already seen the conclusion. On one hand, that's great because we have a foundation of hope. But on the other hand, we fail to respond to the unfolding drama of the story. We don't enjoy or even acknowledge the suspense that the authors built in.

Because we see the crucifixion of Jesus through the lens of the Resurrection, we often fail to realize the depth of defeat and despair that was present on that initial Good Friday.

Death was the final form of Chaos that needed to be defeated.

It would be natural to assume that when the Romans tried to crucify Jesus, it simply wouldn't work. The Gospels had been leading us to conclude that death wouldn't work on Jesus. Imagine a Jesus who was immune to the effect of death. Imagine *that* crucifixion scene with a death-resistant, death-proof Jesus.

That is how many of us think we win against chaos.

We think the goal is to become impervious to chaos. However, Jesus threw a curveball with the Crucifixion. He died—He was defeated by Chaos and swallowed by death. For the first time, Jesus was defeated, and Chaos was victorious. And the gospel writers let us know.

Luke writes, "It was now about noon, and *darkness* came over the whole land until three in the afternoon, while *the sun's light failed;* and the curtain of the temple was torn in two" (23:44–45, NRSV).

The darkness that Yahweh conquered from the Chaos of pre-creation was back. The darkness that He gave boundaries to when He spoke light into existence had returned with a vengeance. This is chaos language.

The light failed.
The sun failed.
Darkness won.
Chaos prevailed.

Matthew's gospel records that "Jesus cried out again with a loud voice, and yielded up His spirit. Then, behold, the veil of the temple was torn in two from top to bottom; and the *earth quaked,* and the *rocks were split*" (27:50–51, NKJV).

This was chaos.

The firm foundation of the earth shook. What was thought to be secure was shaken. The Order of creation was being upended. This was *tohu va-vohu.* It was *Chaos.*

Dr. Michael Heiser points out that "when *darkness,* earthquake, and the tearing of the veil accompanied the *death* of Jesus, Jews of his day would have feared the end of the world—*the victory of chaos.*"[1] The ancient audience would've seen the victory of Chaos. However, modern audiences don't naturally make that connection.

In addition to darkness coming and earthquakes happening, the veil in the temple was torn in two from top to bottom. The temple—the resting place of God, realm of order, microcosm of creation. Not even the temple was immune to the chaos being unleashed on the cosmos.

This wasn't simply the death of Jesus, the Son of God.

This was the death of the old creation and the old temple—the unraveling of the old created order.

The death of Jesus led to the death of *everything.*

The victory of Chaos. The victory of death.

We've seen this before. In the Flood, the Order of creation was undone, chaos swallowed up the cosmos, and creation returned to a state of *tohu va-vohu.* In the plagues of Egypt, the Order of creation was attacked, and Egypt descended into utter chaos. That chaos culminated with the death of Pharaoh's firstborn and the implementation of Passover, because the ultimate form of chaos is *death.*

The death of Jesus on the cross was the new pinnacle of chaos. The victory of death.

Which is precisely what God desired—because you cannot have a new creation without allowing chaos to destroy the old. This is why Paul taught the Corinthians, "None of the rulers of this age understood [the mystery of God's wisdom], for if they had, they would not have crucified the Lord of glory" (1 Corinthians 2:8). The crucifixion of Jesus kick-started a series of events that could not be undone.

The Dragon fell right into the trap.

Chaos couldn't resist the urge.

Death claimed its final victim.

As the Dragon and Chaos celebrated the death of Jesus, they didn't realize that He was a seed. And the true power of a seed can be unlocked only when it dies. They buried Jesus in the earth, and the seed of the new creation was planted in the depth of the old creation.

Jesus had told His disciples that He was a seed. In John 12:24–25, He said, "Unless a kernel of wheat falls to the ground and *dies*, it remains only a single *seed*. But if it dies, it produces many seeds. Anyone who loves their life will lose it, while anyone who hates their life in this world will keep it for eternal life."

Seeds carry life. But the life inside a seed cannot emerge as long as the seed stays intact; the outer shell has to die. Seeds in your hand or in your pocket produce nothing. However, when a seed is buried, moisture from the soil breaks and destroys the seed coat. By killing the seed's covering, the soil and water unlock the true power and life hidden within. The power of life. Ironically, when planted, the seed's "body" has to be broken to spark new life.

Chaos won as Jesus died, and darkness enveloped creation. But Chaos didn't simply kill Jesus. It ruptured the seed of the new creation, placing the power of new life directly in the soil of this old creation.

This is the secret of crushing Chaos—every end is simultaneously a fresh start. Every death is simultaneously a new beginning. Every tomb is simultaneously a womb.

The final secret to crushing Chaos is knowing that sometimes things die, but death is not the end. Sometimes chaos wins. When it does, you must remember that you're also a seed. And your secret superpower as a follower of Jesus is that you're not scared of death.

In the second century, a Christian theologian living in North Africa named Tertullian coined the adage "The blood of the martyrs is the seed of the church." This saying is quite popular, but it's an abridged version of the full statement Tertullian wrote directly to the Roman Empire in response to its persecution of Christians. One translation of the full quote is

"The more you kill the more we are. The blood of the martyrs is the seed of the church."[2]

The Dragon didn't learn the lesson with Jesus. Chaos didn't learn that destroying seeds will always backfire. The more Christians that Rome persecuted, the more Jesus's fame spread. The more seeds Rome buried in the dirt, the more Christianity bore fruit.

This may be the end of a significant season of your life. But you not only have the seeds necessary for what's next—you *are* seed.

Your career may have ended, but you are a seed.
Your ministry may have ended, but you are a seed.
Your marriage may have ended, but you are a seed.
Your business may have ended, but you are a seed.
And the death of one thing prompts the beginning of
     another.

You need not cling to this current iteration of life. You need not cling to anything in this life. For "anyone who loves their life will lose it, while anyone who hates their life in this world will keep it for eternal life" (John 12:25).

That is the secret.
We enter boldly into the belly of the Beast.
And we emerge reborn.
Every time.

Plotting to kill Jesus was the worst mistake the Dragon could've made. Striking the heel of Jesus only prompted the crushing of the Dragon's head. And since the Dragon is a symbol for Chaos, the striking of Jesus's heel prompted the crushing of Chaos.

On Sunday morning, following the victory of Chaos on Friday, Mary Magdalene and a handful of other women went to Jesus's tomb to anoint His body. But when they arrived, the tomb was empty, and the seed was already digging down roots and sprouting new life. Which means that victory over death was found not in being impervious to death but in succumbing to its power and then defeating it by resurrecting from the dead.

On the cross, the Dragon strikes the heel of Jesus.

In the Resurrection, Chaos is utterly decapitated.

You and I have something much more powerful than being impervious to death. We have the power of resurrection life—the truth that from the ashes of death, new life can rise again.

Right before Jesus reveals to His disciples that He's a seed that will produce many seeds, one of His closest friends, Lazarus, gets sick. When Lazarus's two sisters send word to Jesus, He says, "This sickness will not end in death" (John 11:4). Although the text doesn't say for sure, it's likely that the sisters are told about His response.

"This sickness will not *end* in death." Then Lazarus dies. Talk about a curveball.

What do you do when you think Jesus says something won't happen but then it does? Both Martha and Mary are broken and grieving, and they each separately say to Jesus, "Lord, if you had been here, my brother would not have died" (verses 21, 32). They are desperately trying to reconcile what Jesus *said* with what *occurred*. And Jesus is adamant that they need to believe.

Believe? Believe in what exactly? Maybe they need to believe what Jesus said:

"This sickness will not *end* in death."

*End.* Which means if there's death, it must not be the end. For Jesus, even before He went to the cross, death is not a period; it's not synonymous with *end.* Jesus never sees death with the finality that we do.

Yes, there's death. But no, it's not the end. You cannot control death, but you can control whether that death will be final.

Starting over can be chaotic. Unraveling an old life, picking up the pieces, and starting over can be completely daunting. But life is a series of rebirths.

Yes, the chaos of starting over is real. But you have all the tools you need—more tools than you had the last time you had to start over.

The Dragon will tell you to fight for control in the middle of this chaos, but the voice of the One who has gone before you is asking you to trust Him. He has descended into death, and you can follow behind Him. And when you come out, there will be a garden on the other side.

We took a short glimpse at something in the initial section of this book that deserves a deeper look. We need to gaze at the scene in John's gospel as Mary Magdelene finds the resurrected Jesus.

When Mary Magdalene went to the tomb and encountered the risen Lord, "she did not realize that it was Jesus" but thought he "was the gardener" (John 20:14–15). Mary was so wrong yet so right. Jesus wasn't the literal gardener hired to tend and till that property, but He was and still is the figurative gardener who creates new life for you and me. In his commentary series entitled *John for Everyone,* N. T. Wright confirms that:

Mary's intuitive guess, that he must be the gardener, was wrong at one level and right, deeply right, at another.

> This is the new creation. Jesus is the beginning of it. . . .
> Here he is: the new Adam, *the gardener,* charged with
> bringing the chaos of God's creation into new order,
> into flower, into fruitfulness.[3]

Gardens may just be the most powerful symbol in the entire Bible. Everything in the entire biblical narrative is rooted in what took place in the original garden with Adam, Eve, the Dragon, and God Himself. John has already brought us to the Garden of Gethsemane in his gospel, but now Mary discovers Jesus in the garden of new creation.

In the original creation, God planted a garden called Eden. In the garden of new creation, Jesus stands as the firstfruits. Proof that the new creation is active and able to turn death, loss, and pain into life. Again, Mary didn't recognize whom she was talking to, but something within her seemed to recognize the vocation Jesus was fulfilling and properly saw Him as the gardener—the one who prepares a place for humans to flourish and thrive and find rest.

How do I know there's a well-ordered garden on the other side of whatever chaos you're dealing with? Because Mary Magdalene encounters the resurrected Jesus on the other side of His chaos, and He's standing in a garden.

Once humanity sinned in the original garden, not only were they expelled, but also the garden's entrance was guarded. Genesis 3:24 tells us that God "placed on the east side of the Garden of Eden cherubim and a flaming sword flashing back and forth to guard the way to the tree of life." God made His garden inaccessible to this corrupted creation. However, since Jesus was willing to be swallowed up by Death and Chaos—and therefore the garden of the old creation was swallowed up as well—His sacrifice created access to a new garden where God and fallen humanity could dwell together and the Creator could commune with His image-bearing creation. Jesus Christ has become the new Tree of Life by surrendering His life on a tree of death.[4]

So of course Jesus is standing in a garden.

Of course He is mistaken as a Gardener.

The Bible is showing, not telling.

Jesus has made the Garden of Eden accessible again. The way to the Garden of Eden is no longer guarded. Adam and Eve were cast out into the wilderness of the old creation, but Mary Magdalene and others enter the garden of the new creation.

Why would Mary Magdalene suppose that Jesus was the gardener? Because Jesus and Mary are in a garden. Which proves there's a garden on the other side of this chaos.

We crush chaos by surrendering, dying, and sacrificing. We crush it by trusting God and relinquishing our need for control. We crush chaos by allowing it to momentarily crush us so we can enter the garden and enjoy the order on the other side.

The Château du Champ de Bataille in Normandy, France, sits on over three hundred hectares of land and was built in the 1650s by the same royal architect that designed the Palace of Versailles.[5] The property is filled with priceless art and souvenirs from history—like four vases that are said to have been gifts from the King of Sweden to Napoleon. Pretty baller. It's almost impossible to put a price tag on a piece of property like this. But for frame of reference, a few years ago, the château's current owner declined an offer for the property that was well above ten figures.[6] That's over a billion dollars for anyone counting on their fingers.

What's shocking is that the gardens are the most breathtaking part of this massive, opulent piece of property. They make up a major portion of the grounds, making this one of Europe's largest private parks. Over one hundred acres of the château's property are solely dedicated to lush and intricately designed garden spaces,[7] and fifteen of the best gardeners in all of Europe maintain them.[8]

Why all this attention given to a garden area? Why this massive investment of resources for some landscaping? Because when this property was designed and built, kings and royal houses demonstrated their power over nature by subduing it into ordered and symmetrical man-made designs.[9] *A garden wasn't just a garden.* It was the result of men and women imposing order and symmetry over wild and untamed land— a display of authority and power. Order is the only thing that separates a garden from the wilderness.

Square hedges are not natural.

Hedge mazes don't just appear.

If there's a garden, there must be a gardener.

Order never happens by accident, and it doesn't happen organically. Order requires the authority to subdue what is *naturally wild.* It requires intentional and intelligent design. Order requires persistence and focused effort.

The human body doesn't naturally get itself into shape.

Thoughts and ideas don't naturally organize themselves.

The human soul and psyche aren't naturally healthy.

Relationships don't naturally have boundaries.

Nothing in life naturally and organically finds order, even though at times our culture idolizes what is natural. We even call our "natural" selves our authentic selves. However, this is a deeply secular line of reasoning. Because life is naturally wild. *We* are naturally wild. Order must be imposed on us. Yet this is not bondage but freedom. For a train is freest when it's on the tracks.

I hope that is the lesson you've learned by reading this book. I hope that you've become open to the power of the Holy Spirit landscaping your soul and transforming your life from a chaotic wilderness into a well-ordered garden. I hope you can die to your natural self so that you can be born again as the most-ordered version of you.

If you read Genesis closely, you can observe two very small yet important details. First, you'll see that the entirety of Eden isn't a garden. Instead, God plants a garden within a wider space of land known as Eden. Here's exactly what the Bible says in Genesis 2:8: "The LORD God had planted a garden in the east, in Eden; and there he put the man he had formed."

The garden is in Eden. Just like Boston is in Massachusetts.

Eden has a garden, but Eden is not, in its entirety, a garden.

What is the Bible showing us? Adam and Eve are in a garden but surrounded by wilderness—an ordered system surrounded by chaos. In the same way that they must choose whether to eat of the tree of the knowledge of good and evil, they must choose whether they want the garden or the wilderness. We, like our fallen forebears, are constantly making the same choice.

The second detail you'll realize is that Adam isn't formed from the dirt of the garden. He is formed from the dirt outside the garden and then graciously placed inside. Meaning that the garden isn't a space he is entitled to and that the fabric of Adam's humanity is naturally wild, not ordered. Not naturally sinful but naturally chaotic and wild. Yet he's placed within the garden and invited to choose Order over Chaos.

The soil of his soul comes from the realm of Chaos. The Dragon could tempt Adam and Eve with Chaos because something in them was drawn to it. This is why the order of the garden must be imposed on us. This is why humans don't naturally choose order.

We must *unnaturally* embrace discipline.
Restraint. Self-sacrifice.
Divine Order.

It is both natural and logical for Yahweh to send Adam back into the wilderness once Adam brings Chaos into Yahweh's garden.

Ordered humanity gets to occupy ordered space.

Wild humanity gets banished into wild space.

During the French Revolution, the Château du Champ de Bataille was raided, and the furniture was sold all throughout France. The property switched hands several times and ultimately fell into desolation and disrepair. *And nature ran its course.* What was once one of the most beautiful gardens in all of Europe became an overgrown, unkempt, deserted wilderness. This once elegant and beautiful piece of property descended into chaos. The château was defeated by the natural power of *tohu va-vohu.* Until Jacques Garcia purchased the property in 1992 and undertook the overwhelming task of bringing this garden back from the depths of chaos and the death grip of nature and the wilderness.

When he bought the château, Garcia discovered sketches of the original garden. He went to work to scrupulously reproduce them into designs so that gardeners from across Europe could bring the original vision back to life. Garcia believed that the Château du Champ de Bataille and its garden spaces could be *resurrected*.[10]

Garcia believed that the original garden could thrive again. Flourish. Grow. Prosper. Bear fruit again. Order could be imposed again, and beauty could blossom.

He believed that the way to the original garden wasn't guarded. Rather, a blueprint would unlock the order that chaos had utterly defeated and bring back the beauty that had been destroyed.

That's the gospel. God planted a garden. Chaos replaced it with a wilderness. For three years of earthly ministry, Jesus worked tirelessly to landscape His Father's vineyard and restore the Order that had been lost and nearly forgotten. Then in a shocking turn of events, Chaos defeated the second Adam, the Gardener, on the cross as darkness and death prevailed. But in killing Jesus, Chaos planted the seed of new creation into the soil of this earth.

On that Sunday morning, Jesus stood in the garden ready to invite humans made from chaotic soil back into the only space where we truly flourish: the garden of God. And to ensure that we don't allow the chaos of life back into His garden, we die. We die to our old selves, to who we were, to the patterns and systems of the old earth. And we learn to rebuild our lives based on the blueprints and designs that the Gardener of our souls managed to recover.

We die to ourselves.

We enter the garden.

We learn the blueprints.

We maintain Order.

And we crush the Chaos.

# Acknowledgments

This book wouldn't be nearly as creative or comprehensive without Dr. Scot McKnight allowing me the freedom to explore these ideas during my doctoral studies at Northern Seminary. My doctoral thesis laid the groundwork for many of the ideas explored and conclusions discovered in this book. Also, thank you so much, Scot, for writing the foreword. Studying with you was one of the best decisions I've ever made. Thanks.

Massive thanks to Hakeem Bradley, whose research for ARMA has been beyond helpful and who directly contributed to the biblical foundation of this book. So grateful for you, Hakeem.

As providence would have it, BibleProject released a twenty-part podcast series on chaos dragons just months after we went under contract for this manuscript. The insights, nuance, and creativity of that series influenced the quality of this project greatly, and I'm grateful.

The very first time I mentioned the idea for this book to Alexander Field, his face immediately lit up, and his excitement was the affirmation I needed to see this project to its full potential. From the very first Zoom call with Drew Dixon and the WaterBrook & Multnomah team, I knew in my gut that he was going to be the perfect editor for this idea. And Drew, you did not disappoint, and you helped me become a far better writer in this process. To Alex and Drew—thanks for all your wisdom in this process and for caring about this project as if it were your own.

To Jesse Summers, Elijah Gaither, Tiffani Thompson, and Lashawn Thompson, thank you so much for reading countless chapters of this book and providing helpful feedback. Each of you helped bring my writing into focus and added clarity. You saw the ultrasound version of this baby and identified features to help me bring shape to this creative process. Love you all. Thankful for each of you.

Last, but certainly not least—Tia Christine Arango—you fell asleep many nights to the click-clack of my keyboard and woke up many mornings to me wanting to read chapters to you before anything else started in the day. You gave feedback on messaging, word choice, chapter length, the order of particular chapters, book titles, fonts, book covers. Without your feedback, this project would not have been possible. Many times, it felt like we were writing this together. Thank you. I love you, and I'm eternally grateful for you, not simply because of this book but because of every project we've ever worked on together. We can take the world, Tia.

# Notes

**Foreword**

1. Karl Menninger, *Whatever Became of Sin?* (Portland, Ore.: Hawthorne Books, 1973).

**Chapter 1: Panic in the Lobby**

1. *Enhanced Brown-Driver-Briggs Hebrew and English Lexicon,* ed. Francis Brown, Samuel Rolles Driver, and Charles Augustus Briggs (Oak Harbor, Wash.: Logos Library System, 2000), s.v. "*tohu.*"

2. *Enhanced Brown-Driver-Briggs Lexicon,* s.v. "*va-vohu.*"

3. *Gesenius' Hebrew-Chaldee Lexicon,* s.v. "H8414 – *tou,*" Blue Letter Bible, accessed August 21, 2024, www.blueletterbible.org/lexicon/h8414/kjv/wlc/0-1.

4. *Gesenius' Hebrew-Chaldee Lexicon,* s.v. "H922 – *bou,*" Blue Letter Bible, accessed August 21, 2024, www.blueletterbible.org/lexicon/h922/kjv/wlc/0-1.

5. Blue Letter Bible, s.v. "H8414 – *tou,*" accessed August 21, 2024, www.blueletterbible.org/lexicon/h8414/niv/wlc/0-1.

6. *Enhanced Brown-Driver-Briggs Lexicon,* s.v. "*tehom.*"

7. United States Census Bureau, "Census Bureau Releases New Report on Living Arrangements of Children," press

release no. CB22-TPS.10, February 3, 2022, www.census
.gov/newsroom/press-releases/2022/living-arrangements
-of-chldren.html.

8. Jack Brewer, "Issue Brief: Fatherlessness and Its Effects on American Society," America First Policy Institute, May 15, 2023, https://americafirstpolicy.com/latest/issue-brief -fatherlessness-and-its-effects-on-american-society.

9. Brewer, "Issue Brief."

10. Edward Kruk, "Father Absence, Father Deficit, Father Hunger," *Psychology Today,* May 23, 2012, www.psychology today.com/intl/blog/co-parenting-after-divorce/201205/ father-absence-father-deficit-father-hunger.

11. *Lexham Research Lexicon of the Hebrew Bible,* ed. Rick Brannan (Bellingham, Wash.: Lexham, 2020), s.v. "*ada-mah.*"

## Chapter 2: Peace in the Temple

1. John H. Walton, *The Lost World of Genesis One: Ancient Cosmology and the Origins Debate* (Downers Grove, Ill.: IVP Academic, 2009), 71.

2. Hiebert cites Nehemiah 9:6; Psalm 90:2; Proverbs 8:22–31; and Hebrews 11:3 as evidence of this theme. Robert J. V. Hiebert, "Create, Creation," in *Evangelical Dictionary of Biblical Theology,* ed. Walter A. Elwell (Grand Rapids, Mich.: Baker, 1996), 1:133.

3. *The Westminster Shorter Catechism: With Scripture Proofs,* 3rd ed. (Bellingham, Wash.: Faithlife, 1996).

4. Walton, *Lost World of Genesis One,* 52, emphasis added.

5. Psalm 121:4.

6. Walton, *Lost World of Genesis One,* 74.

### Chapter 3: Monsters in the Bible

1. *Enhanced Brown-Driver-Briggs Hebrew and English Lexicon,* ed. Francis Brown, Samuel Rolles Driver, and Charles Augustus Briggs (Oak Harbor, Wash.: Logos Library System, 2000), s.v. *"tannin."*

2. Bernhard W. Anderson, *From Creation to New Creation* (Eugene, Ore.: Wipf and Stock, 2005), 196.

3. Trent C. Butler and Douglas Mangum, "Dragon and Sea," in *The Lexham Bible Dictionary,* ed. John D. Barry (Bellingham, Wash.: Lexham, 2016).

4. Jaap Dekker, "God and the Dragons in the Book of Isaiah," in *Playing with Leviathan: Interpretation and Reception of Monsters from the Biblical World,* ed. Koert van Bekkum et al. (Leiden, The Netherlands: Brill, 2017), 19–39.

5. Lowell K. Handy, "Tiamat (Deity)," in *The Anchor Yale Bible Dictionary,* ed. David Noel Freedman (New York: Doubleday, 1992), 546.

6. Anderson, *From Creation to New Creation,* 20.

7. K. A. Kitchen, "Serpent," in *New Bible Dictionary,* ed. D. R. W. Wood (Downers Grove, Ill.: InterVarsity, 1996), 1081.

8. "Re in the Form of a Cat Slays Apep," Egypt Museum, accessed August 16, 2024, https://egypt-museum.com/re-in-the-form-of-a-cat-slays-apep/.

9. Ken Hemphill, *The Names of God* (Nashville: Broadman & Holman, 2001), 144, 207.

### Chapter 4: A Dragon in the Garden

1. John Carey, *A Little History of Poetry* (New Haven, Conn.: Yale University Press, 2021), 1.

2.  Katie Hunt and Lex Harvey, "A Cave Drawing of Humans and a Pig Is the World's Oldest Known Narrative Art," CNN Science, July 4, 2024, www.cnn.com/2024/07/04/science/indonesia-oldest-narrative-cave-art-scn-intl-hnk/index.html.

3.  Jerome, *The Homilies of Saint Jerome,* trans. Sister Marie Ligouri Ewald, vol. 1, *1–59 on the Psalms* (Washington, D.C.: Catholic University of America Press, 2001), 228.

## Chapter 5: Rolling in the Deep

1.  "Titan Submersible: Timeline of Vessel's Voyage," June 22, 2023, *The Guardian* (US edition), www.theguardian.com/world/2023/jun/21/titanic-sub-timeline-titan-submersible-missing-vessel.

2.  "Titan Submersible."

3.  Holly Margerrison, "Update: Family of Victim Killed in Titan Submersible Disaster Sues OceanGate for $50M," BOAT International, August 13, 2024, www.boatinternational.com/yachts/news/oceangate-titan-disaster-implosion-lawsuit-latest-news-2023-submarine-submersible.

4.  *Enhanced Brown-Driver-Briggs Hebrew and English Lexicon,* ed. Francis Brown, Samuel Rolles Driver, and Charles Augustus Briggs (Oak Harbor, Wash.: Logos Library System, 2000), s.v. "*tehom.*"

5.  *Lexham Research Lexicon of the Hebrew Bible,* ed. Rick Brannan (Bellingham, Wash.: Lexham, 2020), s.v. "*tehom.*"

6.  *Enhanced Brown-Driver-Briggs Lexicon,* s.v. "*mayim.*"

7.  *Enhanced Brown-Driver-Briggs Lexicon,* s.v. "*tehom.*"

8.  *The Lexham Bible Dictionary,* ed. John D. Barry (Bellingham, Wash.: Lexham, 2016), s.v. "*tehom.*"

## Chapter 6: Drowning in the Darkness

1. "La Vida Adirondack Expeditions," La Vida at Gordon College, accessed August 19, 2024, https://lavidacenter .org/adk.

## Chapter 7: Adapting to the Desert

1. *Baker Encyclopedia of the Bible,* ed. Walter A. Elwell, vol. 1 (Grand Rapids, Mich.: Baker, 1988), s.v. "Desert."

2. Melody Wilding, "Why 'Dysfunctional' Families Create Great Entrepreneurs," *Forbes,* September 19, 2016, www .forbes.com/sites/melodywilding/2016/09/19/why -dysfunctional-families-create-great-entrepreneurs.

3. Steve Blank, "Founders and Dysfunctional Families," *Steve Blank,* May 18, 2009, https://steveblank.com/2009/ 05/18/founders-and-dysfunctional-families.

4. Wilding, "Why 'Dysfunctional' Families."

5. Blank, "Founders and Dysfunctional Families."

6. *Gesenius' Hebrew-Chaldee Lexicon,* s.v. "H922 – *bou*," Blue Letter Bible, accessed August 21, 2024, www .blueletterbible.org/lexicon/h922/kjv/wlc/0-1/.

7. *Enhanced Brown-Driver-Briggs Hebrew and English Lexi- con,* ed. Francis Brown, Samuel Rolles Driver, and Charles Augustus Briggs (Oxford: Clarendon Press, 1977), 1062.

## Chapter 9: Hagar and Her Wild Ass

1. "How Old Was Isaac When Abraham Almost Sacrificed Him?," Got Questions, accessed August 22, 2024, www .gotquestions.org/how-old-was-Isaac.html.

2. *Lexham Research Lexicon of the Hebrew Bible,* ed. Rick Brannan (Bellingham, Wash.: Lexham, 2020), s.v. "*aqeb.*"

### Chapter 10: A Ladder in Luz

1. Stephen De Young, "Jacob's Ziggurat," *The Whole Counsel of God: An Introduction to Your Bible* (blog), Ancient Faith Ministries, April 1, 2019, https://blogs.ancientfaith .com/wholecounsel/2019/04/01/jacobs-ziggurat/.

2. James Swanson, *A Dictionary of Biblical Languages with Semantic Domains: Hebrew (Old Testament)* (Oak Harbor, Wash.: Logos Research Systems, 1997), emphasis added.

### Chapter 12: Caged but Not a Beast

1. Bible Hub, s.v. "2455. Ioudas," accessed August 23, 2024, https://biblehub.com/greek/2455.htm.

2. Nelson Mandela, *Long Walk to Freedom: The Autobiography of Nelson Mandela* (Boston: Back Bay Books, 1995), 624.

### Chapter 13: Pierced Ears and Empty Stomachs

1. David Fohrman, *The Beast That Crouches at the Door: Adam and Eve, Cain and Abel, and Beyond; A Biblical Exploration* (New Madrid, Conn.: Maggid Books/Aleph Beta, 2021), 35–36.

2. Fohrman, *Beast That Crouches,* 37.

3. Fohrman, *Beast That Crouches,* 37.

4. Fohrman, *Beast That Crouches,* 38.

5. *A Greek-English Lexicon of the New Testament,* trans. Joseph Henry Thayer (New York: Harper & Brothers, 1889), s.v. "*doulos.*"

6. James Swanson, *A Dictionary of Biblical Languages with Semantic Domains: Greek (New Testament)* (Oak Harbor, Wash.: Logos Research Systems, 1997), s.v. "*doulos.*"

7. Brian J. Tabb, "Deacon," in *The Lexham Bible Diction-ary,* ed. John D. Barry (Bellingham, Wash.: Lexham, 2016).

## Chapter 15: The Context of Chaos

1. *Enhanced Brown-Driver-Briggs Hebrew and English Lexi-con,* ed. Francis Brown, Samuel Rolles Driver, and Charles Augustus Briggs (Oak Harbor, Wash.: Logos Library System, 2000), s.v. "*dun.*"

2. James Swanson, *A Dictionary of Biblical Languages with Semantic Domains: Hebrew (Old Testament)* (Oak Harbor: Logos Research Systems, 1997), s.v. "*dun.*"

3. Michael O. Wise, Martin G. Abegg, Jr., and Edward M. Cook, *The Dead Sea Scrolls: A New Translation* (San Francisco: HarperSanFrancisco, 2005), 353.

4. *Enhanced Brown-Driver-Briggs Lexicon,* s.v. "*sahat.*"

5. *Lexham Research Lexicon of the Hebrew Bible,* ed. Rick Brannan (Bellingham, Wash.: Lexham, 2020), s.v. "*sahat.*"

6. Swanson, *Dictionary of Biblical Languages,* s.v. "*sahat.*"

7. Wikipedia, s.v. "Galileo affair," last modified July 25, 2024, 08:37, https://en.wikipedia.org/wiki/Galileo_affair#cite_ref-Trial_Galileo_Essential_2-0.

8. Bruce Gourley, "Yes, the Civil War Was About Slavery," *Baptists and the American Civil War* (blog), February 8, 2017, https://civilwarbaptists.com/slavery/.

9. Mark A. Noll, *The Civil War as a Theological Crisis* (Chapel Hill: University of North Carolina Press, 2006), 50.

10. Richard Furman, "Exposition of the Views of the Baptists Relative to the Coloured Population of the United States in a Communication to the Governor of South Carolina," in *Richard Furman: Life and Legacy,* James A.

Rogers (Macon, Ga.: Mercer University Press, 1985), 277.

11. John H. Walton and Tremper Longman III, *The Lost World of the Flood: Mythology, Theology, and the Deluge Debate* (Downers Grove, Ill.: IVP Academic, 2018), 61–62.

### Chapter 16: Noah's Temple

1. Gordon J. Wenham, "Genesis," *Eerdmans Commentary on the Bible,* ed. James D. G. Dunn and John W. Rogerson (Grand Rapids, Mich.; Cambridge, U.K.: William B. Eerdmans Publishing Company, 2003), 44.

2. *Lexham Research Lexicon of the Hebrew Bible,* ed. Rick Brannan (Bellingham, Wash.: Lexham, 2020), s.v. "*tevah*"; Wilhelm Gesenius, *Gesenius' Hebrew and Chaldee Lexicon to the Old Testament Scriptures,* trans. Samuel Prideaux Tregelles (Bellingham, Wash.: Logos Bible Software, 2003), s.v. "*tevah*."

3. Blue Letter Bible, s.v. "H8322 – *tēḇâ*," accessed August 26, 2024, www.blueletterbible.org/lexicon/h8392/nkjv/wlc/0-1/.

4. Abraham S. Yahuda, *The Language of the Pentateuch in Its Relation to Egyptian,* vol. 1 (London: Oxford University Press, 1933), 262.

5. Yahuda, *Language of the Pentateuch,* 263.

6. *Enhanced Brown-Driver-Briggs Hebrew and English Lexicon,* ed. Francis Brown, Samuel Rolles Driver, and Charles Augustus Briggs (Oak Harbor, Wash.: Logos Library System, 2000), s.v. "*yanah*."

7. Gesenius, *Gesenius' Hebrew and Chaldee Lexicon,* s.v. "Noah."

### Chapter 17: Passive Wrath and Active Grace

1. *Enhanced Brown-Driver-Briggs Hebrew and English Lexicon*, ed. Francis Brown, Samuel Rolles Driver, and Charles Augustus Briggs (Oak Harbor, Wash.: Logos Library System, 2000), s.v. "*qeset.*"

2. *Enhanced Brown-Driver-Briggs Lexicon*, s.v. "*qeset.*"

3. Leonard J. Coppes, "2093 קֶשֶׁת," in *Theological Wordbook of the Old Testament*, ed. R. Laird Harris, Gleason L. Archer, Jr., and Bruce K. Waltke (Chicago: Moody, 1999), 819.

4. Wikipedia, s.v. "Juneteenth," last modified August 20, 2024, 13:55, https://en.wikipedia.org/wiki/Juneteenth.

### Chapter 18: Moses and His Dragon

1. "The History of Berenstain Bears," The Berenstain Bears, accessed August 26, 2024, https://berenstainbears.com/about/.

2. Jacopo Prisco, "The 'Mandela Effect' Describes the False Memories Many of Us Share. But Why Can't Scientists Explain It?," CNN World, September 18, 2023, www.cnn.com/2023/09/18/world/mandela-effect-collective-false-memory-scn/index.html.

3. Prisco, "'Mandela Effect' Describes."

4. *Enhanced Brown-Driver-Briggs Hebrew and English Lexicon*, ed. Francis Brown, Samuel Rolles Driver, and Charles Augustus Briggs (Oak Harbor, Wash.: Logos Library System, 2000), s.v. "*arum.*"

5. Ronald B. Allen, "1698 עָרֹם," in *Theological Wordbook of the Old Testament*, ed. R. Laird Harris, Gleason L. Archer, Jr., and Bruce K. Waltke (Chicago: Moody, 1999), 697.

6. Klaas Spronk, "Rahab," in *Dictionary of Demons and Deities in the Bible,* ed. Karel van der Toorn, Bob Becking, and Pieter W. van der Horst, 2nd ed. (Grand Rapids, Mich.: Wm. B. Eerdmans, 1999), 684–86.

## Chapter 19: Plagues of Chaos

1. *Theological Wordbook of the Old Testament,* ed. R. Laird Harris, Gleason L. Archer, Jr., and Bruce K. Waltke (Chicago: Moody, 1999), s.v. "1995a מִקְוֶה (*miqweh*)."

## Chapter 20: A Portal Back to Eden

1. The seven sections of tabernacle instructions in Exodus are found here: (a) 25:1–30:10; (b) 30:11–16; (c) 30:17–21; (d) 30:22–33; (e) 30:34–38; (f) 31:1–11; and (g) 31:12–17.

2. Peter Enns, *Exodus,* The NIV Application Commentary (Grand Rapids, Mich.: Zondervan, 2000), 509.

## Chapter 21: Breaking the Cycle of Chaos

1. *Enhanced Brown-Driver-Briggs Hebrew and English Lexicon,* ed. Francis Brown, Samuel Rolles Driver, and Charles Augustus Briggs (Oak Harbor, Wash.: Logos Library System, 2000), s.v. "*ruach.*"

2. Matthew 3:13–17.

## Chapter 22: Plunder the Dragon

1. "Fafnir: The Dragon-Dwarf and Curse of Avarice," Norsegarde, accessed August 29, 2024, www.norsegarde .com/blogs/lore-and-mythology/fafnir-the-dragon-dwarf -and-curse-of-avarice.

2. "Fafnir: The Dragon-Dwarf."

3. Sandra Unerman, "Dragons in Twentieth-Century Fiction," *Folklore* 113, no. 1 (April 2002): 96, www.jstor.org/stable/1261010.

4. Lynnette Porter, *Tarnished Heroes, Charming Villains, and Modern Monsters: Science Fiction in Shades of Gray on 21st Century Television* (Jefferson, N.C.: McFarland, 2010), 37.

5. Anne C. Petty, *Dragons of Fantasy* (Cold Spring Harbor, N.Y.: Cold Spring, 2004), 46.

6. Tom Shippey, *The Road to Middle-Earth: How J. R. R. Tolkien Created a New Mythology* (New York: Houghton Mifflin, 2003), 102–4.

7. Verlyn Flieger, "Frodo and Aragorn: The Concept of the Hero," in *Understanding the Lord of the Rings: The Best of Tolkien Criticism,* ed. Rose A. Zimbardo and Neil D. Isaacs (New York: Houghton Mifflin, 2004), 141–44.

8. Craig S. Keener, *IVP Bible Background Commentary: New Testament,* 2nd ed. (Downers Grove, Ill.: IVP Academic, 2014), 130, emphasis added.

9. *Baker Encyclopedia of the Bible,* ed. Walter A. Elwell (Grand Rapids, Mich.: Baker, 1988), s.v. "desert."

10. J. R. R. Tolkien, *The Hobbit* (Boston: Mariner Books, 2012), 207, emphasis added.

11. Interlinear Study Bible, s.v. "Genesis 3:24," StudyLight.org, accessed August 29, 2024, www.studylight.org/interlinear-study-bible/greek/genesis/3-24.html.

12. *A Greek-English Lexicon of the New Testament,* trans. Joseph Henry Thayer (New York: Harper & Brothers, 1889), s.v. "*phimoō.*"

### Chapter 23: The Tempter and the Tempest

1. James Strong, *A Concise Dictionary of the Words in the Greek Testament and the Hebrew Bible* (Bellingham, Wash.: Logos Bible Software, 2009), s.v. "*phimoō.*"

2. *A Greek-English Lexicon,* comp. Henry George Liddell and Robert Scott (Oxford: Clarendon, 1996), s.v. "*phimoō.*"

3. *A Greek-English Lexicon of the New Testament,* trans. Joseph Henry Thayer (New York: Harper & Brothers, 1889), s.v. "*phimoō.*"


### Chapter 24: One Small Step for Man

1. Christopher Mitra, "Breaking Barriers: How the 4-Minute Mile Taught Us to Embrace the Impossible," LinkedIn, April 20, 2023, www.linkedin.com/pulse/breaking-barriers -how-4-minute-mile-taught-us-embrace-mitra-/.

2. Mitra, "Breaking Barriers."

3. Bill Taylor, "What Breaking the 4-Minute Mile Taught Us About the Limits of Conventional Thinking," Harvard Business Review, March 9, 2018, https://hbr.org/ 2018/03/what-breaking-the-4-minute-mile-taught-us -about-the-limits-of-conventional-thinking.

4. "The Sub-4 Alphabetical Register," National Union of Track Statisticians, accessed August 30, 2024, https:// nuts.org.uk/sub-4/Sub-4%20register%206%20June %202022.pdf.


### Chapter 25: Pregnant with a Prophet

1. *A Greek-English Lexicon of the New Testament,* trans. Joseph Henry Thayer (New York: Harper & Brothers, 1889), s.v. "*kētos.*"

2. *World History Encyclopedia,* s.v. "Sea Monster Ketos (Cetus)," December 17, 2014, www.worldhistory.org/image/3363/sea-monster-ketos-cetus/#google_vignette.

3. Among those words are *ichthys* (ἰχθύς), *ichthydion* (ἰχθύδιον), and *opsarion* (ὀψάριον). *Cetus* (κῆτος) does not mean "fish." It is best translated "sea monster."

### Chapter 26: The Genesis of Jesus

1. There are two quick things about John's gospel that you should know. First, it is quite different from Matthew, Mark, and Luke. Second, John is obsessed with the book of Genesis.

### Chapter 28: The Jesus Judas Thought He Knew

1. For a few of the many examples, see Matthew 16:21–28; 20:17–19; 26:1–2; Mark 8:31–38; 9:9–12, 30–32; 10:32–45; and Luke 9:43–45; 18:31–34.

2. *A Concise Hebrew and Aramaic Lexicon of the Old Testament,* William L. Holladay (Leiden: Brill, 2000), s.v. "messiah."

3. Peter Stanford, *Judas: The Most Hated Name in History* (Berkeley, Calif.: Counterpoint, 2015), 25–26.

### Chapter 29: The Chaos Crusher

1. Michael S. Heiser, *The Bible Unfiltered: Approaching Scripture on Its Own Terms* (Bellingham, Wash.: Lexham Press, 2017), 161, emphasis added.

2. Tertullian, *Apologeticus,* quoted in Nicholas LaBanca, "Blood of the Martyrs Is Still Seed for the Church," Ascension, September 17, 2018, https://media.ascensionpress

.com/2018/09/17/blood-of-the-martyrs-is-still-seed-for
-the-church/.

3.  Tom Wright, *John for Everyone: Part 2; Chapters 11–21*
(London: Society for Promoting Christian Knowledge,
2004), 146.

4.  "Christ redeemed us from the curse of the law by becoming a curse for us—for it is written, 'Cursed is everyone
who is hanged on a tree'" (Galatians 3:13, ESV).

5.  "The Battlefield Castle," Domaine du Champ de Bataille,
accessed September 2, 2024, www.chateauduchamp
debataille.com/le-chateau/.

6.  Erik Van Conover, "Touring the Most Expensive House
in the World: Normandy, France," YouTube video, No-
vember 24, 2023, www.youtube.com/watch?app=desktop
&v=VXOok5J_M3M&t=151.

7.  "Tourism in Normandy: Champ de Bataille," McArthur-
Glen Designer Outlet Paris-Giverny, accessed September 2, 2024, www.mcarthurglen.com/en/outlets/fr/designer
-outlet-paris-giverny/tourism/normandy-travel-diary
-champdebataille/.

8.  Van Conover, "Touring the Most Expensive House."

9.  Van Conover, "Touring the Most Expensive House."

10.  "The Gardens," Domaine du Champ de Bataille, accessed
September 2, 2024, www.chateauduchampdebataille
.com/les-jardins/.

@ ANDREW CHEW

Manny Arango is a Bible nerd and founder of ARMA Courses—an online educational platform that helps Christians become biblically literate. The platform has grown to thousands of monthly subscribers since launching in 2020.

Born in Boston, Massachusetts, Manny was a teaching pastor at Social Dallas under pastors Robert and Taylor Madu, and is now the lead pastor, along with his wife, Tia, of The Garden in Houston, Texas. He graduated from Northern Seminary in June 2024 with a doctorate in New Testament studies.

Manny has been married to his beautiful wife for more than a decade, and they have a son named Theophilus.

Instagram: @mannyarango

TikTok: @manny_arango

## About the Type

This book was set in Minion, a 1990 Adobe Originals typeface by Robert Slimbach. Minion is inspired by classical, old-style typefaces of the late Renaissance, a period of elegant and beautiful type designs. Created primarily for text setting, Minion combines the aesthetic and functional qualities that make text type highly readable with the versatility of digital technology.

# Also from author and pastor
## MANNY ARANGO

A deeply biblical and fresh look at how an ancient reading of the Bible leads to lasting peace, inviting followers of Jesus to join Him in bringing order to the chaos of their lives and the world.

In this compelling companion guide to the book *Crushing Chaos*, engage with key questions, dig into the Bible, and complete activities that will help you chart a path through the chaos to a life of order, joy, and peace.